CONTENTS

INTRODUCTION

The Air fryer oven is an easy way to cook delicious healthy meals. Rather than cooking the food in oil and hot fat that may affect your health, the machine uses rapid hot air to circulate around and cook meals. This allows the outside of your food to be crispy and also makes sure that the inside layers are cooked through.

Air fryer oven allows us to cook almost everything and a lot of dishes. We can use the Air fryer oven to cook Meat, vegetables, poultry, fruit, fish and a wide variety of desserts. It is possible to prepare your entire meals, starting from appetizers to main courses as well as desserts. Not to mention, Air fryer oven also allows home prepared preserves or even delicious sweets and cakes.

How Does Air fryer oven Works?

The technology of the Air fryer oven is very simple. Fried foods get their crunchy texture because hot oil heats foods quickly and evenly on their surface. Oil is an excellent heat conductor, which helps with fast and simultaneous cooking across all of the ingredients. For decades cooks have used convection ovens to try to mimic the effects of frying or cooking the whole surface of food. But the air never circulates quickly enough to achieve that delicious surface crisp we all love in fried foods.

With this mechanism the air is circulated on high degrees, up to 200° C, to "air fry" any food such as fish, chicken or chips etc. This technology has changed the whole idea of cooking by reducing the fat up to 80% compared to old-fashioned deep fat frying.

The Air fryer oven cooking releases the heat through a heating element which cooks the food in a healthier and more appropriate way. There's also an exhaust fan right above the cooking chamber which provides the food required airflow. This way food is cooked with constant heated air. This leads to the same heating temperature reaching every single part of the food that is being cooked. So, this is only grill and the exhaust fan that is helping the Air fryer oven to boost air at a constantly high speed in order to cook healthy food with less fat.

The internal pressure increases the temperature that will then be controlled by the exhaust system. Exhaust fan also releases filtered extra air to cook the food in a much healthier way. Air fryer oven has no odor at all and it is absolutely harmless making it user and environment friendly.

Benefits of the Air fryer oven

- Healthier, oil-free meals
- It eliminates cooking odors through internal air filters
- Makes cleaning easier due to lack of oil grease
- Air Fryers are able to bake, grill, roast and fry providing more options
- Safer method of cooking compared to deep frying with exposed hot oil
- Has the ability to set and leave as most models and it includes a digital timer

The Air fryer oven is an all-in-one that allows cooking to be easy and quick. It also leads to a lot of possibilities once you get to know it. Once you learn the basics and become familiar with your Air fryer oven, you can feel free to experiment and modify the recipes in the way you prefer. You can prepare a wide number of dishes in the Air fryer oven and you can adapt your favorite stove-top dish so it becomes air fryer–friendly. It all boils down to variety and lots of options, right?

Cooking perfect and delicious as well as healthy meals has never been easier. You can see how this recipe collection proves itself.

Enjoy!

APPETIZERS AND SIDE DISHES

1. Scalloped Potatoes

Servings: 6
Cooking Time: 45 Minutes
Ingredients:
- 4 sweet potatoes, peeled
- 1/4 cup olive oil
- 1/2 tsp paprika
- 1 tbsp maple syrup
- 1/2 cup fresh orange juice
- 1/2 tsp orange zest
- 1 tsp salt

Directions:
1. Fit the oven with the rack in position
2. Slice sweet potatoes 1/16-inch thick using a slicer.
3. Arrange sweet potato slices in a greased 8*8-inch baking dish.
4. In a bowl, whisk together the remaining ingredients and pour over sweet potatoes.
5. Set to bake at 350 F for 50 minutes. After 5 minutes place the baking dish in the preheated oven.
6. Serve and enjoy.
- **Nutrition Info:** Calories: 130 Fat: 8.5 g Carbohydrates 13.8 g Sugar 3.9 g Protein 0.7 g Cholesterol 0 mg

2. Cinnamon Sweet Potatoes

Servings: 4
Cooking Time: 30 Minutes
Ingredients:
- 2 large sweet potatoes, peel and cut into cubes
- 2 tbsp brown sugar
- 1/4 cup maple syrup
- 2 tbsp olive oil
- 1/4 tsp cinnamon
- Salt

Directions:
1. Fit the oven with the rack in position
2. Add sweet potatoes, oil, cinnamon, brown sugar, maple syrup, and salt into the large mixing bowl and toss well.
3. Spread sweet potatoes in a parchment-lined baking pan.
4. Set to bake at 400 F for 35 minutes. After 5 minutes place the baking pan in the preheated oven.
5. Serve and enjoy.
- **Nutrition Info:** Calories: 188 Fat: 7.1 g Carbohydrates 31.7 g Sugar 16.3 g Protein 0.8 g Cholesterol 0 mg

3. Buttery Garlic Croutons

Servings:4
Cooking Time: 20 Minutes
Ingredients:
- 2 cups bread, cubed
- 2 tbsp butter, melted
- Garlic salt and black pepper to taste

Directions:
1. In a bowl, toss the bread cubes with butter, garlic salt, and pepper until well-coated. Place them in a baking tray. Select AirFry function, adjust the temperature to 400 F, and press Start. Cook for 12 minutes until golden brown and crispy. Serve in salads or soups.

4. Garlic & Olive Oil Spring Vegetables

Servings: 4
Cooking Time: 20 Minutes
Ingredients:
- 1 pound assorted spring vegetables (such as carrots, asparagus, radishes, spring onions, or sugar snap peas)
- 4 unpeeled garlic cloves
- 2 tablespoons olive oil
- Salt and pepper to taste

Directions:
1. Start by preheating toaster oven to 450°F.
2. Combine vegetables, garlic, oil, salt, and pepper in a bowl and toss.
3. Roast for 20 minutes or until vegetables start to brown.
- **Nutrition Info:** Calories: 105, Sodium: 255 mg, Dietary Fiber: 4.4 g, Total Fat: 7.3 g, Total Carbs: 9.1 g, Protein: 1.8 g.

5. Green Beans

Servings: 4
Cooking Time: 20 Minutes
Ingredients:
- 6 cups green beans; trimmed
- 1 tbsp. hot paprika
- 2 tbsp. olive oil
- A pinch of salt and black pepper

Directions:
1. Take a bowl and mix the green beans with the other ingredients, toss, put them in the air fryer's basket and cook at 370°F for 20 minutes
2. Divide between plates and serve as a side dish.
- **Nutrition Info:** Calories: 120; Fat: 5g; Fiber: 1g; Carbs: 4g; Protein: 2g

6. Spicy Tortilla Chips

Servings: 4
Cooking Time: 5 Minutes
Ingredients:
- ½ teaspoon ground cumin
- ½ teaspoon paprika
- ½ teaspoon chili powder
- ½ teaspoon salt

- Pinch cayenne pepper
- 8 (6-inch) corn tortillas, each cut into 6 wedges
- Cooking spray

Directions:
1. Lightly spritz the air fryer basket with cooking spray.
2. Stir together the cumin, paprika, chili powder, salt, and pepper in a small bowl.
3. Place the tortilla wedges in the basket in a single layer. Lightly mist them with cooking spray. Sprinkle the seasoning mixture on top of the tortilla wedges.
4. Put the air fryer basket on the baking pan and slide into Rack Position 2, select Air Fry, set temperature to 375ºF (190ºC), and set time to 5 minutes.
5. Stir the tortilla wedges halfway through the cooking time.
6. When cooking is complete, the chips should be lightly browned and crunchy. Remove from the oven. Let the tortilla chips cool for 5 minutes and serve.

7.   French Fries

Servings: 4
Cooking Time: 10 Minutes
Ingredients:
- ¼ teaspoon baking soda Oil for frying
- Salt, to taste
- 8 medium potatoes, peeled, cut into medium matchsticks, and patted dry
- 1 cup water

Directions:
1. Put the water in the Instant Pot, add the salt and baking soda and mix. Place the potatoes in the steam basket and place them in the Instant Pot, cover and cook with manual adjustment for 3 minutes.
2. Release the pressure naturally, remove the chips from the Instant Pot and place them in a bowl. Heat a pan with enough oil over medium-high heat, add the potatoes, spread and cook until they are golden brown.
3. Transfer the potatoes to the paper towels to drain the excess fat and place them in a bowl. Salt, mix well and serve.
- **Nutrition Info:** Calories: 300, Fat: 10, Fiber: 3.7, Carbohydrate: 41, Proteins: 3.4

8.   Homemade French Fries

Servings:2
Cooking Time: 25 Minutes
Ingredients:
- 2 russet potatoes, cut into strips
- 2 tbsp olive oil
- Salt and black pepper to taste

Directions:

1. In a bowl, toss the strips with olive oil and season with salt and pepper. Arrange them on the frying basket. Select AirFry function, adjust the temperature to 400 F, and press Start. Cook for 18-22 minutes. Check for crispiness and serve with aioli, ketchup, or crumbled feta cheese.

9.   Whole Chicken With Bbq Sauce

Servings: 3
Cooking Time: 25 Minutes
Ingredients:
- 1 whole small chicken, cut into pieces
- 1 tsp salt
- 1 tsp smoked paprika
- 1 tsp garlic powder
- 1 cup BBQ sauce

Directions:
1. Coat the chicken with salt, paprika, and garlic. Place the chicken pieces skin-side down in the greased baking tray. Cook in the oven for around 15 minutes at 400 F on Bake function until slightly golden. Remove to a plate and brush with barbecue sauce. Return the chicken to the oven skin-side up and cook for 5 minutes at 340 F. Serve with more barbecue sauce.

10.   Rice Broccoli Casserole

Servings: 8
Cooking Time: 40 Minutes
Ingredients:
- 2 cups brown rice, cooked
- 3 cups broccoli florets
- 1 tbsp olive oil
- 2 garlic cloves, minced
- 1 onion, chopped
- For sauce:
- 1 tbsp onion, chopped
- 1/4 cup nutritional yeast flakes
- 1 cup of water
- 1 garlic clove, minced
- 1 tbsp tapioca starch
- 1 cup cashews
- 1 1/2 tsp salt

Directions:
1. Fit the oven with the rack in position
2. For the sauce: add all sauce ingredients into the blender and blend until smooth.
3. Heat oil in a pan over medium-high heat.
4. Add garlic and onion and sauté until onion is softened.
5. Add broccoli and cook for a minute.
6. Add rice and sauce and stir to combine.
7. Transfer broccoli rice mixture into the greased casserole dish.
8. Set to bake at 400 F for 45 minutes. After 5 minutes place the casserole dish in the preheated oven.

9. Serve and enjoy.
- **Nutrition Info:** Calories: 327 Fat: 11.4 g Carbohydrates 49.2 g Sugar 2.1 g Protein 9.7 g Cholesterol 0 mg

11. Rosemary Chickpeas

Servings:4
Cooking Time: 20 Minutes
Ingredients:
- 2 (14.5-ounce) cans chickpeas, rinsed
- 2 tbsp olive oil
- 1 tsp dried rosemary
- ½ tsp dried thyme
- ¼ tsp dried sage
- ¼ tsp salt

Directions:
1. In a bowl, mix together chickpeas, oil, rosemary, thyme, sage, and salt. Transfer to a baking pan. Select Bake function, adjust the temperature to 380 F, and press Start. Cook for 15 minutes.

12. Creamy Fennel(1)

Servings: 4
Cooking Time: 20 Minutes
Ingredients:
- 2 big fennel bulbs; sliced
- ½ cup coconut cream
- 2 tbsp. butter; melted
- Salt and black pepper to taste.

Directions:
1. In a pan that fits the air fryer, combine all the ingredients, toss, introduce in the machine and cook at 370°F for 12 minutes
2. Divide between plates and serve as a side dish.
- **Nutrition Info:** Calories: 151; Fat: 3g; Fiber: 2g; Carbs: 4g; Protein: 6g

13. Spinach And Goat Cheese Risotto

Servings: 6
Cooking Time: 10 Minutes
Ingredients:
- ¾ cup yellow onion, chopped
- 1½ cups Arborio rice
- 12 ounces spinach, chopped
- 3½ cups hot vegetable stock
- ½ cup white wine
- 2 garlic cloves, peeled and minced
- 2 tablespoons extra virgin olive oil
- Salt and ground black pepper, to taste
- ⅓ cup pecans, toasted and chopped
- 4 ounces goat cheese, soft and crumbled
- 2 tablespoons lemon juice

Directions:
1. Put the Instant Pot in the sauté mode, add the oil and heat. Add garlic and onion, mix and cook for 5 minutes.

2. Add the rice, mix and cook for 1 minute. Add wine, stir and cook until it is absorbed. Add 3 cups of stock, cover the Instant Pot and cook the rice for 4 minutes.
3. Release the pressure, uncover the Instant Pot, add the spinach, stir and cook for 3 minutes in Manual mode. Add salt, pepper, the rest of the stock, lemon juice and goat cheese and mix. Divide between plates, decorate with nuts and serve.
- **Nutrition Info:** Calories: 340, Fat: 23, Fiber: 4.5, Carbohydrate: 24, Proteins: 18.9

14. Puffed Asparagus Spears

Servings: 10
Cooking Time: 10 Minutes
Ingredients:
- Nonstick cooking spray
- 3 oz. prosciutto, sliced thin & cut in 30 long strips
- 30 asparagus spears, trimmed
- 10 (14 x 9-inch) sheets phyllo dough, thawed

Directions:
1. Place baking pan in position 2 of the oven.
2. Wrap each asparagus spear with a piece of prosciutto, like a barber pole.
3. One at a time, place a sheet of phyllo on a work surface and cut into 3 4 1/2x9-inch rectangles.
4. Place an asparagus spear across a short end and roll up. Place in a single layer in the fryer basket. Spray with cooking spray.
5. Place the basket in the oven and set to air fry on 450°F for 10 minutes. Cook until phyllo is crisp and golden, about 8-10 minutes, turning over halfway through cooking time. Repeat with remaining ingredients. Serve warm.
- **Nutrition Info:** Calories: 74, Total Fat: 2g, Saturated Fat: 0g, Total Carbs 11g, Net Carbs 10g, Protein 3g, Sugar 0g, Fiber 1g, Sodium 189mg, Potassium 60mg, Phosphorus 33mg

15. Air Fryer Corn

Servings: 2
Cooking Time: 10 Minutes
Ingredients:
- 2 fresh ears of corn, remove husks, wash, and pat dry
- 1 tbsp fresh lemon juice
- 2 tsp oil
- Pepper
- Salt

Directions:
1. Fit the oven with the rack in position 2.
2. Cut the corn to fit in the air fryer basket.

3. Drizzle oil over the corn. Season with pepper and salt.
4. Place corn in the air fryer basket then places an air fryer basket in the baking pan.
5. Place a baking pan on the oven rack. Set to air fry at 400 F for 10 minutes.
6. Serve and enjoy.
7. Drizzle lemon juice over corn and serve.
- **Nutrition Info:** Calories: 122 Fat: 5.6 g Carbohydrates 18.2 g Sugar 4.2 g Protein 3.1 g Cholesterol 0 mg

16. Mini Salmon Quiches

Servings: 15
Cooking Time: 20 Minutes
Ingredients:
- 15 mini tart cases
- 4 eggs, lightly beaten
- ½ cup heavy cream
- Salt and black pepper
- 3 oz smoked salmon, chopped
- 6 oz feta cheese, crumbled
- 2 tsp fresh dill, chopped

Directions:
1. Mix together eggs and heavy cream in a bowl. Arrange the tarts on a greased baking tray. Fill them with the egg mixture, about halfway up the side and top with salmon and feta cheese. Cook for 10 minutes at 360 F on Bake function, regularly checking to avoid overcooking. Sprinkle with dill and serve chilled.

17. Herbed Radish Sauté(2)

Servings: 4
Cooking Time: 20 Minutes
Ingredients:
- 2 bunches red radishes; halved
- 2 tbsp. parsley; chopped.
- 2 tbsp. balsamic vinegar
- 1 tbsp. olive oil
- Salt and black pepper to taste.

Directions:
1. Take a bowl and mix the radishes with the remaining ingredients except the parsley, toss and put them in your air fryer's basket.
2. Cook at 400°F for 15 minutes, divide between plates, sprinkle the parsley on top and serve as a side dish
- **Nutrition Info:** Calories: 180; Fat: 4g; Fiber: 2g; Carbs: 3g; Protein: 5g

18. Red Beans And Rice

Servings: 6
Cooking Time: 25 Minutes
Ingredients:
- 1 teaspoon vegetable oil
- 1 pound red kidney beans, soaked overnight and drained

- Salt, to taste
- 1 pound smoked sausage, cut into wedges
- 1 yellow onion, peeled and chopped
- 4 garlic cloves, peeled and chopped
- 1 celery stalk, chopped
- 1 green bell pepper, seeded and chopped
- 1 teaspoon dried thyme
- 5 cups water
- 2 bay leaves
- Long grain rice already cooked
- 2 tablespoons parsley, minced, for serving
- Hot sauce, for serving
- 2 green onions, minced, for serving

Directions:
1. Put the Instant Pot in the sauté mode, add the oil and heat. Add sausage, onion, pepper, celery, garlic, thyme and salt, mix and cook for 8 minutes.
2. Add beans, bay leaves and water, stir, cover the Instant Pot and cook for 15 minutes.
3. Release the pressure naturally for 20 minutes, discard the bay leaves and put 2 cups of beans and a little liquid in the mixer. Clean them well and return to the plate.
4. Divide the rice between the dishes, add the beans, sausage and vegetables on top, sprinkle with chives and parsley and serve with a hot sauce.
- **Nutrition Info:** Calories: 160, Fat: 3.8, Fiber: 3.4, Carbohydrate: 24, Proteins: 4.6

19. Lemony Broccoli

Servings: 6
Cooking Time: 15 Minutes
Ingredients:
- Salt and ground black pepper, to taste
- 5 lemon slices
- 1 head of broccoli, separated into florets
- 1 cup water

Directions:
1. Pour the water into the Instant Pot. Season the broccoli with salt and pepper to taste and add them to the instant pot, add the lemon slices and mix gently.
2. Cover the pan instantly and cook for 15 minutes. Relieve the pressure, divide the broccoli between the plates and serve.
- **Nutrition Info:** Calories: 55, Fat: 0.5, Fiber: 5, Carbohydrate: 11, Proteins: 3.4

20. Garlic Asparagus

Servings: 4
Cooking Time: 10 Minutes
Ingredients:
- 1 pound (454 g) asparagus, woody ends trimmed
- 2 tablespoons olive oil
- 1 tablespoon balsamic vinegar
- 2 teaspoons minced garlic

- Salt and freshly ground black pepper, to taste
- In a large shallow bowl, toss the asparagus with the olive oil, balsamic vinegar, garlic, salt, and pepper until thoroughly coated. Put the asparagus in the baking pan.
- Slide the baking pan into Rack Position 1, select Convection Bake, set temperature to 350ºF (180ºC), and set time to 10 minutes.
- Flip the asparagus with tongs halfway through the cooking time.
- When cooking is complete, the asparagus should be crispy. Remove from the oven and serve warm.

Directions:
1. Spicy Cabbage
2. Prep time: 5 minutes | Cooking Time: 7 minutes | Servings: 4
3. head cabbage, sliced into 1-inch-thick ribbons
4. tablespoon olive oil
5. teaspoon garlic powder
6. teaspoon red pepper flakes
7. teaspoon salt
8. teaspoon freshly ground black pepper
9. Toss the cabbage with the olive oil, garlic powder, red pepper flakes, salt, and pepper in a large mixing bowl until well coated.
10. Transfer the cabbage to the baking pan.
11. Slide the baking pan into Rack Position 1, select Convection Bake, set temperature to 350ºF (180ºC), and set time to 7 minutes.
12. Flip the cabbage with tongs halfway through the cooking time.
13. When cooking is complete, the cabbage should be crisp. Remove from the oven to a plate and serve warm.

21. Jicama Fries(3)

Servings: 4
Cooking Time: 20 Minutes
Ingredients:
- 1 small jicama; peeled.
- ¼ tsp. onion powder.
- ¾tsp. chili powder
- ¼ tsp. ground black pepper
- ¼ tsp. garlic powder.

Directions:
1. Cut jicama into matchstick-sized pieces.
2. Place pieces into a small bowl and sprinkle with remaining ingredients. Place the fries into the air fryer basket
3. Adjust the temperature to 350 Degrees F and set the timer for 20 minutes. Toss the basket two or three times during cooking. Serve warm.
- **Nutrition Info:** Calories: 37; Protein: 8g; Fiber: 7g; Fat: 1g; Carbs: 7g

22. Baked Vegetables

Servings: 6
Cooking Time: 30 Minutes
Ingredients:
- 2 zucchini, sliced
- 2 tomatoes, quartered
- 6 fresh basil leaves, sliced
- 2 tsp Italian seasoning
- 2 tbsp olive oil
- 1 eggplant, sliced
- 1 onion, sliced
- 1 bell pepper, cut into strips
- Pepper
- Salt

Directions:
1. Fit the oven with the rack in position
2. Add all ingredients except basil leaves into the bowl and toss well.
3. Transfer vegetable mixture in parchment-lined baking pan.
4. Set to bake at 400 F for 35 minutes. After 5 minutes place the baking pan in the preheated oven.
5. Garnish with basil and serve.
- **Nutrition Info:** Calories: 96 Fat: 5.5 g Carbohydrates 11.7 g Sugar 6.4 g Protein 2.3 g Cholesterol 1 mg

23. Gourmet Beef Sticks

Servings: 3
Cooking Time: 10 Minutes + Chilling Time
Ingredients:
- 1 lb ground beef
- 3 tbsp sugar
- A pinch garlic powder
- A pinch chili powder
- Salt to taste
- 1 tsp liquid smoke

Directions:
1. Place the beef, sugar, garlic powder, chili powder, salt and liquid smoke in a bowl. Mix well. Mold out 4 sticks with your hands, place them on a plate, and refrigerate for 30 minutes.
2. Remove and cook in the oven at 350 F for 10 minutes on Bake function. Flip and continue cooking for another 5 minutes until browned.

24. Sweet Carrot Puree

Servings: 4
Cooking Time: 5 Minutes
Ingredients:
- Salt, to taste
- 1 cup water
- 1 teaspoon brown sugar
- 1½ pounds carrots, peeled and chopped
- 1 tablespoon butter, softened

- 1 tablespoon honey

Directions:

1. Place the carrots in the Instant Pot, add the water, cover and cook for 4 minutes in the Manual setting.
2. Release the pressure naturally, drain the carrots and place them in a bowl.
3. Mix with an immersion blender, add the butter, salt and honey. Mix again, add the sugar on top and serve.

- **Nutrition Info:** Calories: 50, Fat: 1, Fiber: 3, Carbohydrate: 11, Proteins: 1

25. Green Bean Casserole(1)

Servings: 4
Cooking Time: 20 Minutes
Ingredients:

- 1 lb. fresh green beans, edges trimmed
- ½ oz. pork rinds, finely ground
- 1 oz. full-fat cream cheese
- ½ cup heavy whipping cream.
- ¼ cup diced yellow onion
- ½ cup chopped white mushrooms
- ½ cup chicken broth
- 4 tbsp. unsalted butter.
- ¼ tsp. xanthan gum

Directions:

1. In a medium skillet over medium heat, melt the butter. Sauté the onion and mushrooms until they become soft and fragrant, about 3–5 minutes.
2. Add the heavy whipping cream, cream cheese and broth to the pan. Whisk until smooth. Bring to a boil and then reduce to a simmer. Sprinkle the xanthan gum into the pan and remove from heat
3. Chop the green beans into 2-inch pieces and place into a 4-cup round baking dish. Pour the sauce mixture over them and stir until coated. Top the dish with ground pork rinds. Place into the air fryer basket
4. Adjust the temperature to 320 Degrees F and set the timer for 15 minutes. Top will be golden and green beans fork tender when fully cooked. Serve warm.

- **Nutrition Info:** Calories: 267; Protein: 3.6g; Fiber: 3.2g; Fat: 23.4g; Carbs: 9.7g

26. Pancetta & Goat Cheese Bombs With Almonds

Servings:4
Cooking Time: 25 Minutes
Ingredients:

- 16 oz soft goat cheese
- 2 tbsp fresh rosemary, finely chopped
- 1 cup almonds, chopped into small pieces
- Salt and black pepper
- 15 dried plums, chopped
- 15 pancetta slices

Directions:

1. Line the frying basket with baking paper. In a bowl, add cheese, rosemary, almonds, salt, pepper and plums and stir well. Roll into balls and wrap with pancetta slices. Arrange the bombs on the frying basket. Select AirFry function, adjust the temperature to 400 F, and press Start. Cook for 10 minutes. Check at the 5-minute mark to avoid overcooking. Serve with toothpicks.

27. Maple Shrimp With Coconut

Servings: 3
Cooking Time: 30 Minutes
Ingredients:

- 1 lb jumbo shrimp, peeled and deveined
- ¾ cup shredded coconut
- 1 tbsp maple syrup
- ½ cup breadcrumbs
- ⅓ cup cornstarch
- ½ cup milk

Directions:

1. Pour the cornstarch in a zipper bag, add shrimp, zip the bag up and shake vigorously to coat with the cornstarch. Mix the syrup and milk in a bowl and set aside.
2. In a separate bowl, mix the breadcrumbs and shredded coconut. Open the zipper bag and remove each shrimp while shaking off excess starch. Dip shrimp in the milk mixture and then in the crumb mixture while pressing loosely to trap enough crumbs and coconut.
3. Place in the basket without overcrowding and fit in the baking tray. Cook for 12 minutes at 350 F on Air Fry function, flipping once halfway through until golden brown. Serve warm.

28. Roasted Garlic(1)

Servings: 12 Cloves
Cooking Time: 20 Minutes
Ingredients:

- 1 medium head garlic
- 2 tsp. avocado oil

Directions:

1. Remove any hanging excess peel from the garlic but leave the cloves covered. Cut off ¼ of the head of garlic, exposing the tips of the cloves
2. Drizzle with avocado oil. Place the garlic head into a small sheet of aluminum foil, completely enclosing it. Place it into the air fryer basket. Adjust the temperature to 400 Degrees F and set the timer for 20 minutes. If your garlic head is a bit smaller, check it after 15 minutes
3. When done, garlic should be golden brown and very soft

4. To serve, cloves should pop out and easily be spread or sliced. Store in an airtight container in the refrigerator up to 5 days.
5. You may also freeze individual cloves on a baking sheet, then store together in a freezer-safe storage bag once frozen.
- **Nutrition Info:** Calories: 11; Protein: 0.2g; Fiber: 0.1g; Fat: 0.7g; Carbs: 1.0g

29. Tasty Bok Choy Crisps

Servings:2
Cooking Time: 10 Minutes
Ingredients:
- 2 tbsp olive oil
- 4 cups packed bok choy
- 1 tsp Italian seasoning
- 1 tbsp yeast flakes
- Sea salt to taste

Directions:
1. In a bowl, mix olive oil, bok choy, yeast, and Italian seasoning. Dump the coated kale in frying basket. Set the temperature of toaster oven to 360 F on AirFry function and press Start. Cook for 5-8 minutes until crispy. Serve sprinkled with sea salt.

30. Bok Choy And Butter Sauce(4)

Servings: 4
Cooking Time: 8 Minutes
Ingredients:
- 2 bok choy heads; trimmed and cut into strips
- 1 tbsp. butter; melted
- 2 tbsp. chicken stock
- 1 tsp. lemon juice
- 1 tbsp. olive oil
- A pinch of salt and black pepper

Directions:
1. In a pan that fits your air fryer, mix all the ingredients, toss, introduce the pan in the air fryer and cook at 380°F for 15 minutes.
2. Divide between plates and serve as a side dish
- **Nutrition Info:** Calories: 141; Fat: 3g; Fiber: 2g; Carbs: 4g; Protein: 3g

31. Potato Chips With Lemony Dip

Servings: 3
Cooking Time: 25 Minutes
Ingredients:
- 3 large potatoes, sliced
- 1 cup sour cream
- 2 scallions, white part minced
- 3 tbsp olive oil.
- ½ tsp lemon juice
- salt and black pepper

Directions:
1. Preheat on Air Fry function to 350 F. Place the potatoes into the AirFryer basket and

fit in the baking tray. Cook for 15 minutes, flipping once. Season with salt and pepper. Mix sour cream, olive oil, scallions, lemon juice, salt, and pepper and serve with chips.

32. Preparation Time: 20 Minutes

Servings: 2
Cooking Time: 20 Minutes
Ingredients:
- 2 bell peppers, tops and seeds removed
- Salt and pepper, to taste
- 2/3 cup cream cheese
- 2 tablespoons mayonnaise
- 1 tablespoon fresh celery stalks, chopped

Directions:
1. Arrange the peppers in the lightly greased cooking basket. Cook in the preheated Air Fryer at 400 degrees F for 15 minutes, turning them over halfway through the cooking time.
2. Season with salt and pepper.
3. Then, in a mixing bowl, combine the cream cheese with the mayonnaise and chopped celery. Stuff the pepper with the cream cheese mixture and serve.
- **Nutrition Info:** 378 Calories; 38g Fat; 6g Carbs; 5g Protein; 1g Sugars; 6g Fiber

33. Ham And Cheese Grilled Sandwich

Servings: 2
Cooking Time: 15 Minutes
Ingredients:
- 4 slices bread
- ¼ cup butter
- 2 slices ham
- 2 slices cheese

Directions:
1. Preheat on Air Fry function to 360 F. Place 2 bread slices on a flat surface. Spread butter on the exposed surfaces. Lay cheese and ham on two of the slices. Cover with the other 2 slices to form sandwiches. Place the sandwiches in the cooking basket and cook for 5 minutes on Bake function. For additional crispiness, set on Toast function for 2 minutes.

34. Black Beans

Servings: 8
Cooking Time: 5 Minutes
Ingredients:
- ⅔ cup saltwater, to taste
- 1 cup of black beans, soaked overnight, drained and washed
- 1 piece of dried seaweed
- 1 tablespoon of coriander seed tea
- ½ teaspoon of cumin seeds
- 2 garlic cloves, peeled and chopped

Directions:

1. In the Instant Pot, mix the beans with the seaweed, water, garlic, coriander and cumin. Stir, cover the Instant Pot and cook for 5 minutes in the Bean / Chili setting.
2. Relieve the pressure, remove the seaweed and coriander seeds, divide the beans between the dishes, season with salt and serve.
- **Nutrition Info:** Calories: 330, Fat: 1, Fiber: 16, Carbohydrate: 23, Proteins: 21

35. Baked Artichoke Hearts

Servings: 6
Cooking Time: 25 Minutes
Ingredients:
- 15 oz frozen artichoke hearts, defrosted
- 1 tbsp olive oil
- Pepper
- Salt

Directions:
1. Fit the oven with the rack in position
2. Arrange artichoke hearts in baking pan and drizzle with olive oil. Season with pepper and salt.
3. Set to bake at 400 F for 30 minutes. After 5 minutes place the baking pan in the preheated oven.
4. Serve and enjoy.
- **Nutrition Info:** Calories: 53 Fat: 2.4 g Carbohydrates 7.5 g Sugar 0.7 g Protein 2.3 g Cholesterol 0 mg

36. Spicy Broccoli With Hot Sauce

Servings:6
Cooking Time: 14 Minutes
Ingredients:
- Broccoli:
- 1 medium-sized head broccoli, cut into florets
- 1½ tablespoons olive oil
- 1 teaspoon shallot powder
- 1 teaspoon porcini powder
- ½ teaspoon freshly grated lemon zest
- ½ teaspoon hot paprika
- ½ teaspoon granulated garlic
- $^1/_3$ teaspoon fine sea salt
- $^1/_3$ teaspoon celery seeds
- Hot Sauce:
- ½ cup tomato sauce
- 1 tablespoon balsamic vinegar
- ½ teaspoon ground allspice

Directions:
1. In a mixing bowl, combine all the ingredients for the broccoli and toss to coat. Transfer the broccoli to the air fryer basket.
2. Put the air fryer basket on the baking pan and slide into Rack Position 2, select Air Fry, set temperature to 360ºF (182ºC), and set time to 14 minutes.

3. Meanwhile, make the hot sauce by whisking together the tomato sauce, balsamic vinegar, and allspice in a small bowl.
4. When cooking is complete, remove the broccoli from the oven and serve with the hot sauce.

37. Cheddar Cheese Cauliflower Casserole

Servings: 8
Cooking Time: 35 Minutes
Ingredients:
- 4 cups cauliflower florets
- 1 1/2 cups cheddar cheese, shredded
- 1 cup sour cream
- 4 bacon slices, cooked and crumbled
- 3 green onions, chopped

Directions:
1. Fit the oven with the rack in position
2. Boil water in a large pot. Add cauliflower in boiling water and cook for 8-10 minutes or until tender. Drain well.
3. Transfer cauliflower in a large bowl.
4. Add half bacon, half green onion, 1 cup cheese, and sour cream in cauliflower bowl and mix well.
5. Transfer mixture into a greased baking dish and sprinkle with remaining cheese.
6. Set to bake at 350 F for 30 minutes. After 5 minutes place the baking dish in the preheated oven.
7. Garnish with remaining green onion and bacon.
8. Serve and enjoy.
- **Nutrition Info:** Calories: 213 Fat: 17.1 g Carbohydrates 4.7 g Sugar 1.5 g Protein 10.8 g Cholesterol 45 mg

38. Homemade Cheesy Sticks

Servings: 12
Cooking Time: 5 Minutes
Ingredients:
- 6 (6 oz) bread cheese
- 2 tbsp butter
- 2 cups panko crumbs

Directions:
1. Put the butter in a bowl and melt in the microwave for 2 minutes; set aside. With a knife, cut the cheese into equal-sized sticks. Brush each stick with butter and dip into panko crumbs. Arrange the sticks in a single layer in the basket. Fit in the baking tray and cook in the at 390 F for 10 minutes on Air Fry function. Flip halfway through. Serve warm.

39. Homemade Cod Fingers

Servings: 3
Cooking Time: 25 Minutes
Ingredients:

- 2 cups flour
- Salt and black pepper to taste
- 1 tsp seafood seasoning
- 2 whole eggs, beaten
- 1 cup cornmeal
- 1 pound cod fillets, cut into fingers
- 2 tbsp milk
- 2 eggs, beaten
- 1 cup breadcrumbs
- 1 lemon, cut into wedges

Directions:
1. Preheat on Air Fryer function to 400 F. In a bowl, mix beaten eggs with milk. In a separate bowl, combine flour, cornmeal, and seafood seasoning. In another mixing bowl, mix spices with the eggs. In a third bowl, pour the breadcrumbs.
2. Dip cod fingers in the seasoned flour mixture, followed by a dip in the egg mixture, and finally coat with breadcrumbs. Place the fingers in your Air Fryer basket and fit in the baking tray. Cook for 10 minutes until golden brown. Serve with lemon wedges.

40. Mexican Rice

Servings: 8
Cooking Time: 4 Minutes
Ingredients:
- ½ cup chopped fresh cilantro
- 1 cup of long grain rice
- 1 cup of vegetable broth
- ¼ cup of hot green sauce
- ½ avocado, salt, peeled and chopped
- Salt and freshly ground black pepper, to taste

Directions:
1. Put the rice in the instant pot, add the broth, stir, cover and cook for 4 minutes.
2. Release the pressure naturally for 10 minutes, uncover the Instant Pot, fluff it with a fork and transfer it to a bowl.
3. In a food processor, mix the avocado with the hot sauce and the cilantro and mash until smooth.
4. Pour over the rice, mix well, add salt and pepper, stir again, divide between the plates and serve.
- **Nutrition Info:** Calories: 100, Fat: 2, Fiber: 1, Carbohydrate: 18, Proteins: 2

41. Lime Pumpkin Wedges

Servings:4
Cooking Time: 30 Minutes
Ingredients:
- 1 lb pumpkin, cut into wedges
- 1 tbsp paprika
- 1 whole lime, squeezed
- 1 cup paleo dressing

- 1 tbsp balsamic vinegar
- Salt and black pepper to taste
- 1 tsp turmeric

Directions:
1. Preheat on AirFry function to 360 F. Add the pumpkin wedges in a baking tray and press Start. Cook for 20 minutes. In a bowl, mix lime juice, vinegar, turmeric, salt, pepper, and paprika. Pour the mixture over pumpkin and cook for 5 more minutes. Serve.

42. Cheese & Zucchini Cake With Yogurt

Servings:4
Cooking Time: 20 Minutes
Ingredients:
- 1 ½ cups flour
- 1 tsp cinnamon
- 3 eggs
- 1 tsp baking powder
- 2 tbsp sugar
- 1 cup milk
- 2 tbsp butter, melted
- 1 tbsp yogurt
- ½ cup zucchini, shredded
- A pinch of salt
- 2 tbsp cream cheese, softened

Directions:
1. In a bowl, whisk eggs with sugar, salt, cinnamon, cream cheese, flour, and baking powder. In another bowl, combine all of the liquid ingredients. Gently combine the dry and liquid mixtures.
2. Stir in zucchini. Line the muffin tins with baking paper and pour in the batter. Arrange on a baking tray and place in the oven. Press Start and cook for 15 minutes. Serve chilled.

43. Turmeric Mushroom(1)

Servings: 4
Cooking Time: 20 Minutes
Ingredients:
- 1 lb. brown mushrooms
- 4 garlic cloves; minced
- ¼ tsp. cinnamon powder
- 1 tsp. olive oil
- ½ tsp. turmeric powder
- Salt and black pepper to taste.

Directions:
1. In a bowl, combine all the ingredients and toss.
2. Put the mushrooms in your air fryer's basket and cook at 370°F for 15 minutes
3. Divide the mix between plates and serve as a side dish.
- **Nutrition Info:** Calories: 208; Fat: 7g; Fiber: 3g; Carbs: 5g; Protein: 7g

44. Potato Croquettes

Servings: 4
Cooking Time: 8 Minutes
Ingredients:
- 2 medium Russet potatoes, peeled and cubed
- 2 tablespoons all-purpose flour
- ½ cup Parmesan cheese, grated
- 1 egg yolk
- 2 tablespoons chives, minced
- Pinch of ground nutmeg Salt and freshly ground black pepper, as needed
- 2 eggs
- ½ cup breadcrumbs
- 2 tablespoons vegetable oil

Directions:
1. In a pan of a boiling water, add the potatoes and cook for about 15 minutes.
2. Drain the potatoes well and transfer into a large bowl.
3. With a potato masher, mash the potatoes and set aside to cool completely.
4. In the bowl of mashed potatoes, add the flour, Parmesan cheese, egg yolk, chives, nutmeg, salt, and black pepper and mix until well combined.
5. Make small equal-sized balls from the mixture.
6. Now, roll each ball into a cylinder shape.
7. In a shallow dish, crack the eggs and beat well.
8. In another dish, mix together the breadcrumbs, and oil.
9. Dip the croquettes in egg mixture and then coat with the breadcrumbs mixture.
10. Press "Power Button" of Air Fry Oven and turn the dial to select the "Air Fry" mode.
11. Press the Time button and again turn the dial to set the cooking time to 8 minutes.
12. Now push the Temp button and rotate the dial to set the temperature at 390 degrees F.
13. Press "Start/Pause" button to start.
14. When the unit beeps to show that it is preheated, open the lid.
15. Arrange the croquettes in "Air Fry Basket" and insert in the oven.
16. Serve warm.
- **Nutrition Info:** Calories 283 Total Fat: 13.4 g Saturated Fat: 3.8 g Cholesterol 142 mg Sodium 263mg Total Carbs 29.9 g Fiber 3.3 g Sugar 2.3 g Protein 11.5 g

45. Sausage Mushroom Caps(3)

Servings: 2
Cooking Time: 8 Minutes
Ingredients:
- ½ lb. Italian sausage
- 6 large Portobello mushroom caps
- ¼ cup grated Parmesan cheese.
- ¼ cup chopped onion
- 2 tbsp. blanched finely ground almond flour
- 1 tsp. minced fresh garlic

Directions:
1. Use a spoon to hollow out each mushroom cap, reserving scrapings.
2. In a medium skillet over medium heat, brown the sausage about 10 minutes or until fully cooked and no pink remains. Drain and then add reserved mushroom scrapings, onion, almond flour, Parmesan and garlic.
3. Gently fold ingredients together and continue cooking an additional minute, then remove from heat
4. Evenly spoon the mixture into mushroom caps and place the caps into a 6-inch round pan. Place pan into the air fryer basket
5. Adjust the temperature to 375 Degrees F and set the timer for 8 minutes. When finished cooking, the tops will be browned and bubbling. Serve warm.
- **Nutrition Info:** Calories: 404; Protein: 24.3g; Fiber: 4.5g; Fat: 25.8g; Carbs: 18.2g

46. Goat Cheese & Pancetta Bombs

Servings: 10
Cooking Time: 25 Minutes
Ingredients:
- 16 oz soft goat cheese
- 2 tbsp fresh rosemary, finely chopped
- 1 cup almonds, chopped into small pieces
- Salt and black pepper
- 15 dried plums, chopped
- 15 pancetta slices

Directions:
1. Line the Air Fryer tray with parchment paper. In a bowl, add goat cheese, rosemary, almonds, salt, pepper, and plums; stir well. Roll into balls and wrap with pancetta slices. Arrange the bombs on the tray and cook for 10 minutes at 400 F. Let cool before serving.

47. Yogurt Masala Cashew

Servings: 2
Cooking Time: 25 Minutes
Ingredients:
- 8 oz Greek yogurt
- 2 tbsp mango powder
- 8¾ oz cashew nuts
- Salt and black pepper to taste
- 1 tsp coriander powder
- ½ tsp masala powder
- ½ tsp black pepper powder

Directions:
1. Preheat on Air Fry function to 350 F. In a bowl, mix all powders, salt, and pepper. Add in cashews and toss to coat thoroughly. Place the cashews in your Air Fryer baking

pan and cook for 15 minutes, shaking every 5 minutes. Serve.

48. Traditional Indian Kofta

Servings: 4
Cooking Time: 20 Minutes
Ingredients:
- Veggie Balls:
- 3/4-pound zucchini, grated and well drained
- 1/4-pound kohlrabi, grated and well drained
- 2 cloves garlic, minced
- 1 tablespoon Garam masala
- 1 cup paneer, crumbled
- 1/4 cup coconut flour
- 1/2 teaspoon chili powder
- Himalayan pink salt and ground black pepper, to taste
- Sauce:
- 1 tablespoon sesame oil
- 1/2 teaspoon cumin seeds
- 2 cloves garlic, roughly chopped
- 1 onion, chopped
- 1 Kashmiri chili pepper, seeded and minced
- 1 (1-inchpiece ginger, chopped
- 1 teaspoon paprika
- 1 teaspoon turmeric powder
- 2 ripe tomatoes, pureed
- 1/2 cup vegetable broth
- 1/4 full fat coconut milk

Directions:
1. Start by preheating your Air Fryer to 360 degrees F. Thoroughly combine the zucchini, kohlrabi, garlic, Garam masala, paneer, coconut flour, chili powder, salt and ground black pepper.
2. Shape the vegetable mixture into small balls and arrange them in the lightly greased cooking basket.
3. Cook in the preheated Air Fryer at 360 degrees F for 15 minutes or until thoroughly cooked and crispy. Repeat the process until you run out of ingredients.
4. Heat the sesame oil in a saucepan over medium heat and add the cumin seeds. Once the cumin seeds turn brown, add the garlic, onions, chili pepper, and ginger. Sauté for 2 to 3 minutes.
5. Add the paprika, turmeric powder, tomatoes, and broth; let it simmer, covered, for 4 to 5 minutes, stirring occasionally.
6. Add the coconut milk. Heat off; add the veggie balls and gently stir to combine.
- **Nutrition Info:** 259 Calories; 11g Fat; 1g Carbs; 19g Protein; 3g Sugars; 4g Fiber

49. Baked Turnip & Sweet Potato

Servings: 4
Cooking Time: 30 Minutes
Ingredients:
- 1 1/2 lbs sweet potato, sliced 1/4-inch thick
- 2 tbsp olive oil
- 1 lb turnips, sliced 1/4-inch thick
- 1 tbsp thyme, chopped
- 1 tsp paprika
- 1/4 tsp pepper
- 1/2 tsp sea salt

Directions:
1. Fit the oven with the rack in position
2. Add sliced sweet potatoes and turnips in a bowl and toss with seasoning and olive oil.
3. Arrange sliced sweet potatoes and turnips in baking dish.
4. Set to bake at 425 F for 35 minutes. After 5 minutes place the baking dish in the preheated oven.
5. Garnish with thyme and serve.
- **Nutrition Info:** Calories: 250 Fat: 7.4 g Carbohydrates 43.5 g Sugar 15.8 g Protein 4.5 g Cholesterol 0 mg

50. Simple Cauliflower Poppers

Servings: 4
Cooking Time: 8 Minutes
Ingredients:
- ½ large head cauliflower, cut into bite-sized florets
- 1 tablespoon olive oil
- Salt and ground black pepper, as required

Directions:
1. In a bowl, add all the ingredients and toss to coat well.
2. Press "Power Button" of Air Fry Oven and turn the dial to select the "Air Fry" mode.
3. Press the Time button and again turn the dial to set the cooking time to 8 minutes.
4. Now push the Temp button and rotate the dial to set the temperature at 390 degrees F.
5. Press "Start/Pause" button to start.
6. When the unit beeps to show that it is preheated, open the lid.
7. Arrange the cauliflower florets in "Air Fry Basket" and insert in the oven.
8. Toss the cauliflower florets once halfway through.
9. Serve warm.
- **Nutrition Info:** Calories 38 Total Fat: 23.5 g Saturated Fat: 0.5 g Cholesterol 0 mg Sodium 49 mg Total Carbs 1.8 g Fiber 0.8 g Sugar 0.8 g Protein 0.7 g

51. Savory Parsley Crab Cakes

Servings: 6
Cooking Time: 20 Minutes
Ingredients:
- 1 lb crab meat, shredded
- 2 eggs, beaten

- ½ cup breadcrumbs
- ⅓ cup finely chopped green onion
- ¼ cup parsley, chopped
- 1 tbsp mayonnaise
- 1 tsp sweet chili sauce
- ½ tsp paprika
- Salt and black pepper to taste

Directions:
1. In a bowl, add crab meat, eggs, crumbs, green onion, parsley, mayo, chili sauce, paprika, salt and black pepper; mix well with your hands.
2. Shape into 6 cakes and grease them lightly with oil. Arrange them in the fryer basket without overcrowding. Fit in the baking tray and cook for 8 minutes at 400 F on Air Fry function, turning once halfway through.

52. Creamy Broccoli Casserole

Servings: 6
Cooking Time: 30 Minutes
Ingredients:
- 16 oz frozen broccoli florets, defrosted and drained
- 1/2 tsp onion powder
- 10.5 oz can cream of mushroom soup
- 1 cup cheddar cheese, shredded
- 1/3 cup almond milk
- For topping:
- 1 tbsp butter, melted
- 1/2 cup cracker crumbs

Directions:
1. Fit the oven with the rack in position
2. Add all ingredients except topping ingredients into the 1.5-qt casserole dish.
3. In a small bowl, mix together cracker crumbs and melted butter and sprinkle over the casserole dish mixture.
4. Set to bake at 350 F for 35 minutes. After 5 minutes place the casserole dish in the preheated oven.
5. Serve and enjoy.
- **Nutrition Info:** Calories: 203 Fat: 13.5 g Carbohydrates 11.9 g Sugar 3.6 g Protein 6.9 g Cholesterol 26 mg

53. Cajun Shrimp

Servings:3
Cooking Time: 15 Minutes
Ingredients:
- ½ pound shrimp, deveined
- ½ tsp Cajun seasoning
- Salt and black pepper to taste
- 1 tbsp olive oil

Directions:
1. Preheat on AirFry function to 390 F. In a bowl, make the marinade by mixing salt, pepper, olive oil, and seasoning. Add in the shrimp and toss to coat. Transfer the

prepared shrimp to the frying basket and place in the oven. Press Start and cook for 10-12 minutes.

54. Spicy Brussels Sprouts(2)

Servings: 4
Cooking Time: 15 Minutes
Ingredients:
- 1 lb Brussels sprouts, cut in half
- 1 1/2 tbsp olive oil
- 1 tbsp gochujang
- 1/2 tsp salt

Directions:
1. Fit the oven with the rack in position 2.
2. In a large mixing bowl, mix together olive oil, gochujang, and salt.
3. Add Brussels sprouts into the bowl and toss until well coated.
4. Transfer Brussels sprouts in air fryer basket then place air fryer basket in baking pan.
5. Place a baking pan on the oven rack. Set to air fry at 360 F for 20 minutes.
6. Serve and enjoy.
- **Nutrition Info:** Calories: 98 Fat: 5.6 g Carbohydrates 11.2 g Sugar 3 g Protein 4 g Cholesterol 0 mg

55. Easy Parsnip Fries

Servings: 3
Cooking Time: 15 Minutes
Ingredients:
- 4 parsnips, sliced
- ¼ cup flour
- ¼ cup olive oil
- ¼ cup water
- A pinch of salt

Directions:
1. Preheat on Air Fry function to 390 F. In a bowl, add the flour, olive oil, water, and parsnips; mix to coat. Line the fries in the greased Air Fryer basket and fit in the baking tray. Cook for 15 minutes. Serve with yogurt and garlic dip.

56. Cod Nuggets

Servings: 5
Cooking Time: 8 Minutes
Ingredients:
- 1 cup all-purpose flour
- 2 eggs
- ¾ cup breadcrumbs
- Pinch of salt
- 2 tablespoons olive oil
- 1 lb. cod, cut into 1x2½-inch strips

Directions:
1. In a shallow dish, place the flour.
2. Crack the eggs in a second dish and beat well.

3. In a third dish, mix together the breadcrumbs, salt, and oil.
4. Coat the nuggets with flour, then dip into beaten eggs and finally, coat with the breadcrumbs.
5. Press "Power Button" of Air Fry Oven and turn the dial to select the "Air Fry" mode.
6. Press the Time button and again turn the dial to set the cooking time to 8 minutes.
7. Now push the Temp button and rotate the dial to set the temperature at 390 degrees F.
8. Press "Start/Pause" button to start.
9. When the unit beeps to show that it is preheated, open the lid.
10. Arrange the nuggets in "Air Fry Basket" and insert in the oven.
11. Serve warm.
- **Nutrition Info:** Calories 323 Total Fat: 9.2 g Saturated Fat: 1.7 g Cholesterol 115 mg Sodium 245 mg Total Carbs 30.9 g Fiber 1.4 g Sugar 1.2 g Protein 27.7 g

57. Spicy Brussels Sprouts(1)

Servings: 2

Cooking Time: 15 Minutes

Ingredients:
- 1/2 lb Brussels sprouts, trimmed and halved
- 1 tbsp chives, chopped
- 1/4 tsp cayenne
- 1/2 tsp chili powder
- 1/2 tbsp olive oil
- Pepper
- Salt

Directions:
1. Fit the oven with the rack in position
2. Add all ingredients into the large bowl and toss well.
3. Spread Brussels sprouts in baking pan.
4. Set to bake at 370 F for 20 minutes. After 5 minutes place the baking pan in the preheated oven.
5. Serve and enjoy.
- **Nutrition Info:** Calories: 82 Fat: 4.1 g Carbohydrates 10.9 g Sugar 2.6 g Protein 4 g Cholesterol 0 mg

BREAKFAST RECIPES

58. Apple Fritter Loaf

Servings: 10
Cooking Time: 1 Hour
Ingredients:
- Butter flavored cooking spray
- 1/3 cup brown sugar, packed
- 1 tsp. cinnamon, divided
- 1 ½ cups apples, chopped
- 2/3 cup + 1 tsp. sugar, divided
- ½ cup + ½ tbsp. butter, soft, divided
- 2 eggs
- 2 ¼ tsp. vanilla, divided
- 1 ½ cups flour
- 2 tsp baking powder
- ¼ tsp salt
- ½ cup + 2 tbsp. milk
- 1/2 cup powdered sugar

Directions:
1. Place rack in position 1 of the oven. Spray an 8-inch loaf pan with cooking spray.
2. In a small bowl, combine brown sugar and ½ teaspoon cinnamon.
3. Place apples in a medium bowl and sprinkle with remaining cinnamon and 1 teaspoon sugar, toss to coat.
4. In a large bowl, beat remaining sugar and butter until smooth.
5. Beat in eggs and 2 teaspoons vanilla until combined. Stir in flour, baking powder, and salt until combined.
6. Add ½ cup milk and beat until smooth. Pour half the batter in the prepared pan. Add half the apples then remaining batter. Add the remaining apples over the top, pressing lightly. Sprinkle brown sugar mixture over the apples.
7. Set oven to convection bake at 325°F for 5 minutes. Once timer goes, off place bread on the rack and set timer to 1 hour. Bread is done when it passes the toothpick test.
8. Let cool in pan 10 minutes, then invert onto wire rack to cool.
9. In a small bowl, whisk together powdered sugar and butter until smooth. Whisk in remaining milk and vanilla and drizzle over cooled bread.
- **Nutrition Info:** Calories: 418, Total Fat: 14g, Saturated Fat: 8g, Total Carbs 44g, Net Carbs 43g, Protein 4g, Sugar 28g, Fiber 1g, Sodium 85mg, Potassium 190mg, Phosphorus 128mg

59. Sausage Omelet

Servings: 2
Cooking Time: 13 Minutes
Ingredients:
- 4 eggs
- 1 bacon slice, chopped
- 2 sausages, chopped
- 1 yellow onion, chopped

Directions:
1. In a bowl, crack the eggs and beat well.
2. Add the remaining ingredients and gently, stir to combine.
3. Place the mixture into a baking pan.
4. Press "Power Button" of Air Fry Oven and turn the dial to select the "Air Fry" mode.
5. Press the Time button and again turn the dial to set the cooking time to 13 minutes.
6. Now push the Temp button and rotate the dial to set the temperature at 320 degrees F.
7. Press "Start/Pause" button to start.
8. When the unit beeps to show that it is preheated, open the lid.
9. Arrange pan over the "Wire Rack" and insert in the oven.
10. Cut into equal-sized wedges and serve hot.
- **Nutrition Info:** Calories 325 Total Fat: 23.1 g Saturated Fat: 7.4 g Cholesterol 368 mg Sodium 678 mg Total Carbs 6 g Fiber 1.2 g Sugar 3 g Protein 22.7 g

60. Herby Mushrooms With Vermouth

Servings:4
Cooking Time: 20 Minutes
Ingredients:
- 2 lb portobello mushrooms, sliced
- 2 tbsp vermouth
- ½ tsp garlic powder
- 1 tbsp olive oil
- 2 tsp herbs
- 1 tbsp duck fat, softened

Directions:
1. Mix duck fat, garlic powder, and herbs in a bowl. Pour the mixture over the mushrooms and top with vermouth. Place the mushrooms in a baking dish and press Start. Cook for 15 minutes on Bake function at 350 F. Serve warm.

61. Green Cottage Omelet

Servings:1
Cooking Time: 20 Minutes
Ingredients:
- 3 eggs
- 3 tbsp cottage cheese
- 3 tbsp kale, chopped
- ½ tbsp fresh parsley, chopped
- Salt and black pepper to taste
- 1 tsp olive oil

Directions:
1. Beat the eggs with a pinch of salt and black pepper in a bowl. Stir in the rest of the ingredients. Drizzle a baking pan with olive oil. Pour the pan into the oven and press

Start. Cook for 15 minutes on Bake function at 360 F until slightly golden and set. Serve warm.

62. Berry Breakfast Oatmeal

Servings: 4
Cooking Time: 20 Minutes
Ingredients:

- 1 egg
- 2 cups old fashioned oats
- 1 cup blueberries
- 1/4 cup maple syrup
- 1 1/2 cups milk
- 1/2 cup blackberries
- 1/2 cup strawberries, sliced
- 1 1/2 tsp baking powder
- 1/2 tsp salt

Directions:

1. Fit the oven with the rack in position
2. In a bowl, mix together oats, salt, and baking powder.
3. Add vanilla, egg, maple syrup, and milk and stir well. Add berries and fold well.
4. Pour mixture into the greased baking dish.
5. Set to bake at 375 F for 25 minutes. After 5 minutes place the baking dish in the preheated oven.
6. Serve and enjoy.
- **Nutrition Info:** Calories: 461 Fat: 8.4 g Carbohydrates 80.7 g Sugar 23.4 g Protein 15 g Cholesterol 48 mg

63. Whole Wheat Carrot Bread

Servings: 10
Cooking Time: 50 Minutes
Ingredients:

- 1 egg
- 3/4 cup whole wheat flour
- 1 cup carrots, shredded
- 3/4 tsp vanilla
- 3/4 cup all-purpose flour
- 1/2 cup brown sugar
- 1 tsp baking powder
- 1/2 tsp nutmeg
- 1 1/2 tsp cinnamon
- 3/4 cup yogurt
- 3 tbsp vegetable oil
- 1 tsp baking soda

Directions:

1. Fit the oven with the rack in position
2. In a large bowl, mix all dry ingredients and set aside.
3. In a separate bowl, whisk the egg with vanilla, sugar, yogurt, and oil.
4. Add carrots and fold well.
5. Add dry ingredient mixture and stir until just combined.
6. Pour mixture into the 9*5-inch greased loaf pan.

7. Set to bake at 350 F for 55 minutes, after 5 minutes, place the loaf pan in the oven.
8. Slice and serve.
- **Nutrition Info:** Calories: 159 Fat: 5 g Carbohydrates 24.4 g Sugar 9 g Protein 3.7 g Cholesterol 17 mg

64. Creamy Bacon & Egg Wraps With Spicy Salsa

Servings: 3
Cooking Time: 15 Minutes
Ingredients:

- 3 tortillas
- 2 previously scrambled eggs
- 3 slices bacon, cut into strips
- 3 tbsp salsa
- 3 tbsp cream cheese, divided
- 1 cup grated pepper Jack cheese

Directions:

1. Preheat on Air Fry to 390 F. Spread cream cheese onto tortillas. Divide the eggs and bacon between the tortillas. Top with salsa. Sprinkle with cheese. Roll up the tortillas. Place in a greased baking pan and cook for 10 minutes. Serve.

65. Potato Egg Casserole

Servings: 6
Cooking Time: 35 Minutes
Ingredients:

- 5 eggs
- 2 medium potatoes, cut into 1/2-inch cubes
- 1 green bell pepper, diced
- 1 small onion, chopped
- 1 tbsp olive oil
- 1/2 cup cheddar cheese, shredded
- 3/4 tsp pepper
- 3/4 tsp salt

Directions:

1. Fit the oven with the rack in position
2. Spray 9*9-inch casserole dish with cooking spray and set aside.
3. Heat oil in a pan over medium heat.
4. Add onion and sauté for 1 minute. Add potatoes, bell peppers, 1/2 tsp pepper, and 1/2 tsp salt and sauté for 4 minutes.
5. Transfer sautéed vegetables to the prepared casserole dish and spread evenly.
6. In a bowl, whisk eggs with remaining pepper and salt.
7. Pour egg mixture over sautéed vegetables in a casserole dish. Sprinkle cheese on top.
8. Set to bake at 350 F for 40 minutes. After 5 minutes place the casserole dish in the preheated oven.
9. Serve and enjoy.
- **Nutrition Info:** Calories: 171 Fat: 9.2 g Carbohydrates 14.3 g Sugar 2.6 g Protein 8.5 g Cholesterol 146 mg

66. Turkey Sliders With Chive Mayo

Servings:6
Cooking Time: 15 Minutes
Ingredients:
- 12 burger buns
- Cooking spray
- Turkey Sliders:
- ¾ pound (340 g) turkey, minced
- 1 tablespoon oyster sauce
- ¼ cup pickled jalapeno, chopped
- 2 tablespoons chopped scallions
- 1 tablespoon chopped fresh cilantro
- 1 to 2 cloves garlic, minced
- Sea salt and ground black pepper, to taste
- Chive Mayo:
- 1 tablespoon chives
- 1 cup mayonnaise
- Zest of 1 lime
- 1 teaspoon salt

Directions:
1. Spritz the air fryer basket with cooking spray.
2. Combine the ingredients for the turkey sliders in a large bowl. Stir to mix well. Shape the mixture into 6 balls, then bash the balls into patties.
3. Arrange the patties in the pan and spritz with cooking spray.
4. Put the air fryer basket on the baking pan and slide into Rack Position 2, select Air Fry, set temperature to 365ºF (185ºC) and set time to 15 minutes.
5. Flip the patties halfway through the cooking time.
6. Meanwhile, combine the ingredients for the chive mayo in a small bowl. Stir to mix well.
7. When cooked, the patties will be well browned.
8. Smear the patties with chive mayo, then assemble the patties between two buns to make the sliders. Serve immediately.

67. Walnuts And Mango Oatmeal

Servings: 4
Cooking Time: 20 Minutes
Ingredients:
- 2 cups almond milk
- ½ cup walnuts, chopped
- 1 teaspoon vanilla extract
- 1 cup mango, peeled and cubed
- 3 tablespoons sugar
- ½ cup steel cut oats

Directions:
1. In your air fryer, combine the almond milk with the oats and the other ingredients, toss and cook at 360 degrees F for 20 minutes.
2. Divide the mix into bowls and serve for breakfast.

- **Nutrition Info:** calories 141, Fat: 4, fiber 7, carbs 8, protein 5

68. Shrimp And Zucchini Curry Potstickers

Servings:10
Cooking Time: 5 Minutes
Ingredients:
- ½ pound (227 g) peeled and deveined shrimp, finely chopped
- 1 medium zucchini, coarsely grated
- 1 tablespoon fish sauce
- 1 tablespoon green curry paste
- 2 scallions, thinly sliced
- ¼ cup basil, chopped
- 30 round dumpling wrappers
- Cooking spray

Directions:
1. Combine the chopped shrimp, zucchini, fish sauce, curry paste, scallions, and basil in a large bowl. Stir to mix well.
2. Unfold the dumpling wrappers on a clean work surface, dab a little water around the edges of each wrapper, then scoop up 1 teaspoon of filling in the middle of each wrapper.
3. Make the potstickers: Fold the wrappers in half and press the edges to seal.
4. Spritz the air fryer basket with cooking spray.
5. Transfer the potstickers to the pan and spritz with cooking spray.
6. Put the air fryer basket on the baking pan and slide into Rack Position 2, select Air Fry, set temperature to 350ºF (180ºC) and set time to 5 minutes.
7. Flip the potstickers halfway through the cooking time.
8. When cooking is complete, the potstickers should be crunchy and lightly browned.
9. Serve immediately.

69. Latkes

Servings: 5
Cooking Time: 7 Minutes
Ingredients:
- 1 large onion
- 5 large potatoes peeled
- 4 large eggs
- ¼ cup potato starch
- 2 tsp kosher salt
- ½ tsp baking powder
- Olive oil

Directions:
1. Scrub your potatoes well and place them in a food processor. Besides, place the shredded potatoes in a bowl of cool water and set it aside.

2. Rinse the food in the processor and grate the onions. Place your grated onions in a paper towel and squeeze out the liquid.
3. In a medium sized bowl whisk your eggs and add matzo, pepper, 1 tsp potato starch, baking powder and grated onion. Drain the water from the potatoes and save the starch that remains in your bowl.
4. Scoop the starch from the potato bowl and add to the latke mixture. Form latkes from the mixture in flat circles and dip into dry potato starch. Add oil and place them in an air fryer
5. Air fry your latkes at 360-degree Fahrenheit for 8 minutes
6. and turn in the middle once it indicates turn food.
7. Serve while hot.
- **Nutrition Info:** Calories 68 Fat: 4g, Carbohydrates 6g, Protein 2g.

70. Buttery Orange Toasts

Servings:6
Cooking Time: 15 Minutes
Ingredients:
- 12 bread slices
- ½ cup sugar
- 1 stick butter
- 1 ½ tbsp vanilla extract
- 1 ½ tbsp cinnamon
- 2 oranges, zested

Directions:
1. Mix butter, sugar, and vanilla extract and microwave the mixture for 30 seconds until it melts. Add in orange zest. Spread the mixture onto bread slices. Lay the bread slices on the cooking basket and cook in the oven for 5 minutes at 400 F on Toast function. Serve warm.

71. Bacon And Cheddar Cheese Frittata

Servings:x
Cooking Time:x
Ingredients:
- 8 slices bacon, chopped
- ½ cup grated cheddar cheese
- 12 large eggs
- 3 Tbsp milk
- Coarse salt, freshly ground pepper, to taste
- ¼ cup Romano cheese
- Dash of hot sauce

Directions:
1. Preheat oven to 375°F.
2. Heat oven and cook bacon over medium heat, stirring until crisp.
3. Set aside on a plate.
4. In a bowl, whisk eggs, milk, salt, pepper, cheeses and hot sauce.
5. Add cooked bacon to egg mixture.

6. Pour eggs into oven. When eggs are half set and edges begin to
7. pull away, place frittata in oven and bake for about 10 minutes, or until
8. center is no longer jiggly.
9. Cut into wedges inside pot or slide out onto serving plate.

72. Easy Apple Pie Baked Oatmeal

Servings: 4
Cooking Time: 30 Minutes
Ingredients:
- 1 cup rolled oats
- 1/4 tsp nutmeg
- 2 tsp cinnamon
- 2 tbsp maple syrup
- 1/4 cup milk
- 1/2 cup raisins
- 1 banana, sliced
- 2 apples, diced
- 1 cup boiling water

Directions:
1. Fit the oven with the rack in position
2. Add oats and boiling water in a mixing bowl and let sit for 10 minutes.
3. After 10 minutes add remaining ingredients to the bowl and mix well.
4. Pour mixture into the greased baking dish.
5. Set to bake at 350 F for 35 minutes. After 5 minutes place the baking dish in the preheated oven.
6. Serve and enjoy.
- **Nutrition Info:** Calories: 253 Fat: 2.1 g Carbohydrates 58.8 g Sugar 32.8 g Protein 4.4 g Cholesterol 1 mg

73. Cinnamon Sweet Potato Chips

Servings: 6 To 8 Slices
Cooking Time: 8 Minutes
Ingredients:
- 1 small sweet potato, cut into ⅜ inch-thick slices
- 2 tablespoons olive oil
- 1 to 2 teaspoon ground cinnamon

Directions:
1. Add the sweet potato slices and olive oil in a bowl and toss to coat. Fold in the cinnamon and stir to combine.
2. Lay the sweet potato slices in a single layer in the air fryer basket.
3. Put the air fryer basket on the baking pan and slide into Rack Position 2, select Air Fry, set temperature to 390ºF (199ºC), and set time to 8 minutes.
4. Stir the potato slices halfway through the cooking time.
5. When cooking is complete, the chips should be crisp. Remove the pan from the oven. Allow to cool for 5 minutes before serving.

74. Banana And Oat Bread Pudding

Servings:4
Cooking Time: 16 Minutes
Ingredients:

- 2 medium ripe bananas, mashed
- ½ cup low-fat milk
- 2 tablespoons maple syrup
- 2 tablespoons peanut butter
- 1 teaspoon vanilla extract
- 1 teaspoon ground cinnamon
- 2 slices whole-grain bread, cut into bite-sized cubes
- ¼ cup quick oats
- Cooking spray

Directions:

1. Spritz the baking pan lightly with cooking spray.
2. Mix the bananas, milk, maple syrup, peanut butter, vanilla, and cinnamon in a large mixing bowl and stir until well incorporated.
3. Add the bread cubes to the banana mixture and stir until thoroughly coated. Fold in the oats and stir to combine.
4. Transfer the mixture to the baking pan. Wrap the baking pan in aluminum foil.
5. Slide the baking pan into Rack Position 2, select Air Fry, set temperature to 350ºF (180ºC) and set time to 16 minutes.
6. After 10 minutes, remove the pan from the oven. Remove the foil. Return the pan to the oven and continue to cook for another 6 minutes.
7. When done, the pudding should be set.
8. Let the pudding cool for 5 minutes before serving.

75. Beans And Pork Mix

Servings: 4
Cooking Time: 20 Minutes
Ingredients:

- 1-pound pork stew meat, ground
- 1 red onion, chopped
- 1 tablespoon olive oil
- 1 cup canned kidney beans, drained and rinsed
- 1 teaspoon chili powder
- Salt and black pepper to the taste
- ¼ teaspoon cumin, ground

Directions:

1. Heat up your air fryer at 360 degrees F, add the meat and the onion and cook for 5 minutes.
2. Add the beans and the rest of the ingredients, toss and cook for 15 minutes more.
3. Divide everything into bowls and serve for breakfast.
- **Nutrition Info:** calories 203, Fat: 4, fiber 6, carbs 12, protein 4

76. Almond & Cinnamon Berry Oat Bars

Servings: 10
Cooking Time: 40 Minutes
Ingredients:

- 3 cups rolled oats
- ½ cup ground almonds
- ½ cup flour
- 1 tsp baking powder
- 1 tsp ground cinnamon
- 3 eggs, lightly beaten
- ½ cup canola oil
- ⅓ cup milk
- 2 tsp vanilla extract
- 2 cups mixed berries

Directions:

1. Spray the baking pan with cooking spray. In a bowl, add oats, almonds, flour, baking powder and cinnamon into and stir well. In another bowl, whisk eggs, oil, milk, and vanilla.
2. Stir the wet ingredients gently into the oat mixture. Fold in the berries. Pour the mixture in the pan and place in the toaster oven. Cook for 15-20 minutes at 350 F on Bake function until is nice and soft. Let cool and cut into bars to serve.

77. Mushroom & Pepperoncini Omelet

Servings: 2
Cooking Time: 20 Minutes
Ingredients:

- 3 large eggs
- ¼ c milk
- Salt and ground black pepper, as required
- ½ cup cheddar cheese, shredded
- ¼ cup cooked mushrooms
- 3 pepperoncini peppers, sliced thinly
- ½ tablespoon scallion, sliced thinly

Directions:

1. In a bowl, add the eggs, milk, salt and black pepper and beat well.
2. Place the mixture into a greased baking pan.
3. Press "Power Button" of Air Fry Oven and turn the dial to select the "Air Bake" mode.
4. Press the Time button and again turn the dial to set the cooking time to 20 minutes.
5. Now push the Temp button and rotate the dial to set the temperature at 350 degrees F.
6. Press "Start/Pause" button to start.
7. When the unit beeps to show that it is preheated, open the lid.
8. Arrange pan over the "Wire Rack" and insert in the oven.
9. Cut into equal-sized wedges and serve hot.
- **Nutrition Info:** Calories 254 Total Fat: 17.5 g Saturated Fat: 8.7 g Cholesterol 311 mg Sodium 793 mg Total Carbs 7.3 g Fiber 0.1 g Sugar 3.8 g Protein 8.2 g

78. Mushroom Leek Frittata

Servings: 4
Cooking Time: 32 Minutes
Ingredients:
- 6 eggs
- 6 oz mushrooms, sliced 1 cup leeks, sliced
- Salt

Directions:
1. Preheat the air fryer to 325 F.
2. Spray air fryer baking dish with cooking spray and set aside.
3. Heat another pan over medium heat. Spray pan with cooking spray.
4. Add mushrooms, leeks, and salt in a pan sauté for 6 minutes.
5. Break eggs in a bowl and whisk well.
6. Transfer sautéed mushroom and leek mixture into the prepared baking dish.
7. Pour egg over mushroom mixture.
8. Place dish in the air fryer and cook for 32 minutes.
9. Serve and enjoy.
- **Nutrition Info:** Calories 116 Fat: 7 g Carbohydrates 5.1 g Sugar 2.1 g Protein 10 g Cholesterol 245 mg

79. Blueberry Cake

Servings:8
Cooking Time: 10 Minutes
Ingredients:
- 1½ cups Bisquick
- ¼ cup granulated sugar
- 2 large eggs, beaten
- ¾ cup whole milk
- 1 teaspoon vanilla extract
- ½ teaspoon lemon zest
- Cooking spray
- 2 cups blueberries

Directions:
1. Stir together the Bisquick and sugar in a medium bowl. Stir together the eggs, milk, vanilla and lemon zest. Add the wet ingredients to the dry ingredients and stir until well combined.
2. Spritz the baking pan with cooking spray and line with parchment paper, pressing it into place. Spray the parchment paper with cooking spray. Pour the batter into the pan and spread it out evenly. Sprinkle the blueberries evenly over the top.
3. Slide the baking pan into Rack Position 1, select Convection Bake, set temperature to 375ºF (190ºC) and set time to 10 minutes.
4. When cooking is complete, the cake should be pulling away from the edges of the pan and the top should be just starting to turn golden brown.
5. Let the cake rest for a minute before cutting into 16 squares. Serve immediately.

80. Avocado And Tomato Egg Rolls

Servings:5
Cooking Time: 5 Minutes
Ingredients:
- 10 egg roll wrappers
- 3 avocados, peeled and pitted
- 1 tomato, diced
- Salt and ground black pepper, to taste
- Cooking spray

Directions:
1. Spritz the air fryer basket with cooking spray.
2. Put the tomato and avocados in a food processor. Sprinkle with salt and ground black pepper. Pulse to mix and coarsely mash until smooth.
3. Unfold the wrappers on a clean work surface, then divide the mixture in the center of each wrapper. Roll the wrapper up and press to seal.
4. Transfer the rolls to the pan and spritz with cooking spray.
5. Put the air fryer basket on the baking pan and slide into Rack Position 2, select Air Fry, set temperature to 350ºF (180ºC) and set time to 5 minutes.
6. Flip the rolls halfway through the cooking time.
7. When cooked, the rolls should be golden brown.
8. Serve immediately.

81. Quick Cheddar Omelet

Servings:1
Cooking Time: 15 Minutes
Ingredients:
- 2 eggs, beaten
- 1 cup cheddar cheese, shredded
- 1 whole onion, chopped
- 2 tbsp soy sauce

Directions:
1. Preheat on AirFry function to 340 F. Drizzle soy sauce over the chopped onions. Sauté the onions ina greased pan over medium heat for 5 minutes; turn off the heat.
2. In a bowl, mix the eggs with salt and pepper. Pour the egg mixture over onions and cook in the for 6 minutes. Top with cheddar cheese and bake for 4 more minutes. Serve and enjoy!

82. Corned Beef Hash With Eggs

Servings:4
Cooking Time: 25 Minutes
Ingredients:
- 2 medium Yukon Gold potatoes, peeled and cut into ¼-inch cubes
- 1 medium onion, chopped
- $1/3$ cup diced red bell pepper

- 3 tablespoons vegetable oil
- ½ teaspoon dried thyme
- ½ teaspoon kosher salt, divided
- ½ teaspoon freshly ground black pepper, divided
- ¾ pound (340 g) corned beef, cut into ¼-inch pieces
- 4 large eggs

Directions:
1. In a large bowl, stir together the potatoes, onion, red pepper, vegetable oil, thyme, ¼ teaspoon of the salt and ¼ teaspoon of the pepper. Spread the vegetable mixture into the baking pan in an even layer.
2. Slide the baking pan into Rack Position 2, select Roast, set temperature to 375ºF (190ºC) and set time to 25 minutes.
3. After 15 minutes, remove the pan from the oven and add the corned beef. Stir the mixture to incorporate the corned beef. Return the pan to the oven and continue cooking.
4. After 5 minutes, remove the pan from the oven. Using a large spoon, create 4 circles in the hash to hold the eggs. Gently crack an egg into each circle. Season the eggs with the remaining ¼ teaspoon of the salt and ¼ teaspoon of the pepper. Return the pan to the oven. Continue cooking for 3 to 5 minutes, depending on how you like your eggs.
5. When cooking is complete, remove the pan from the oven. Serve immediately.

83. Honey Banana Pastry With Berries

Servings: 2
Cooking Time: 15 Minutes
Ingredients:
- 3 bananas, sliced
- 3 tbsp honey
- 2 puff pastry sheets, cut into thin strips
- Fresh berries to serve

Directions:
1. Preheat on Bake function to 340 F. Place the banana slices into a baking dish. Cover with the pastry strips and top with honey. Cook for 12 minutes. Serve with berries.

84. Avocado Oil Gluten Free Banana Bread Recipe

Servings:x
Cooking Time:x
Ingredients:
- 1/2 cup Granulated Sugar
- 1 cup Mashed Banana
- 1/2 cup Light Brown Sugar
- 1/3 cup Avocado Oil, (or canola oil)
- 2 cups All-Purpose Gluten Free Flour, (see notes)

- 3/4 teaspoon Xanthan Gum, (omit if your flour blend contains it)
- 1 teaspoon Baking Powder
- 1/2 teaspoon Baking Soda
- 1/2 teaspoon Fine Sea Salt
- 2 large Eggs, room temperature
- 2/3 cup Milk, (dairy free or regular milk), room temperature
- 1 teaspoon Pure Vanilla Extract

Directions:
1. Preheat oven to 350°F and spray a 9x9 inch square pan with non-stick spray and line with parchment paper.
2. In a large bowl, whisk together the flour, xanthan gum, baking powder, baking soda, salt, and granulated sugar.
3. In a separate bowl, whisk together the mashed banana, brown sugar, oil, eggs, milk, and vanilla extract. Pour the wet ingredients into the dry ingredients and stir to combine.
4. Pour the batter into the prepared pan and bake at 350°F for 25-30 minutes or until a toothpick or cake tester comes out clean or with a few moist crumbs attached. Cooking time will vary depending on your oven - mine took 29 minutes.
5. Cool the bread in the pan on a cooling rack. Cut into 16 pieces and serve slightly warm or room temperature.
6. To store, wrap tightly in foil or store slices in an air-tight container. It will stay fresh up to 3 days. This bread also freezes well. To freeze, slice into individual pieces and freeze in a freezer bag.

85. Cheesy Hash Brown Cups

Servings:6
Cooking Time: 9 Minutes
Ingredients:
- 4 eggs, beaten
- 2¼ cups frozen hash browns, thawed
- 1 cup diced ham
- ½ cup shredded Cheddar cheese
- ½ teaspoon Cajun seasoning
- Cooking spray

Directions:
1. Lightly spritz a 12-cup muffin tin with cooking spray.
2. Combine the beaten eggs, hash browns, diced ham, cheese, and Cajun seasoning in a medium bowl and stir until well blended.
3. Spoon a heaping 1½ tablespoons of egg mixture into each muffin cup.
4. Put the muffin tin into Rack Position 1, select Convection Bake, set temperature to 350ºF (180ºC) and set time to 9 minutes.
5. When cooked, the muffins will be golden brown.

6. Allow to cool for 5 to 10 minutes on a wire rack and serve warm.

86. Mediterranean Spinach Frittata

Servings: 6
Cooking Time: 20 Minutes
Ingredients:
- 6 eggs
- 1/2 cup frozen spinach, drained the excess liquid
- 1/4 cup feta cheese, crumbled
- 1/4 cup olives, chopped
- 1/4 cup kalamata olives, chopped
- 1/2 cup tomatoes, diced
- 1/2 tsp garlic powder
- 1 tsp oregano
- 1/4 cup milk
- 1/2 tsp pepper
- 1/4 tsp salt

Directions:
1. Fit the oven with the rack in position
2. Spray 9-inch pie pan with cooking spray and set aside.
3. In a bowl, whisk eggs with oregano, garlic powder, milk, pepper, and salt until well combined.
4. Add olives, feta cheese, tomatoes, and spinach and mix well.
5. Pour egg mixture into the prepared pie pan.
6. Set to bake at 400 F for 25 minutes. After 5 minutes place the pie pan in the preheated oven.
7. Serve and enjoy.
- **Nutrition Info:** Calories: 103 Fat: 7.2 g Carbohydrates 2.9 g Sugar 1.5 g Protein 7.2 g Cholesterol 170 mg

87. Cashew Granola With Cranberries

Servings:6
Cooking Time: 12 Minutes
Ingredients:
- 3 cups old-fashioned rolled oats
- 2 cups raw cashews
- 1 cup unsweetened coconut chips
- ½ cup honey
- ¼ cup vegetable oil
- $^1/_3$ cup packed light brown sugar
- ¼ teaspoon kosher salt
- 1 cup dried cranberries

Directions:
1. In a large bowl, stir together all the ingredients, except for the cranberries. Spread the mixture in the baking pan in an even layer.
2. Slide the baking pan into Rack Position 1, select Convection Bake, set temperature to 325ºF (163ºC) and set time to 12 minutes.

3. After 5 to 6 minutes, remove the pan and stir the granola. Return the pan to the oven and continue cooking.
4. When cooking is complete, remove the pan. Let the granola cool to room temperature. Stir in the cranberries before serving.

88. Wheat &seed Bread

Servings: 4
Cooking Time: 18 Minutes
Ingredients:
- 31/2 ounces of flour
- 1 tsp. of yeast
- 1 tsp. of salt
- 3 &1/2 ounces of wheat flour ¼ cup of pumpkin seeds

Directions:
1. Mix the wheat flour, yeast, salt, seeds and the plain flour together in a large bowl. Stir in ¾ cup of lukewarm water and keep stirring until dough becomes soft.
2. Knead for another 5 minutes until the dough becomes elastic and smooth. Mold into a ball and cover with a plastic bag. Set aside for 30 minutes for it to rise.
3. Heat your air fryer to 392°F.
4. Transfer the dough into a small pizza pan and place in the air fryer. Bake for 18 minutes until golden. Remove and place on a wire rack to cool.
- **Nutrition Info:** Calories 116 Fat: 9.4 g Carbohydrates 0.3 g Sugar 0.2 g Protein 6 g Cholesterol 21 mg

89. Cheesy Hash Brown Casserole

Servings: 8
Cooking Time: 45 Minutes
Ingredients:
- 32 oz hash browns
- 1 stick butter, melted
- 1/3 tsp black pepper
- 16 oz sour cream
- 2 cups cheddar cheese, grated
- 1 small onion, diced
- 10 oz can chicken soup

Directions:
1. Fit the oven with the rack in position
2. Spray 9*13-inch casserole dish with cooking spray and set aside.
3. In a large bowl, add hash browns, 1 1/2 cups cheddar cheese, onion, sour cream, soup, butter, and black pepper and mix until well combined.
4. Transfer hash brown mixture into the prepared casserole dish and spread well.
5. Top with remaining cheese.
6. Set to bake at 350 F for 50 minutes. After 5 minutes place the casserole dish in the preheated oven.

7. Serve and enjoy.
- **Nutrition Info:** Calories: 673 Fat: 49 g Carbohydrates 46 g Sugar 2.5 g Protein 13.3 g Cholesterol 88 mg

90. Buttered Apple & Brie Cheese Sandwich

Servings: 1
Cooking Time: 10 Minutes
Ingredients:
- 2 bread slices
- ½ apple, thinly sliced
- 2 tsp butter
- 2 oz brie cheese, thinly sliced

Directions:
1. Spread butter on the bread slices. Top with apple slices. Place brie slices on top of the apples. Finish with the other slice of bread. Cook in for 5 minutes at 350 F on Bake function.

91. Ham And Cheese Bagel Sandwiches

Servings: 2
Cooking Time: 5 Minutes
Ingredients:
- 2 bagels
- 4 teaspoons honey mustard
- 4 slices cooked honey ham
- 4 slices Swiss cheese

Directions:
1. Start by preheating toaster oven to 400°F.
2. Spread honey mustard on each half of the bagel.
3. Add ham and cheese and close the bagel.
4. Bake the sandwich until the cheese is fully melted, approximately 5 minutes.
- **Nutrition Info:** Calories: 588, Sodium: 1450 mg, Dietary Fiber: 2.3 g, Total Fat: 20.1 g, Total Carbs: 62.9 g, Protein: 38.4 g.

92. Crispy Tilapia Tacos

Servings:4
Cooking Time: 5 Minutes
Ingredients:
- 2 tablespoons milk
- $1/3$ cup mayonnaise
- ¼ teaspoon garlic powder
- 1 teaspoon chili powder
- 1½ cups panko bread crumbs
- ½ teaspoon salt
- 4 teaspoons canola oil
- 1 pound (454 g) skinless tilapia fillets, cut into 3-inch-long and 1-inch-wide strips
- 4 small flour tortillas
- Lemon wedges, for topping
- Cooking spray

Directions:
1. Spritz the air fryer basket with cooking spray.
2. Combine the milk, mayo, garlic powder, and chili powder in a bowl. Stir to mix well.

Combine the panko with salt and canola oil in a separate bowl. Stir to mix well.
3. Dredge the tilapia strips in the milk mixture first, then dunk the strips in the panko mixture to coat well. Shake the excess off.
4. Arrange the tilapia strips in the pan.
5. Put the air fryer basket on the baking pan and slide into Rack Position 2, select Air Fry, set temperature to 400ºF (205ºC) and set time to 5 minutes.
6. Flip the strips halfway through the cooking time.
7. When cooking is complete, the strips will be opaque on all sides and the panko will be golden brown.
8. Unfold the tortillas on a large plate, then divide the tilapia strips over the tortillas. Squeeze the lemon wedges on top before serving.

93. Smart Oven Breakfast Sandwich

Servings:x
Cooking Time:x
Ingredients:
- 1 large egg
- 1 slice cheese
- Salt and pepper, to taste
- 1 English muffin, split

Directions:
1. Coat a small 4-inch round metal pan with cooking oil.
2. Crack egg into prepared pan, poke yolk with a fork or toothpick, and season with salt and pepper.
3. Place pan and split English muffin in the center of the cooking rack in your toaster oven.
4. Select the TOAST setting on DARK and toast for one cycle.
5. Check the egg and muffin and remove if ready. If further cooking is needed, set for another cycle of toasting until desired level of doneness is achieved.
6. Layer egg and cheese inside English muffin and enjoy.

94. Vegetable Quiche

Servings: 6
Cooking Time: 24 Minutes
Ingredients:
- 8 eggs
- cup coconut milk
- 1 cup tomatoes, chopped 1 cup zucchini, chopped 1 tbsp butter
- 1 onion, chopped
- 1 cup Parmesan cheese, grated 1/2 tsp pepper
- tsp salt

Directions:
1. Preheat the air fryer to 370 F.
2. Melt butter in a pan over medium heat then add onion and sauté until onion lightly brown.

3. Add tomatoes and zucchini to the pan and sauté for 4-5 minutes.
4. Transfer cooked vegetables into the air fryer baking dish.
5. Beat eggs with cheese, milk, pepper, and salt in a bowl.
6. Pour egg mixture over vegetables in a baking dish.
7. Place dish in the air fryer and cook for 24 minutes or until eggs are set.
8. Slice and serve.

Nutrition Info: Calories 255 Fat: 16 g Carbohydrates 8 g Sugar 4.2 g Protein 21 g Cholesterol 257 mg

95. Spinach & Kale Balsamic Chicken

Servings: 1
Cooking Time: 20 Minutes
Ingredients:
- ½ cup baby spinach leaves
- ½ cup shredded romaine
- 3 large kale leaves, chopped
- 4 oz chicken breasts, cut into cubes
- 3 tbsp olive oil, divided
- 1 tsp balsamic vinegar
- 1 garlic clove, minced
- Salt and black pepper to taste

Directions:
1. Place the chicken, 1 tbsp of olive oil, and garlic in a bowl. Season with salt and pepper and toss to combine. Put on a lined Air Fryer pan and cook for 14 minutes at 390 F on Bake function.
2. Place the greens in a large bowl. Add the remaining olive oil and balsamic vinegar. Season with salt and pepper and toss to combine. Top with the chicken and serve.

96. Bacon Bread Egg Casserole

Servings: 4
Cooking Time: 20 Minutes
Ingredients:
- 6 eggs
- 1 cup cheddar cheese, shredded
- 1/2 tsp garlic, minced
- 3 tbsp milk
- 2 tbsp green onion, chopped
- 1/3 bell pepper, diced
- 2 bread slices, cubed
- 5 bacon slices, diced
- Pepper
- Salt

Directions:
1. Fit the oven with the rack in position
2. Add all ingredients into the large bowl and stir until well combined.
3. Pour into the greased baking dish.
4. Set to bake at 350 F for 25 minutes. After 5 minutes place the baking dish in the preheated oven.
5. Serve and enjoy.

- **Nutrition Info:** Calories: 231 Fat 26.3 g Carbohydrates 5.2 g Sugar 1.9 g Protein 25 g Cholesterol 302 mg

97. Healthy Squash

Servings: 4
Cooking Time: 25 Minutes
Ingredients:
- 2 lbs yellow squash, cut into half-moons
- 1 tsp Italian seasoning
- ¼ tsp pepper
- 1 tbsp olive oil
- ¼ tsp salt

Directions:
1. Add all ingredients into the large bowl and toss well.
2. Preheat the air fryer to 400 F.
3. Add squash mixture into the air fryer basket and cook for 10 minutes.
4. Shake basket and cook for another 10 minutes.
5. Shake once again and cook for 5 minutes more.

- **Nutrition Info:** Calories: 70, Fat 4 g, Carbohydrates 7 g, Sugar 4 g, Protein 2 g, Cholesterol 1 mg

98. Choco Chip Banana Bread

Servings: 10
Cooking Time: 50 Minutes
Ingredients:
- 2 eggs
- 3 ripe bananas
- 1 tsp vanilla
- 1 cup granulated sugar
- 1/2 cup sour cream
- 1/2 cup butter, melted
- 1/2 cup chocolate chips
- 1 1/2 cups all-purpose flour
- 1 tsp baking soda
- 1 tsp salt

Directions:
1. Fit the oven with the rack in position
2. In a large bowl, add bananas and mash using a fork until smooth.
3. Stir in sour cream and melted butter.
4. Add eggs, vanilla, sugar, and salt and stir well.
5. Add flour, baking soda, and salt and stir until just combined.
6. Add chocolate chips and stir well.
7. Pour batter into the greased 9*8-inch loaf pan.
8. Set to bake at 350 F for 55 minutes, after 5 minutes, place the loaf pan in the oven.
9. Slice and serve.

Nutrition Info: Calories 339 Fat 15.3 g Carbohydrates 48 g Sugar 28.9 g Protein 4.5 g Cholesterol 64 mg

99. Rice, Shrimp, And Spinach Frittata

Servings:4

Cooking Time: 16 Minutes
Ingredients:
- 4 eggs
- Pinch salt
- ½ cup cooked rice
- ½ cup chopped cooked shrimp
- ½ cup baby spinach
- ½ cup grated Monterey Jack cheese
- Nonstick cooking spray

Directions:
1. Spritz the baking pan with nonstick cooking spray.
2. Whisk the eggs and salt in a small bowl until frothy.
3. Place the cooked rice, shrimp, and baby spinach in the baking pan. Pour in the whisked eggs and scatter the cheese on top.
4. Slide the baking pan into Rack Position 1, select Convection Bake, set temperature to 320ºF (160ºC) and set time to 16 minutes.
5. When cooking is complete, the frittata should be golden and puffy.
6. Let the frittata cool for 5 minutes before slicing to serve.

100.Italian Sandwich

Servings:1
Cooking Time: 7 Minutes
Ingredients:
- 2 bread slices
- 4 tomato slices
- 4 mozzarella cheese slices
- 1 tbsp olive oil
- 1 tbsp fresh basil, chopped
- Salt and black pepper to taste

Directions:
1. Preheat on Toast function to 350 F. Place the bread slices in the toaster oven and toast for 5 minutes. Arrange two tomato slices on each bread slice. Season with salt and pepper.
2. Top each slice with 2 mozzarella slices. Return to the oven and cook for 1 more minute. Drizzle the caprese toasts with olive oil and top with chopped basil.

101.Air Fryer Breakfast Frittata

Servings: 2
Cooking Time: 20 Minutes
Ingredients:
- ¼ pound breakfast sausage, fully cooked and crumbled
- 4 eggs, lightly beaten
- ½ cup Monterey Jack cheese, shredded
- 2 tablespoons red bell pepper, diced
- 1 green onion, chopped
- 1 pinch cayenne pepper

Directions:
1. Preheat the Air fryer to 365 °F and grease a nonstick 6x2-inch cake pan.
2. Whisk together eggs with sausage, green onion, bell pepper, cheese and cayenne in a bowl.
3. Transfer the egg mixture in the prepared cake pan and place in the Air fryer.
4. Cook for about 20 minutes and serve warm.

Nutrition Info: Calories: 464, Fat: 33.7g, Carbohydrates: 10.4g, Sugar: 7g, Protein: 30.4g, Sodium: 704mg

102.Egg In A Hole

Servings:1
Cooking Time: 5 Minutes
Ingredients:
- 1 slice bread
- 1 teaspoon butter, softened
- 1 egg
- Salt and pepper, to taste
- 1 tablespoon shredded Cheddar cheese
- 2 teaspoons diced ham

Directions:
1. On a flat work surface, cut a hole in the center of the bread slice with a 2½-inch-diameter biscuit cutter.
2. Spread the butter evenly on each side of the bread slice and transfer to the baking pan.
3. Crack the egg into the hole and season as desired with salt and pepper. Scatter the shredded cheese and diced ham on top.
4. Slide the baking pan into Rack Position 1, select Convection Bake, set temperature to 330ºF (166ºC), and set time to 5 minutes.
5. When cooking is complete, the bread should be lightly browned and the egg should be set. Remove from the oven and serve hot.

103.Cauliflower Tater Tots With Cheddar Cheese

Servings:6
Cooking Time: 35 Minutes
Ingredients:
- 2 lb cauliflower florets, steamed
- 5 oz cheddar cheese, grated
- 1 onion, diced
- 1 cup breadcrumbs
- 1 egg, beaten
- 1 tsp fresh parsley, chopped
- 1 tsp fresh oregano, chopped
- 1 tsp chives, chopped
- 1 tsp garlic powder
- Salt and black pepper to taste

Directions:
1. Mash the cauliflower and place it in a large bowl. Add in the onion, parsley, oregano, chives, garlic powder, cheddar cheese, salt, and pepper. Mix well and form 12 balls out of the mixture.
2. Line a baking sheet with parchment paper. Dip half of the tater tots into the egg and then coat with breadcrumbs. Arrange them on the baking sheet and cook in the

preheated oven at 350 F for 15 minutes on AirFry function. Serve.

104. Fried Potatoes With Peppers And Onions

Servings:4
Cooking Time: 35 Minutes
Ingredients:
- 1 pound (454 g) red potatoes, cut into ½-inch dices
- 1 large red bell pepper, cut into ½-inch dices
- 1 large green bell pepper, cut into ½-inch dices
- 1 medium onion, cut into ½-inch dices
- 1½ tablespoons extra-virgin olive oil
- 1¼ teaspoons kosher salt
- ¾ teaspoon sweet paprika
- ¾ teaspoon garlic powder
- Freshly ground black pepper, to taste

Directions:
1. Mix together the potatoes, bell peppers, onion, oil, salt, paprika, garlic powder, and black pepper in a large mixing and toss to coat.
2. Transfer the potato mixture to the air fryer basket.
3. Put the air fryer basket on the baking pan and slide into Rack Position 2, select Air Fry, set temperature to 350ºF (180ºC) and set time to 35 minutes.
4. Stir the potato mixture three times during cooking.
5. When done, the potatoes should be nicely browned.
6. Remove from the oven to a plate and serve warm.

105. Smart Oven Jalapeño Popper Grilled Cheese Recipe

Servings:x
Cooking Time:x
Ingredients:
- 1 medium Jalapeño
- 2 slices Whole Grain Bread
- 2 teaspoons Mayonnaise
- 1/2-ounce Shredded Mild Cheddar Cheese, (about 2 tablespoons)
- 2 teaspoons Honey
- 1-ounce Cream Cheese, softened
- 1 tablespoon Sliced Green Onions
- dash of Garlic Powder
- 1-ounce Shredded Monterey Jack Cheese, (about 1/4 cup)
- 1/4 cup Corn Flakes Cereal

Directions:
1. Cut jalapeño into 1/4-inch slices. If you want your Classic Sandwich less spicy, use a paring knife to remove the seeds and veins.
2. Adjust cooking rack to the top placement and select the BROIL setting. Place jalapeño slices on a baking sheet, and broil until they

have softened and are just starting to brown, about 2 to 4 minutes. Remove pan and set aside.
3. Adjust the cooking rack to the bottom position. Place an empty sheet pan inside of the toaster oven, and preheat to 400°F on the BAKE setting.
4. Spread one side of each slice of bread with mayonnaise. Place the bread mayo-side-down on a cutting board.
5. In a small bowl, combine the cream cheese, green onion, and garlic powder. Spread each slice of bread with the mixture. Arrange jalapeño slices in an even layer on one slice and distribute the cheese evenly over both pieces of bread.
6. Carefully remove the pan and add the bread, mayo-side-down, to the pan. Return to the oven and bake until the bread is toasted and the cheese is melted and bubbly, about 6 to 7 minutes.
7. Finishing Touches
8. Drizzle the honey over the jalapeño and sprinkle with corn flakes. Immediately top with the remaining cheesy bread slice.

106. Avocado And Zucchini Mix

Servings: 4
Cooking Time: 15 Minutes
Ingredients:
- 2 avocados, peeled, pitted and roughly cubed
- 2 zucchinis, roughly cubed
- 1 tablespoon olive oil
- 2 spring onions, chopped
- 8 eggs, whisked
- 1 teaspoon sweet paprika
- A pinch of salt and black pepper
- 1 tablespoon dill, chopped

Directions:
1. Heat up the air fryer with the oil at 350 degrees F, add the zucchinis and the spring onions and cook for 2 minutes.
2. Add the avocados and the other ingredients, cook the mix for 13 minutes more, divide into bowls and serve.
- **Nutrition Info:** calories 232, fat 12, fiber 2, carbs 10, protein 5

107. Chicken & Zucchini Omelet

Servings: 6
Cooking Time: 35 Minutes
Ingredients:
- 8 eggs
- ½ cup milk
- Salt and ground black pepper, as required
- 1 cup cooked chicken, chopped
- 1 cup Cheddar cheese, shredded
- ½ cup fresh chives, chopped
- ¾ cup zucchini, chopped

Directions:
1. In a bowl, add the eggs, milk, salt and black pepper and beat well.

2. Add the remaining ingredients and stir to combine.
3. Place the mixture into a greased baking pan.
4. Press "Power Button" of Air Fry Oven and turn the dial to select the "Air Bake" mode.
5. Press the Time button and again turn the dial to set the cooking time to 35 minutes.
6. Now push the Temp button and rotate the dial to set the temperature at 315 degrees F.
7. Press "Start/Pause" button to start.
8. When the unit beeps to show that it is preheated, open the lid.
9. Arrange pan over the "Wire Rack" and insert in the oven.
10. Cut into equal-sized wedges and serve hot.
- **Nutrition Info:** Calories 209 Total Fat 13.3 g Saturated Fat 6.3 g Cholesterol 258 mg Sodium 252 mg Total Carbs 2.3 g Fiber 0.3 g Sugar 1.8 g Protein 9.8 g

108.Sweet Potato Chickpeas Hash

Servings: 4
Cooking Time: 30 Minutes
Ingredients:
- 14.5 oz can chickpeas, drained
- 1 tsp paprika
- 1 tsp garlic powder
- 1 sweet potato, peeled and cubed
- 1 tbsp olive oil
- 1 bell pepper, chopped
- 1 onion, diced
- 1/2 tsp ground black pepper
- 1 tsp salt

Directions:
1. Fit the oven with the rack in position
2. Spread sweet potato, chickpeas, bell pepper, and onion in a baking pan.
3. Drizzle with oil and season with paprika, garlic powder, pepper, and salt. Stir well.
4. Set to bake at 390 F for 35 minutes, after 5 minutes, place the baking pan in the oven.
- **Nutrition Info:** Calories: 203 Fat 4.9 g Carbohydrates 34.9 g Sugar 4.7 g Protein 6.5 g Cholesterol 0 mg

109.Meat Lover Omelet With Mozzarella

Servings:2
Cooking Time: 20 Minutes
Ingredients:
- 1 beef sausage, chopped
- 4 slices prosciutto, chopped
- 3 oz salami, chopped
- 1 cup grated mozzarella cheese
- 4 eggs
- 1 tbsp chopped onion
- 1 tbsp ketchup

Directions:
1. Preheat on Bake function to 350 F. Whisk the eggs with ketchup in a bowl. Stir in the onion. Brown the sausage in a greased pan over medium heat for 2 minutes.
2. Combine the egg mixture, mozzarella cheese, salami, and prosciutto. Pour the egg mixture over the sausage and give it a stir. Press Start and cook in the for 15 minutes.

110.Amazing Strawberry Pancake

Servings:4
Cooking Time: 30 Minutes
Ingredients:
- 3 eggs, beaten
- 2 tbsp unsalted butter
- ½ cup flour
- 2 tbsp sugar, powdered
- ½ cup milk
- 1 ½ cups fresh strawberries, sliced

Directions:
1. Preheat to 330 F on Bake function. Add butter to a pan and melt over low heat. In a bowl, mix flour, milk, eggs, and vanilla. Add the mixture to the pan with melted butter.
2. Place the pan in the oven and press Start. Cook for 14-16 minutes until the pancake is fluffy and golden brown. Drizzle powdered sugar and toss sliced strawberries on top.

111.French Toast Sticks

Servings:4
Cooking Time: 12 Minutes
Ingredients:
- 3 slices low-sodium whole-wheat bread, each cut into 4 strips
- 1 tablespoon unsalted butter, melted
- 1 tablespoon 2 percent milk
- 1 tablespoon sugar
- 1 egg, beaten
- 1 egg white
- 1 cup sliced fresh strawberries
- 1 tablespoon freshly squeezed lemon juice

Directions:
1. Arrange the bread strips on a plate and drizzle with the melted butter.
2. In a bowl, whisk together the milk, sugar, egg and egg white.
3. Dredge the bread strips into the egg mixture and place on a wire rack to let the batter drip off. Arrange half the coated bread strips in the air fryer basket.
4. Put the air fryer basket on the baking pan and slide into Rack Position 2, select Air Fry, set temperature to 380ºF (193ºC) and set time to 6 minutes.
5. After 3 minutes, remove from the oven and turn the strips over. Return to the oven to continue cooking.
6. When cooking is complete, the strips should be golden brown. Repeat with the remaining strips.
7. In a small bowl, mash the strawberries with a fork and stir in the lemon juice. Serve the French toast sticks with the strawberry sauce.

112. Aromatic Potato Hash

Servings: 4
Cooking Time: 42 Minutes
Ingredients:
- 2 teaspoons butter, melted
- 1 medium onion, chopped
- ½ of green bell pepper, seeded and chopped
- 1½ pound russet potatoes, peeled and cubed
- 5 eggs, beaten
- ½ teaspoon dried thyme, crushed
- ½ teaspoon dried savory, crushed
- Salt and black pepper, to taste

Directions:
1. Preheat the Air fryer to 390 °F and grease an Air fryer pan with melted butter.
2. Put onion and bell pepper in the Air fryer pan and cook for about 5 minutes.
3. Add the potatoes, thyme, savory, salt and black pepper and cook for about 30 minutes.
4. Meanwhile, heat a greased skillet on medium heat and stir in the beaten eggs.
5. Cook for about 1 minute on each side and remove from the skillet.
6. Cut it into small pieces and transfer the egg pieces into the Air fryer pan.
7. Cook for about 5 more minutes and serve warm.
- **Nutrition Info:** Calories: 229 Cal Total Fat: 7.6 g Saturated Fat: 0 g Cholesterol: 0 mg Sodium: 103 mg Total Carbs: 30.8 g Fiber: 0 g Sugar: 4.2 g Protein: 10.3 g

113. Avocado Cauliflower Toast

Servings: 2
Cooking Time: 30 Minutes
Ingredients:
- 1: 12-oz.steamer bag cauliflower
- ½ cup shredded mozzarella cheese
- 1 large egg.
- 1 ripe medium avocado
- ½ tsp. garlic powder.
- ¼ tsp. ground black pepper

Directions:
1. Cook cauliflower according to package instructions. Remove from bag and place into cheesecloth or clean towel to remove excess moisture.
2. Place cauliflower into a large bowl and mix in egg and mozzarella. Cut a piece of parchment to fit your air fryer basket
3. Separate the cauliflower mixture into two and place it on the parchment in two mounds. Press out the cauliflower mounds into a ¼-inch-thick rectangle. Place the parchment into the air fryer basket.
4. Adjust the temperature to 400 Degrees F and set the timer for 8 minutes
5. Flip the cauliflower halfway through the cooking time
6. When the timer beeps, remove the parchment and allow the cauliflower to cool 5 minutes.
7. Cut open the avocado and remove the pit. Scoop out the inside, place it in a medium bowl and mash it with garlic powder and pepper. Spread onto the cauliflower.
- **Nutrition Info:** Calories: 278; Protein: 14.1g; Fiber: 8.2g; Fat: 15.6g; Carbs: 15.9g

114. Easy Cheese Egg Casserole

Servings: 10
Cooking Time: 40 Minutes
Ingredients:
- 12 eggs
- 8 oz cheddar cheese, shredded
- 1/3 cup milk
- 1/4 tsp pepper
- 1 tsp salt

Directions:
1. Fit the oven with the rack in position
2. Spray 9*13-inch casserole dish with cooking spray and set aside.
3. In a bowl, whisk eggs with milk, pepper, and salt.
4. Add shredded cheese and stir well.
5. Pour egg mixture into the prepared casserole dish.
6. Set to bake at 350 F for 45 minutes. After 5 minutes place the casserole dish in the preheated oven.
7. Serve and enjoy.
- **Nutrition Info:** Calories: 171 Fat 12.9 g Carbohydrates 1.1 g Sugar 0.9 g Protein 12.6 g Cholesterol 221 mg

LUNCH RECIPES

115. Turkey And Mushroom Stew

Servings: 4
Cooking Time: 12 Minutes
Ingredients:

- ½ lb. brown mushrooms; sliced
- 1 turkey breast, skinless, boneless; cubed and browned
- ¼ cup tomato sauce
- 1 tbsp. parsley; chopped.
- Salt and black pepper to taste.

Directions:

1. In a pan that fits your air fryer, mix the turkey with the mushrooms, salt, pepper and tomato sauce, toss, introduce in the fryer and cook at 350°F for 25 minutes
2. Divide into bowls and serve for lunch with parsley sprinkled on top.
- **Nutrition Info:** Calories: 220; Fat: 12g; Fiber: 2g; Carbs: 5g; Protein: 12g

116. Roasted Garlic(2)

Servings: 12 Cloves
Cooking Time: 12 Minutes
Ingredients:

- 1 medium head garlic
- 2 tsp. avocado oil

Directions:

1. Remove any hanging excess peel from the garlic but leave the cloves covered. Cut off ¼ of the head of garlic, exposing the tips of the cloves
2. Drizzle with avocado oil. Place the garlic head into a small sheet of aluminum foil, completely enclosing it. Place it into the air fryer basket. Adjust the temperature to 400 Degrees F and set the timer for 20 minutes. If your garlic head is a bit smaller, check it after 15 minutes
3. When done, garlic should be golden brown and very soft
4. To serve, cloves should pop out and easily be spread or sliced. Store in an airtight container in the refrigerator up to 5 days.
5. You may also freeze individual cloves on a baking sheet, then store together in a freezer-safe storage bag once frozen.
- **Nutrition Info:** Calories: 11; Protein: 2g; Fiber: 1g; Fat: 7g; Carbs: 0g

117. Zucchini And Cauliflower Stew

Servings: 4
Cooking Time: 12 Minutes
Ingredients:

- 1 cauliflower head, florets separated
- 1 ½ cups zucchinis; sliced
- 1 handful parsley leaves; chopped.
- ½ cup tomato puree
- 2 green onions; chopped.
- 1 tbsp. balsamic vinegar
- 1 tbsp. olive oil
- Salt and black pepper to taste.

Directions:

1. In a pan that fits your air fryer, mix the zucchinis with the rest of the ingredients except the parsley, toss, introduce the pan in the air fryer and cook at 380°F for 20 minutes
2. Divide into bowls and serve for lunch with parsley sprinkled on top.
- **Nutrition Info:** Calories: 193; Fat: 5g; Fiber: 2g; Carbs: 4g; Protein: 7g

118. Onion Omelet

Servings: 2
Cooking Time: 15 Minutes
Ingredients:

- 4 eggs
- ¼ teaspoon low-sodium soy sauce
- Ground black pepper, as required
- 1 teaspoon butter
- 1 medium yellow onion, sliced
- ¼ cup Cheddar cheese, grated

Directions:

1. In a skillet, melt the butter over medium heat and cook the onion and cook for about 8-10 minutes.
2. Remove from the heat and set aside to cool slightly.
3. Meanwhile, in a bowl, add the eggs, soy sauce and black pepper and beat well.
4. Add the cooked onion and gently, stir to combine.
5. Place the zucchini mixture into a small baking pan.
6. Press "Power Button" of Air Fry Oven and turn the dial to select the "Air Fry" mode.
7. Press the Time button and again turn the dial to set the cooking time to 5 minutes.
8. Now push the Temp button and rotate the dial to set the temperature at 355 degrees F.
9. Press "Start/Pause" button to start.
10. When the unit beeps to show that it is preheated, open the lid.
11. Arrange pan over the "Wire Rack" and insert in the oven.
12. Cut the omelet into 2 portions and serve hot.
- **Nutrition Info:** Calories: 222 Cal Total Fat: 15.4 g Saturated Fat: 6.9 g Cholesterol: 347 mg Sodium: 264 mg Total Carbs: 6.1 g Fiber: 1.2 g Sugar: 3.1 g Protein: 15.3 g

119. Lamb Gyro

Servings: 4
Cooking Time: 25 Minutes
Ingredients:

- 1 pound ground lamb
- ¼ red onion, minced
- ¼ cup mint, minced
- ¼ cup parsley, minced
- 2 cloves garlic, minced
- ½ teaspoon salt
- ⅛ teaspoon rosemary
- ½ teaspoon black pepper
- 4 slices pita bread
- ¾ cup hummus
- 1 cup romaine lettuce, shredded
- ½ onion sliced
- 1 Roma tomato, diced
- ½ cucumber, skinned and thinly sliced
- 12 mint leaves, minced
- Tzatziki sauce, to taste

Directions:
1. Mix ground lamb, red onion, mint, parsley, garlic, salt, rosemary, and black pepper until fully incorporated.
2. Select the Broil function on the COSORI Air Fryer Toaster Oven, set time to 25 minutes and temperature to 450°F, then press Start/Cancel to preheat.
3. Line the food tray with parchment paper and place ground lamb on top, shaping it into a patty 1-inch-thick and 6 inches in diameter.
4. Insert the food tray at top position in the preheated air fryer toaster oven, then press Start/Cancel.
5. Remove when done and cut into thin slices.
6. Assemble each gyro starting with pita bread, then hummus, lamb meat, lettuce, onion, tomato, cucumber, and mint leaves, then drizzle with tzatziki.
7. Serve immediately.
- **Nutrition Info:** Calories: 409 kcal Total Fat: 14.6 g Saturated Fat: 0 g Cholesterol: 0 mg Sodium: 0 mg Total Carbs: 29.9 g Fiber: 0 g Sugar: 0 g Protein: 39.4 g

120.Perfect Size French Fries

Servings: 1
Cooking Time: 30 Minutes
Ingredients:
- 1 medium potato
- 1 tablespoon olive oil
- Salt and pepper to taste

Directions:
1. Start by preheating your oven to 425°F.
2. Clean the potato and cut it into fries or wedges.
3. Place fries in a bowl of cold water to rinse.
4. Lay the fries on a thick sheet of paper towels and pat dry.
5. Toss in a bowl with oil, salt, and pepper.
6. Bake for 30 minutes.

- **Nutrition Info:** Calories: 284, Sodium: 13 mg, Dietary Fiber: 4.7 g, Total Fat: 14.2 g, Total Carbs: 37.3 g, Protein: 4.3 g.

121.Jicama Fries(1)

Servings: 4
Cooking Time: 12 Minutes
Ingredients:
- 1 small jicama; peeled.
- ¼ tsp. onion powder.
- ¾tsp. chili powder.
- ¼ tsp. ground black pepper
- ¼ tsp. garlic powder.

Directions:
1. Cut jicama into matchstick-sized pieces.
2. Place pieces into a small bowl and sprinkle with remaining ingredients. Place the fries into the air fryer basket
3. Adjust the temperature to 350 Degrees F and set the timer for 20 minutes. Toss the basket two or three times during cooking. Serve warm.
- **Nutrition Info:** Calories: 37; Protein: 8g; Fiber: 7g; Fat: 1g; Carbs: 7g

122.Sweet Potato Rosti

Servings: 2
Cooking Time: 15 Minutes
Ingredients:
- ½ lb. sweet potatoes, peeled, grated and squeezed
- 1 tablespoon fresh parsley, chopped finely
- Salt and ground black pepper, as required
- 2 tablespoons sour cream

Directions:
1. In a large bowl, mix together the grated sweet potato, parsley, salt, and black pepper.
2. Press "Power Button" of Air Fry Oven and turn the dial to select the "Air Fry" mode.
3. Press the Time button and again turn the dial to set the cooking time to 15 minutes.
4. Now push the Temp button and rotate the dial to set the temperature at 355 degrees F.
5. Press "Start/Pause" button to start.
6. When the unit beeps to show that it is preheated, open the lid and lightly, grease the sheet pan.
7. Arrange the sweet potato mixture into the "Sheet Pan" and shape it into an even circle.
8. Insert the "Sheet Pan" in the oven.
9. Cut the potato rosti into wedges.
10. Top with the sour cream and serve immediately.
- **Nutrition Info:** Calories: 160 Cal Total Fat: 2.7 g Saturated Fat: 1.6 g Cholesterol: 5 mg Sodium: 95 mg Total Carbs: 32.3 g Fiber: 4.7 g Sugar: 0.6 g Protein: 2.2 g

123.Air Fried Sausages

Servings: 6
Cooking Time: 13 Minutes
Ingredients:
- 6 sausage
- olive oil spray

Directions:
1. Pour 5 cup of water into Instant Pot Duo Crisp Air Fryer. Place air fryer basket inside the pot, spray inside with nonstick spray and put sausage links inside.
2. Close the Air Fryer lid and steam for about 5 minutes.
3. Remove the lid once done. Spray links with olive oil and close air crisp lid.
4. Set to air crisp at 400°F for 8 min flipping halfway through so both sides get browned.
- **Nutrition Info:** Calories 267, Total Fat 23g, Total Carbs 2g, Protein 13g

124.Amazing Mac And Cheese

Servings:
Cooking Time: 12 Minutes
Ingredients:
- 1 cup cooked macaroni
- 1/2 cup warm milk
- 1 tablespoon parmesan cheese
- 1 cup grated cheddar cheese
- salt and pepper; to taste

Directions:
1. Preheat the Air Fryer to 350 - degrees Fahrenheit. Stir all of the ingredients; except Parmesan, in a baking dish.
2. Place the dish inside the Air Fryer and cook for 10 minutes. Top with the Parmesan cheese.

125.Lemon Chicken Breasts

Servings: 4
Cooking Time: 30 Minutes
Ingredients:
- 1/4 cup olive oil
- 3 tablespoons garlic, minced
- 1/3 cup dry white wine
- 1 tablespoon lemon zest, grated
- 2 tablespoons lemon juice
- 1 1/2 teaspoons dried oregano, crushed
- 1 teaspoon thyme leaves, minced
- Salt and black pepper
- 4 skin-on boneless chicken breasts
- 1 lemon, sliced

Directions:
1. Whisk everything in a baking pan to coat the chicken breasts well.
2. Place the lemon slices on top of the chicken breasts.
3. Spread the mustard mixture over the toasted bread slices.

4. Press "Power Button" of Air Fry Oven and turn the dial to select the "Bake" mode.
5. Press the Time button and again turn the dial to set the cooking time to 30 minutes.
6. Now push the Temp button and rotate the dial to set the temperature at 370 degrees F.
7. Once preheated, place the baking pan inside and close its lid.
8. Serve warm.
- **Nutrition Info:** Calories 388 Total Fat 8 g Saturated Fat 1 g Cholesterol 153mg sodium 339 mg Total Carbs 8 g Fiber 1 g Sugar 2 g Protein 13 g

126.Marinated Chicken Parmesan

Servings: 4
Cooking Time: 20 Minutes
Ingredients:
- 2 cups breadcrumbs
- 1 teaspoon dried oregano
- 1/2 teaspoon garlic powder
- 4 teaspoons paprika
- 1/2 teaspoon salt
- 1/2 teaspoon black pepper
- 2 egg whites
- 1/2 cup skim milk
- 1/2 cup flour
- 4 (6 oz.) chicken breast halves, lb.ed
- Cooking spray
- 1 jar marinara sauce
- 3/4 cup mozzarella cheese, shredded
- 2 tablespoons Parmesan, shredded

Directions:
1. Whisk the flour with all the spices in a bowl and beat the eggs in another.
2. Coat the pounded chicken with flour then dip in the egg whites.
3. Dredge the chicken breast through the crumbs well.
4. Spread marinara sauce in a baking dish and place the crusted chicken on it.
5. Drizzle cheese on top of the chicken.
6. Press "Power Button" of Air Fry Oven and turn the dial to select the "Bake" mode.
7. Press the Time button and again turn the dial to set the cooking time to 20 minutes.
8. Now push the Temp button and rotate the dial to set the temperature at 400 degrees F.
9. Once preheated, place the baking pan inside and close its lid.
10. Serve warm.
- **Nutrition Info:** Calories 361 Total Fat 16.3 g Saturated Fat 4.9 g Cholesterol 114 mg Sodium 515 mg Total Carbs 19.3 g Fiber 0.1 g Sugar 18.2 g Protein 33.3 g

127.Turmeric Mushroom(3)

Servings: 4
Cooking Time: 12 Minutes

Ingredients:
- 1 lb. brown mushrooms
- 4 garlic cloves; minced
- ¼ tsp. cinnamon powder
- 1 tsp. olive oil
- ½ tsp. turmeric powder
- Salt and black pepper to taste.

Directions:
1. In a bowl, combine all the ingredients and toss.
2. Put the mushrooms in your air fryer's basket and cook at 370°F for 15 minutes
3. Divide the mix between plates and serve as a side dish.
- **Nutrition Info:** Calories: 208; Fat: 7g; Fiber: 3g; Carbs: 5g; Protein: 7g

128.Turkey Meatballs With Manchego Cheese

Servings: 4
Cooking Time: 10 Minutes
Ingredients:
- 1 pound ground turkey
- 1/2 pound ground pork
- 1 egg, well beaten
- 1 teaspoon dried basil
- 1 teaspoon dried rosemary
- 1/4 cup Manchego cheese, grated
- 2 tablespoons yellow onions, finely chopped
- 1 teaspoon fresh garlic, finely chopped
- Sea salt and ground black pepper, to taste

Directions:
1. In a mixing bowl, combine all the ingredients until everything is well incorporated.
2. Shape the mixture into 1-inch balls.
3. Cook the meatballs in the preheated Air Fryer at 380 degrees for 7 minutes. Shake halfway through the cooking time. Work in batches.
4. Serve with your favorite pasta.
- **Nutrition Info:** 386 Calories; 24g Fat; 9g Carbs; 41g Protein; 3g Sugars; 2g Fiber

129.Air Fryer Fish

Servings: 4
Cooking Time: 17 Minutes
Ingredients:
- 4-6 Whiting Fish fillets cut in half
- Oil to mist
- Fish Seasoning
- ¾ cup very fine cornmeal
- ¼ cup flour
- 2 tsp old bay
- 1 ½ tsp salt
- 1 tsp paprika
- ½ tsp garlic powder
- ½ tsp black pepper

Directions:
1. Put the Ingredients: for fish seasoning in a Ziplock bag and shake it well. Set aside.
2. Rinse and pat dry the fish fillets with paper towels. Make sure that they still are damp.
3. Place the fish fillets in a ziplock bag and shake until they are completely covered with seasoning.
4. Place the fillets on a baking rack to let any excess flour to fall off.
5. Grease the bottom of the Instant Pot Duo Crisp Air Fryer basket tray and place the fillets on the tray. Close the lid, select the Air Fry option and cook filets on 400°F for 10 minutes.
6. Open the Air Fryer lid and spray the fish with oil on the side facing up before flipping it over, ensure that the fish is fully coated. Flip and cook another side of the fish for 7 minutes. Remove the fish and serve.
- **Nutrition Info:** Calories 193, Total Fat 1g, Total Carbs 27g, Protein 19g

130.Fried Whole Chicken

Servings: 4
Cooking Time: 70 Minutes
Ingredients:
- 1 Whole chicken
- 2 Tbsp or spray of oil of choice
- 1 tsp garlic powder
- 1 tsp onion powder
- 1 tsp paprika
- 1 tsp Italian seasoning
- 2 Tbsp Montreal Steak Seasoning (or salt and pepper to taste)
- 1.5 cup chicken broth

Directions:
1. Truss and wash the chicken.
2. Mix the seasoning and rub a little amount on the chicken.
3. Pour the broth inside the Instant Pot Duo Crisp Air Fryer.
4. Place the chicken in the air fryer basket.
5. Select the option Air Fry and Close the Air Fryer lid and cook for 25 minutes.
6. Spray or rub the top of the chicken with oil and rub it with half of the seasoning.
7. Close the air fryer lid and air fry again at 400°F for 10 minutes.
8. Flip the chicken, spray it with oil, and rub with the remaining seasoning.
9. Again air fry it for another ten minutes.
10. Allow the chicken to rest for 10 minutes.
- **Nutrition Info:** Calories 436, Total Fat 28g, Total Carbs 4g, Protein 42g

131.Dijon And Swiss Croque Monsieur

Servings: 2
Cooking Time: 13 Minutes
Ingredients:

- 4 slices white bread
- 2 tablespoons unsalted butter
- 1 tablespoon all-purpose flour
- 1/2 cup whole milk
- 3/4 cups shredded Swiss cheese
- 1/4 teaspoon freshly ground black pepper
- 1/8 teaspoon salt
- 1 tablespoon Dijon mustard
- 4 slices ham

Directions:
1. Start by cutting crusts off bread and placing them on a pan lined with parchment paper.
2. Melt 1 tablespoon of butter in a sauce pan, then dab the top sides of each piece of bread with butter.
3. Toast bread inoven for 3-5 minutes until each piece is golden brown.
4. Melt the second tablespoon of butter in the sauce pan and add the flour, mix together until they form a paste.
5. Add the milk and continue to mix until the sauce begins to thicken.
6. Remove from heat and mix in 1 tablespoon of Swiss cheese, salt, and pepper; continue stirring until cheese is melted.
7. Flip the bread over in the pan so the untoasted side is facing up.
8. Set two slices aside and spread Dijon on the other two slices.
9. Add ham and sprinkle 1/4 cup Swiss over each piece.
10. Broil for about 3 minutes.
11. Top the sandwiches off with the other slices of bread, soft-side down.
12. Top with sauce and sprinkle with remaining Swiss. Toast for another 5 minutes or until the cheese is golden brown.
13. Serve immediately.
- **Nutrition Info:** Calories: 452, Sodium: 1273 mg, Dietary Fiber: 1.6 g, Total Fat: 30.5 g, Total Carbs: 19.8 g, Protein: 24.4 g.

132.Lime And Mustard Marinated Chicken

Servings: 4
Cooking Time: 10 Minutes
Ingredients:
- 1/2 teaspoon stone-ground mustard
- 1/2 teaspoon minced fresh oregano
- 1/3 cup freshly squeezed lime juice
- 2 small-sized chicken breasts, skin-on
- 1 teaspoon kosher salt
- 1teaspoon freshly cracked mixed peppercorns

Directions:
1. Preheat your Air Fryer to 345 degrees F.
2. Toss all of the above ingredients in a medium-sized mixing dish; allow it to marinate overnight.

3. Cook in the preheated Air Fryer for 26 minutes.
- **Nutrition Info:** 255 Calories; 15g Fat; 7g Carbs; 33g Protein; 8g Sugars; 3g Fiber

133.Kale And Pine Nuts

Servings: 4
Cooking Time: 12 Minutes
Ingredients:
- 10 cups kale; torn
- 1/3 cup pine nuts
- 2 tbsp. lemon zest; grated
- 1 tbsp. lemon juice
- 2 tbsp. olive oil
- Salt and black pepper to taste.

Directions:
1. In a pan that fits the air fryer, combine all the ingredients, toss, introduce the pan in the machine and cook at 380°F for 15 minutes
2. Divide between plates and serve as a side dish.
- **Nutrition Info:** Calories: 121; Fat: 9g; Fiber: 2g; Carbs: 4g; Protein: 5g

134.Coriander Artichokes(3)

Servings: 4
Cooking Time: 12 Minutes
Ingredients:
- 12 oz. artichoke hearts
- 1 tbsp. lemon juice
- 1 tsp. coriander, ground
- ½ tsp. cumin seeds
- ½ tsp. olive oil
- Salt and black pepper to taste.

Directions:
1. In a pan that fits your air fryer, mix all the ingredients, toss, introduce the pan in the fryer and cook at 370°F for 15 minutes
2. Divide the mix between plates and serve as a side dish.
- **Nutrition Info:** Calories: 200; Fat: 7g; Fiber: 2g; Carbs: 5g; Protein: 8g

135.Sweet Potato And Eggplant Mix

Servings: 4
Cooking Time: 20 Minutes
Ingredients:
- 2 sweet potatoes, peeled and cut into medium wedges
- 2 eggplants, roughly cubed
- 1 tablespoon avocado oil
- Juice of 1 lemon
- 4 garlic cloves, minced
- 1 teaspoon nutmeg, ground
- Salt and black pepper to the taste
- 1 tablespoon rosemary, chopped

Directions:

1. In your air fryer, combine the potatoes with the eggplants and the other Ingredients:, toss and cook at 370 degrees F for 20 minutes.
2. Divide the mix between plates and serve as a side dish.
- **Nutrition Info:** Calories 182, fat 6, fiber 3, carbs 11, protein 5

136.Okra And Green Beans Stew

Servings: 4
Cooking Time: 12 Minutes
Ingredients:
- 1 lb. green beans; halved
- 4 garlic cloves; minced
- 1 cup okra
- 3 tbsp. tomato sauce
- 1 tbsp. thyme; chopped.
- Salt and black pepper to taste.

Directions:
1. In a pan that fits your air fryer, mix all the ingredients, toss, introduce the pan in the air fryer and cook at 370°F for 15 minutes
2. Divide the stew into bowls and serve.
- **Nutrition Info:** Calories: 183; Fat: 5g; Fiber: 2g; Carbs: 4g; Protein: 8g

137.Barbecue Air Fried Chicken

Servings: 10
Cooking Time: 26 Minutes
Ingredients:
- 1 teaspoon Liquid Smoke
- 2 cloves Fresh Garlic smashed
- 1/2 cup Apple Cider Vinegar
- 3 pounds Chuck Roast well-marbled with intramuscular fat
- 1 Tablespoon Kosher Salt
- 1 Tablespoon Freshly Ground Black Pepper
- 2 teaspoons Garlic Powder
- 1.5 cups Barbecue Sauce
- 1/4 cup Light Brown Sugar + more for sprinkling
- 2 Tablespoons Honey optional and in place of 2 TBL sugar

Directions:
1. Add meat to the Instant Pot Duo Crisp Air Fryer Basket, spreading out the meat.
2. Select the option Air Fry.
3. Close the Air Fryer lid and cook at 300 degrees F for 8 minutes. Pause the Air Fryer and flip meat over after 4 minutes.
4. Remove the lid and baste with more barbecue sauce and sprinkle with a little brown sugar.
5. Again Close the Air Fryer lid and set the temperature at 400°F for 9 minutes. Watch meat though the lid and flip it over after 5 minutes.

- **Nutrition Info:** Calories 360, Total Fat 16g, Total Carbs 27g, Protein 27g

138.Bbq Chicken Breasts

Servings: 4
Cooking Time: 15 Minutes
Ingredients:
- 4 boneless skinless chicken breast about 6 oz each
- 1-2 Tbsp bbq seasoning

Directions:
1. Cover both sides of chicken breast with the BBQ seasoning. Cover and marinate the in the refrigerator for 45 minutes.
2. Choose the Air Fry option and set the temperature to 400°F. Push start and let it preheat for 5 minutes.
3. Upon preheating, place the chicken breast in the Instant Pot Duo Crisp Air Fryer basket, making sure they do not overlap. Spray with oil.
4. Cook for 13-14 minutes
5. flipping halfway.
6. Remove chicken when the chicken reaches an internal temperature of 160°F. Place on a plate and allow to rest for 5 minutes before slicing.
- **Nutrition Info:** Calories 131, Total Fat 3g, Total Carbs 2g, Protein 24g

139.Carrot And Beef Cocktail Balls

Servings: 10
Cooking Time: 20 Minutes
Ingredients:
- 1-pound ground beef
- 2 carrots
- 1 red onion, peeled and chopped
- 2 cloves garlic
- 1/2 teaspoon dried rosemary, crushed
- 1/2 teaspoon dried basil
- 1 teaspoon dried oregano
- 1 egg
- 3/4 cup breadcrumbs
- 1/2 teaspoon salt
- 1/2 teaspoon black pepper, or to taste
- 1 cup plain flour

Directions:
1. Preparing the ingredients. Place ground beef in a large bowl.
2. In a food processor, pulse the carrot, onion and garlic; transfer the vegetable mixture to a large-sized bowl.
3. Then, add the rosemary, basil, oregano, egg, breadcrumbs, salt, and black pepper.
4. Shape the mixture into even balls; refrigerate for about 30 minutes.
5. Roll the balls into the flour.
6. Air frying. Close air fryer lid.

7. Then, air-fry the balls at 350 degrees f for about 20 minutes, turning occasionally; work with batches. Serve with toothpicks.
- **Nutrition Info:** Calories 284 Total fat 7.9 g Saturated fat 1.4 g Cholesterol 36 mg Sodium 704 mg Total carbs 46 g Fiber 3.6 g Sugar 5.5 g Protein 17.9 g

140.Greek Lamb Meatballs

Servings: 12
Cooking Time: 12 Minutes
Ingredients:
- 1 pound ground lamb
- ½ cup breadcrumbs
- ¼ cup milk
- 2 egg yolks
- 1 teaspoon ground coriander
- 1 teaspoon ground cumin
- 3 garlic cloves, minced
- 1 teaspoon dried oregano
- ½ teaspoon salt
- ½ teaspoon black pepper
- 1 lemon, juiced and zested
- ¼ cup fresh parsley, chopped
- ½ cup crumbled feta cheese
- Olive oil, for shaping
- Tzatziki, for dipping

Directions:
1. Combine all ingredients except olive oil in a large mixing bowl and mix until fully incorporated.
2. Form 12 meatballs, about 2 ounces each. Use olive oil on your hands so they don't stick to the meatballs. Set aside.
3. Select the Broil function on the COSORI Air Fryer Toaster Oven, set time to 12 minutes, then press Start/Cancel to preheat.
4. Place the meatballs on the food tray, then insert the tray at top position in the preheated air fryer toaster oven. Press Start/Cancel.
5. Take out the meatballs when done and serve with a side of tzatziki.
- **Nutrition Info:** Calories: 129 kcal Total Fat: 6.4 g Saturated Fat: 0 g Cholesterol: 0 mg Sodium: 0 mg Total Carbs: 4.9 g Fiber: 0 g Sugar: 0 g Protein: 12.9 g

141.Beef Steaks With Beans

Servings: 4
Cooking Time: 10 Minutes
Ingredients:
- 4 beef steaks, trim the fat and cut into strips
- 1 cup green onions, chopped
- 2 cloves garlic, minced
- 1 red bell pepper, seeded and thinly sliced
- 1 can tomatoes, crushed
- 1 can cannellini beans
- 3/4 cup beef broth

- 1/4 teaspoon dried basil
- 1/2 teaspoon cayenne pepper
- 1/2 teaspoon sea salt
- 1/4 teaspoon ground black pepper, or to taste

Directions:
1. Preparing the ingredients. Add the steaks, green onions and garlic to the instant crisp air fryer basket.
2. Air frying. Close air fryer lid. Cook at 390 degrees f for 10 minutes, working in batches.
3. Stir in the remaining ingredients and cook for an additional 5 minutes.
- **Nutrition Info:** Calories 284 Total fat 7.9 g Saturated fat 1.4 g Cholesterol 36 mg Sodium 704 mg Total carbs 46 g Fiber 3.6 g Sugar 5.5 g Protein 17.9 g

142.Roasted Delicata Squash With Kale

Servings: 2
Cooking Time: 10 Minutes
Ingredients:
- 1 medium delicata squash
- 1 bunch kale
- 1 clove garlic
- 2 tablespoons olive oil
- Salt and pepper

Directions:
1. Start by preheating toaster oven to 425°F.
2. Clean squash and cut off each end. Cut in half and remove the seeds. Quarter the halves.
3. Toss the squash in 1 tablespoon of olive oil.
4. Place the squash on a greased baking sheet and roast for 25 minutes, turning halfway through.
5. Rinse kale and remove stems. Chop garlic.
6. Heat the leftover oil in a medium skillet and add kale and salt to taste.
7. Sauté the kale until it darkens, then mix in the garlic.
8. Cook for another minute then remove from heat and add 2 tablespoons of water.
9. Remove squash from oven and lay it on top of the garlic kale.
10. Top with salt and pepper to taste and serve.
- **Nutrition Info:** Calories: 159, Sodium: 28 mg, Dietary Fiber: 1.8 g, Total Fat: 14.2 g, Total Carbs: 8.2 g, Protein: 2.6 g.

143.Seven-layer Tostadas

Servings: 6
Cooking Time: 5 Minutes
Ingredients:
- 1 (16-ounce) can refried pinto beans
- 1-1/2 cups guacamole
- 1 cup light sour cream
- 1/2 teaspoon taco seasoning

- 1 cup shredded Mexican cheese blend
- 1 cup chopped tomatoes
- 1/2 cup thinly sliced green onions
- 1/2 cup sliced black olives
- 6-8 whole wheat flour tortillas small enough to fit in your oven
- Olive oil

Directions:
1. Start by placing baking sheet into toaster oven while preheating it to 450°F. Remove pan and drizzle with olive oil.
2. Place tortillas on pan and cook in oven until they are crisp, turn at least once, this should take about 5 minutes or less.
3. In a medium bowl, mash refried beans to break apart any chunks, then microwave for 2 1/2 minutes.
4. Stir taco seasoning into the sour cream. Chop vegetables and halve olives.
5. Top tortillas with ingredients in this order: refried beans, guacamole, sour cream, shredded cheese, tomatoes, onions, and olives.
- **Nutrition Info:** Calories: 657, Sodium: 581 mg, Dietary Fiber: 16.8 g, Total Fat: 31.7 g, Total Carbs: 71.3 g, Protein: 28.9 g.

144.Parmigiano Reggiano And Prosciutto Toasts With Balsamic Glaze

Servings: 8
Cooking Time: 15 Minutes
Ingredients:
- 3 ounces thinly sliced prosciutto, cut crosswise into 1/4-inch-wide strips
- 1 (3-ounce) piece Parmigiano Reggiano cheese
- 1/2 cup balsamic vinegar
- 1 medium red onion, thinly sliced
- 1 loaf ciabatta, cut into 3/4-inch-thick slices
- 1 tablespoon extra-virgin olive oil
- 1 clove garlic
- Black pepper to taste

Directions:
1. Preheat toaster oven to 350°F.
2. Place onion in a bowl of cold water and let sit for 10 minutes.
3. Bring vinegar to a boil, then reduce heat and simmer for 5 minutes.
4. Remove from heat completely and set aside to allow the vinegar to thicken.
5. Drain the onion.
6. Brush the tops of each bun with oil, rub with garlic, and sprinkle with pepper.
7. Use a vegetable peeler to make large curls of Parmigiano Reggiano cheese and place them on the bun.
8. Bake for 15 minutes or until the bread just starts to crisp.

9. Sprinkle prosciutto and onions on top, then drizzle vinegar and serve.
- **Nutrition Info:** Calories: 154, Sodium: 432 mg, Dietary Fiber: 1.0 g, Total Fat: 5.6 g, Total Carbs: 17.3 g, Protein: 8.1 g.

145.Easy Turkey Breasts With Basil

Servings: 4
Cooking Time: 10 Minutes
Ingredients:
- 2 tablespoons olive oil
- 2 pounds turkey breasts, bone-in skin-on
- Coarse sea salt and ground black pepper, to taste
- 1 teaspoon fresh basil leaves, chopped
- 2 tablespoons lemon zest, grated

Directions:
1. Rub olive oil on all sides of the turkey breasts; sprinkle with salt, pepper, basil, and lemon zest.
2. Place the turkey breasts skin side up on a parchment-lined cooking basket.
3. Cook in the preheated Air Fryer at 330 degrees F for 30 minutes. Now, turn them over and cook an additional 28 minutes.
4. Serve with lemon wedges, if desired.
- **Nutrition Info:** 416 Calories; 26g Fat; 0g Carbs; 49g Protein; 0g Sugars; 2g Fiber

146.Ricotta Toasts With Salmon

Servings: 2
Cooking Time: 4 Minutes
Ingredients:
- 4 bread slices
- 1 garlic clove, minced
- 8 oz. ricotta cheese
- 1 teaspoon lemon zest
- Freshly ground black pepper, to taste
- 4 oz. smoked salmon

Directions:
1. In a food processor, add the garlic, ricotta, lemon zest and black pepper and pulse until smooth.
2. Spread ricotta mixture over each bread slices evenly.
3. Press "Power Button" of Air Fry Oven and turn the dial to select the "Air Fry" mode.
4. Press the Time button and again turn the dial to set the cooking time to 4 minutes.
5. Now push the Temp button and rotate the dial to set the temperature at 355 degrees F.
6. Press "Start/Pause" button to start.
7. When the unit beeps to show that it is preheated, open the lid and lightly, grease the sheet pan.
8. Arrange the bread slices into "Air Fry Basket" and insert in the oven.
9. Top with salmon and serve.

- **Nutrition Info:** Calories: 274 Cal Total Fat: 12 g Saturated Fat: 6.3 g Cholesterol: 48 mg Sodium: 1300 mg Total Carbs: 15.7 g Fiber: 0.5 g Sugar: 1.2 g Protein: 24.8 g

147.Baked Shrimp Scampi

Servings: 4
Cooking Time: 10 Minutes
Ingredients:
- 1 lb large shrimp
- 8 tbsp butter
- 1 tbsp minced garlic (use 2 for extra garlic flavor)
- 1/4 cup white wine or cooking sherry
- 1/2 tsp salt
- 1/4 tsp cayenne pepper
- 1/4 tsp paprika
- 1/2 tsp onion powder
- 3/4 cup bread crumbs

Directions:
1. Take a bowl and mix the bread crumbs with dry seasonings.
2. On the stovetop (or in the Instant Pot on saute), melt the butter with the garlic and the white wine.
3. Remove from heat and add the shrimp and the bread crumb mix.
4. Transfer the mix to a casserole dish.
5. Choose the Bake operation and add food to the Instant Pot Duo Crisp Air Fryer. Close the lid and Bake at 350°F for 10 minutes or until they are browned.
6. Serve and enjoy.
- **Nutrition Info:** Calories 422, Total Fat 26g, Total Carbs 18g, Protein 29 g

148.Chicken Wings With Prawn Paste

Servings: 6
Cooking Time: 8 Minutes
Ingredients:
- Corn flour, as required
- 2 pounds mid-joint chicken wings
- 2 tablespoons prawn paste
- 4 tablespoons olive oil
- 1½ teaspoons sugar
- 2 teaspoons sesame oil
- 1 teaspoon Shaoxing wine
- 2 teaspoons fresh ginger juice

Directions:
1. Preheat the Air fryer to 360 degree F and grease an Air fryer basket.
2. Mix all the ingredients in a bowl except wings and corn flour.
3. Rub the chicken wings generously with marinade and refrigerate overnight.
4. Coat the chicken wings evenly with corn flour and keep aside.

5. Set the Air fryer to 390 degree F and arrange the chicken wings in the Air fryer basket.
6. Cook for about 8 minutes and dish out to serve hot.
- **Nutrition Info:** Calories: 416, Fat: 31.5g, Carbohydrates: 11.2g, Sugar: 1.6g, Protein: 24.4g, Sodium: 661mg

149.Chicken And Celery Stew

Servings: 6
Cooking Time: 12 Minutes
Ingredients:
- 1 lb. chicken breasts, skinless; boneless and cubed
- 4 celery stalks; chopped.
- ½ cup coconut cream
- 2 red bell peppers; chopped.
- 2 tsp. garlic; minced
- 1 tbsp. butter, soft
- Salt and black pepper to taste.

Directions:
1. Grease a baking dish that fits your air fryer with the butter, add all the ingredients in the pan and toss them.
2. Introduce the dish in the fryer, cook at 360°F for 30 minutes, divide into bowls and serve
- **Nutrition Info:** Calories: 246; Fat: 12g; Fiber: 2g; Carbs: 6g; Protein: 12g

150.Coconut Shrimp With Dip

Servings: 4
Cooking Time: 9 Minutes
Ingredients:
- 1 lb large raw shrimp peeled and deveined with tail on
- 2 eggs beaten
- ¼ cup Panko Breadcrumbs
- 1 tsp salt
- ¼ tsp black pepper
- ½ cup All-Purpose Flour
- ½ cup unsweetened shredded coconut
- Oil for spraying

Directions:
1. Clean and dry the shrimp. Set it aside.
2. Take 3 bowls. Put flour in the first bowl. Beat eggs in the second bowl. Mix coconut, breadcrumbs, salt, and black pepper in the third bowl.
3. Select the Air Fry option and adjust the temperature to 390°F. Push start and preheating will start.
4. Dip each shrimp in flour followed by the egg and then coconut mixture, ensuring shrimp is covered on all sides during each dip.
5. Once the preheating is done, place shrimp in a single layer on greased tray in the

basket of the Instant Pot Duo Crisp Air Fryer.

6. Spray the shrimp with oil lightly, and then close the Air Fryer basket lid. Cook for around 4 minutes.
7. After 4 minutes
8. open the Air Fryer basket lid and flip the shrimp over. Respray the shrimp with oil, close the Air Fryer basket lid, and cook for five more minutes.
9. Remove shrimp from the basket and serve with Thai Sweet Chili Sauce.
- **Nutrition Info:** Calories 279, Total Fat 11g, Total Carbs 17g, Protein 28g

151.Creamy Chicken Tenders

Servings: 8
Cooking Time: 20 Minutes
Ingredients:
- 2 pounds chicken tenders
- 1 cup feta cheese
- 4 tablespoons olive oil
- 1 cup cream
- Salt and black pepper, to taste

Directions:
1. Preheat the Air fryer to 340 degree F and grease an Air fryer basket.
2. Season the chicken tenders with salt and black pepper.
3. Arrange the chicken tenderloins in the Air fryer basket and drizzle with olive oil.\
4. Cook for about 15 minutes and set the Air fryer to 390 degree F.
5. Cook for about 5 more minutes and dish out to serve warm.
6. Repeat with the remaining mixture and dish out to serve hot.
- **Nutrition Info:** Calories: 344, Fat: 21.1g, Carbohydrates: 1.7g, Sugar: 1.4g, Protein: 35.7g, Sodium: 317mg

152.Roasted Fennel, Ditalini, And Shrimp

Servings: 4
Cooking Time: 30 Minutes
Ingredients:
- 1 pound extra large, thawed, tail-on shrimp
- 1 teaspoon fennel seeds
- 1 teaspoon salt
- 1 fennel bulb, halved and sliced crosswise
- 4 garlic cloves, chopped
- 2 tablespoons olive oil
- 1/2 teaspoon freshly ground black pepper
- Grated zest of 1 lemon
- 1/2 pound whole wheat ditalini

Directions:
1. Start by preheating toaster oven to 450°F.
2. Toast the seeds in a medium pan over medium heat for about 5 minutes, then toss with shrimp.

3. Add water and 1/2 teaspoon salt to the pan and bring the mixture to a boil.
4. Reduce heat and simmer for 30 minutes.
5. Combine fennel, garlic, oil, pepper, and remaining salt in a roasting pan.
6. Roast for 20 minutes, then add shrimp mixture and roast for another 5 minutes or until shrimp are cooked.
7. While the fennel is roasting, cook pasta per the directions on the package, drain, and set aside.
8. Remove the shrimp mixture and mix in pasta, roast for another 5 minutes.
- **Nutrition Info:** Calories: 420, Sodium: 890 mg, Dietary Fiber: 4.2 g, Total Fat: 10.2 g, Total Carbs: 49.5 g, Protein: 33.9 g.

153.Turkey-stuffed Peppers

Servings: 6
Cooking Time: 35 Minutes
Ingredients:
- 1 pound lean ground turkey
- 1 tablespoon olive oil
- 2 cloves garlic, minced
- 1/3 onion, minced
- 1 tablespoon cilantro (optional)
- 1 teaspoon garlic powder
- 1 teaspoon cumin powder
- 1/2 teaspoon salt
- Pepper to taste
- 3 large red bell peppers
- 1 cup chicken broth
- 1/4 cup tomato sauce
- 1-1/2 cups cooked brown rice
- 1/4 cup shredded cheddar
- 6 green onions

Directions:
1. Start by preheating toaster oven to 400°F.
2. Heat a skillet on medium heat.
3. Add olive oil to the skillet, then mix in onion and garlic.
4. Sauté for about 5 minutes, or until the onion starts to look opaque.
5. Add the turkey to the skillet and season with cumin, garlic powder, salt, and pepper.
6. Brown the meat until thoroughly cooked, then mix in chicken broth and tomato sauce.
7. Reduce heat and simmer for about 5 minutes, stirring occasionally.
8. Add the brown rice and continue stirring until it is evenly spread through the mix.
9. Cut the bell peppers lengthwise down the middle and remove all of the seeds.
10. Grease a pan or line it with parchment paper and lay all peppers in the pan with the outside facing down.
11. Spoon the meat mixture evenly into each pepper and use the back of the spoon to level.

12. Bake for 30 minutes.
13. Remove pan from oven and sprinkle cheddar over each pepper, then put it back in for another 3 minutes, or until the cheese is melted.
14. While the cheese melts, dice the green onions. Remove pan from oven and sprinkle onions over each pepper and serve.
- **Nutrition Info:** Calories: 394, Sodium: 493 mg, Dietary Fiber: 4.1 g, Total Fat: 12.9 g, Total Carbs: 44.4 g, Protein: 27.7 g.

154.Turkey And Almonds

Servings: 2
Cooking Time: 10 Minutes
Ingredients:
- 1 big turkey breast, skinless; boneless and halved
- 2 shallots; chopped
- 1/3 cup almonds; chopped
- 1 tbsp. sweet paprika
- 2 tbsp. olive oil
- Salt and black pepper to taste.

Directions:
1. In a pan that fits the air fryer, combine the turkey with all the other ingredients, toss.
2. Put the pan in the machine and cook at 370°F for 25 minutes
3. Divide everything between plates and serve.
- **Nutrition Info:** Calories: 274; Fat: 12g; Fiber: 3g; Carbs: 5g; Protein: 14g

155.Easy Prosciutto Grilled Cheese

Servings: 1
Cooking Time: 5 Minutes
Ingredients:
- 2 slices muenster cheese
- 2 slices white bread
- Four thinly-shaved pieces of prosciutto
- 1 tablespoon sweet and spicy pickles

Directions:
1. Set toaster oven to the Toast setting.
2. Place one slice of cheese on each piece of bread.
3. Put prosciutto on one slice and pickles on the other.
4. Transfer to a baking sheet and toast for 4 minutes or until the cheese is melted.
5. Combine the sides, cut, and serve.
- **Nutrition Info:** Calories: 460, Sodium: 2180 mg, Dietary Fiber: 0 g, Total Fat: 25.2 g, Total Carbs: 11.9 g, Protein: 44.2 g.

156.Orange Chicken Rice

Servings: 4
Cooking Time: 55 Minutes
Ingredients:
- 3 tablespoons olive oil
- 1 medium onion, chopped
- 1 3/4 cups chicken broth
- 1 cup brown basmati rice
- Zest and juice of 2 oranges
- Salt to taste
- 4 (6-oz.) boneless, skinless chicken thighs
- Black pepper, to taste
- 2 tablespoons fresh mint, chopped
- 2 tablespoons pine nuts, toasted

Directions:
1. Spread the rice in a casserole dish and place the chicken on top.
2. Toss the rest of the Ingredients: in a bowl and liberally pour over the chicken.
3. Press "Power Button" of Air Fry Oven and turn the dial to select the "Bake" mode.
4. Press the Time button and again turn the dial to set the cooking time to 55 minutes.
5. Now push the Temp button and rotate the dial to set the temperature at 350 degrees F.
6. Once preheated, place the casserole dish inside and close its lid.
7. Serve warm.
- **Nutrition Info:** Calories 231 Total Fat 20.1 g Saturated Fat 2.4 g Cholesterol 110 mg Sodium 941 mg Total Carbs 30.1 g Fiber 0.9 g Sugar 1.4 g Protein 14.6 g

157.Air Fryer Marinated Salmon

Servings: 4
Cooking Time: 12 Minutes
Ingredients:
- 4 salmon fillets or 1 1lb fillet cut into 4 pieces
- 1 Tbsp brown sugar
- ½ Tbsp Minced Garlic
- 6 Tbsps Soy Sauce
- ¼ cup Dijon Mustard
- 1 Green onions finely chopped

Directions:
1. Take a bowl and whisk together soy sauce, dijon mustard, brown sugar, and minced garlic. Pour this mixture over salmon fillets, making sure that all the fillets are covered. Refrigerate and marinate for 20-30 minutes.
2. Remove salmon fillets from marinade and place them in greased or lined on the tray in the Instant Pot Duo Crisp Air Fryer basket, close the lid.
3. Select the Air Fry option and Air Fry for around 12 minutes at 400°F.
4. Remove from Instant Pot Duo Crisp Air Fryer and top with chopped green onions.
- **Nutrition Info:** Calories 267, Total Fat 11g, Total Carbs 5g, Protein 37g

158.Country Comfort Corn Bread

Servings: 12
Cooking Time: 20 Minutes
Ingredients:

- 1 cup yellow cornmeal
- 1-1/2 cups oatmeal
- 1/4 teaspoon salt
- 1/4 cup granulated sugar
- 2 teaspoons baking powder
- 1 cup milk
- 1 large egg
- 1/2 cup applesauce

Directions:
1. Start by blending oatmeal into a fine powder.
2. Preheat toaster oven to 400°F.
3. Mix oatmeal, cornmeal, salt, sugar, and baking powder, and stir to blend.
4. Add milk, egg, and applesauce, and mix well.
5. Pour into a pan and bake for 20 minutes.
- **Nutrition Info:** Calories: 113, Sodium: 71 mg, Dietary Fiber: 1.9 g, Total Fat: 1.9 g, Total Carbs: 21.5 g, Protein: 3.4 g.

159.Sweet Potato And Parsnip Spiralized Latkes

Servings: 12
Cooking Time: 20 Minutes
Ingredients:
- 1 medium sweet potato
- 1 large parsnip
- 4 cups water
- 1 egg + 1 egg white
- 2 scallions
- 1/2 teaspoon garlic powder
- 1/2 teaspoon sea salt
- 1/2 teaspoon ground pepper

Directions:
1. Start by spiralizing the sweet potato and parsnip and chopping the scallions, reserving only the green parts.
2. Preheat toaster oven to 425°F.
3. Bring 4 cups of water to a boil. Place all of your noodles in a colander and pour the boiling water over the top, draining well.
4. Let the noodles cool, then grab handfuls and place them in a paper towel; squeeze to remove as much liquid as possible.
5. In a large bowl, beat egg and egg white together. Add noodles, scallions, garlic powder, salt, and pepper, mix well.
6. Prepare a baking sheet; scoop out 1/4 cup of mixture at a time and place on sheet.
7. Slightly press down each scoop with your hands, then bake for 20 minutes, flipping halfway through.
- **Nutrition Info:** Calories: 24, Sodium: 91 mg, Dietary Fiber: 1.0 g, Total Fat: 0.4 g, Total Carbs: 4.3 g, Protein: 0.9 g.

160.Ranch Chicken Wings

Servings: 3
Cooking Time: 10 Minutes

Ingredients:
- 1/4 cup almond meal
- 1/4 cup flaxseed meal
- 2 tablespoons butter, melted
- 6 tablespoons parmesan cheese, preferably freshly grated
- 1 tablespoon Ranch seasoning mix
- 2 tablespoons oyster sauce
- 6 chicken wings, bone-in

Directions:
1. Start by preheating your Air Fryer to 370 degrees F.
2. In a resealable bag, place the almond meal, flaxseed meal, butter, parmesan, Ranch seasoning mix, andoyster sauce. Add the chicken wings and shake to coat on all sides.
3. Arrange the chicken wings in the Air Fryer basket. Spritz the chicken wings with a nonstick cooking spray.
4. Cook for 11 minutes. Turn them over and cook an additional 11 minutes. Serve warm with your favorite dipping sauce, if desired. Enjoy!
- **Nutrition Info:** 285 Calories; 22g Fat; 3g Carbs; 12g Protein; 5g Sugars; 6g Fiber

161.Air Fryer Beef Steak

Servings: 4
Cooking Time: 15 Minutes
Ingredients:
- 1 tbsp. Olive oil
- Pepper and salt
- 2 pounds of ribeye steak

Directions:
1. Preparing the ingredients. Season meat on both sides with pepper and salt.
2. Rub all sides of meat with olive oil.
3. Preheat instant crisp air fryer to 356 degrees and spritz with olive oil.
4. Air frying. Close air fryer lid. Set temperature to 356°f, and set time to 7 minutes. Cook steak 7 minutes. Flip and cook an additional 6 minutes.
5. Let meat sit 2-5 minutes to rest. Slice and serve with salad.
- **Nutrition Info:** Calories: 233; Fat: 19g; Protein:16g; Sugar:0g

162.Chicken Breast With Rosemary

Servings: 4
Cooking Time: 60 Minutes
Ingredients:
- 4 bone-in chicken breast halves
- 3 tablespoons softened butter
- 1/2 teaspoon salt
- 1/4 teaspoon pepper
- 1 tablespoon rosemary
- 1 tablespoon extra-virgin olive oil

Directions:

1. Start by preheating toaster oven to 400°F.
2. Mix butter, salt, pepper, and rosemary in a bowl.
3. Coat chicken with the butter mixture and place in a shallow pan.
4. Drizzle oil over chicken and roast for 25 minutes.
5. Flip chicken and roast for another 20 minutes.
6. Flip chicken one more time and roast for a final 15 minutes.
- **Nutrition Info:** Calories: 392, Sodium: 551 mg, Dietary Fiber: 0 g, Total Fat: 18.4 g, Total Carbs: 0.6 g, Protein: 55.4 g.

163.Coriander Potatoes

Servings: 4
Cooking Time: 25 Minutes
Ingredients:
- 1 pound gold potatoes, peeled and cut into wedges
- Salt and black pepper to the taste
- 1 tablespoon tomato sauce
- 2 tablespoons coriander, chopped
- ½ teaspoon garlic powder
- 1 teaspoon chili powder
- 1 tablespoon olive oil

Directions:
1. In a bowl, combine the potatoes with the tomato sauce and the other Ingredients:, toss, and transfer to the air fryer's basket.
2. Cook at 370 degrees F for 25 minutes, divide between plates and serve as a side dish.
- **Nutrition Info:** Calories 210, fat 5, fiber 7, carbs 12, protein 5

164.Rosemary Lemon Chicken

Servings: 8
Cooking Time: 45 Minutes
Ingredients:
- 4-lb. chicken, cut into pieces
- Salt and black pepper, to taste
- Flour for dredging 3 tablespoons olive oil
- 1 large onion, sliced
- Peel of ½ lemon
- 2 large garlic cloves, minced
- 1 1/2 teaspoons rosemary leaves
- 1 tablespoon honey
- 1/4 cup lemon juice
- 1 cup chicken broth

Directions:
1. Dredges the chicken through the flour then place in the baking pan.
2. Whisk broth with the rest of the Ingredients: in a bowl.
3. Pour this mixture over the dredged chicken in the pan.

4. Press "Power Button" of Air Fry Oven and turn the dial to select the "Bake" mode.
5. Press the Time button and again turn the dial to set the cooking time to 45 minutes.
6. Now push the Temp button and rotate the dial to set the temperature at 400 degrees F.
7. Once preheated, place the baking pan inside and close its lid.
8. Baste the chicken with its sauce every 15 minutes.
9. Serve warm.
- **Nutrition Info:** Calories 405 Total Fat 22.7 g Saturated Fat 6.1 g Cholesterol 4 mg Sodium 227 mg Total Carbs 26.1 g Fiber 1.4 g Sugar 0.9 g Protein 45.2 g

165.Basic Roasted Tofu

Servings: 4
Cooking Time: 45 Minutes
Ingredients:
- 1 or more (16-ounce) containers extra-firm tofu
- 1 tablespoon sesame oil
- 1 tablespoon soy sauce
- 1 tablespoon rice vinegar
- 1 tablespoon water

Directions:
1. Start by drying the tofu: first pat dry with paper towels, then lay on another set of paper towels or a dish towel.
2. Put a plate on top of the tofu then put something heavy on the plate (like a large can of vegetables). Leave it there for at least 20 minutes.
3. While tofu is being pressed, whip up marinade by combining oil, soy sauce, vinegar, and water in a bowl and set aside.
4. Cut the tofu into squares or sticks. Place the tofu in the marinade for at least 30 minutes.
5. Preheat toaster oven to 350°F. Line a pan with parchment paper and add as many pieces of tofu as you can, giving each piece adequate space.
6. Bake 20–45 minutes; tofu is done when the outside edges look golden brown. Time will vary depending on tofu size and shape.
- **Nutrition Info:** Calories: 114, Sodium: 239 mg, Dietary Fiber: 1.1 g, Total Fat: 8.1 g, Total Carbs: 2.2 g, Protein: 9.5 g.

166.Chili Chicken Sliders

Servings: 4
Cooking Time: 10 Minutes
Ingredients:
- 1/3 teaspoon paprika
- 1/3 cup scallions, peeled and chopped
- 3 cloves garlic, peeled and minced
- 1 teaspoon ground black pepper, or to taste
- 1/2 teaspoon fresh basil, minced

- 1 ½ cups chicken,minced
- 1 ½ tablespoons coconut aminos
- 1/2 teaspoon grated fresh ginger
- 1/2 tablespoon chili sauce
- 1 teaspoon salt

Directions:
1. Thoroughly combine all ingredients in a mixing dish. Then, form into 4 patties.
2. Cook in the preheated Air Fryer for 18 minutes at 355 degrees F.
3. Garnish with toppings of choice.
- **Nutrition Info:** 366 Calories; 6g Fat; 4g Carbs; 66g Protein; 3g Sugars; 9g Fiber

167.Maple Chicken Thighs

Servings: 4
Cooking Time: 30 Minutes
Ingredients:
- 4 large chicken thighs, bone-in
- 2 tablespoons French mustard
- 2 tablespoons Dijon mustard
- 1 clove minced garlic
- 1/2 teaspoon dried marjoram
- 2 tablespoons maple syrup

Directions:
1. Mix chicken with everything in a bowl and coat it well.
2. Place the chicken along with its marinade in the baking pan.
3. Press "Power Button" of Air Fry Oven and turn the dial to select the "Bake" mode.
4. Press the Time button and again turn the dial to set the cooking time to 30 minutes.
5. Now push the Temp button and rotate the dial to set the temperature at 370 degrees F.
6. Once preheated, place the baking pan inside and close its lid.
7. Serve warm.
- **Nutrition Info:** Calories 301 Total Fat 15.8 g Saturated Fat 2.7 g Cholesterol 75 mg Sodium 189 mg Total Carbs 31.7 g Fiber 0.3 g Sugar 0.1 g Protein 28.2 g

168.Juicy Turkey Burgers

Servings: 8
Cooking Time: 25 Minutes
Ingredients:
- 1 lb ground turkey 85% lean / 15% fat
- ¼ cup unsweetened apple sauce
- ½ onion grated
- 1 Tbsp ranch seasoning
- 2 tsp Worcestershire Sauce
- 1 tsp minced garlic
- ¼ cup plain breadcrumbs
- Salt and pepper to taste

Directions:
1. Combine the onion, ground turkey, unsweetened apple sauce, minced garlic, breadcrumbs, ranch seasoning, Worchestire sauce, and salt and pepper. Mix them with your hands until well combined. Form 4 equally sized hamburger patties with them.
2. Place these burgers in the refrigerator for about 30 minutes to have them firm up a bit.
3. While preparing for cooking, select the Air Fry option. Set the temperature of 360°F and the cook time as required. Press start to begin preheating.
4. Once the preheating temperature is reached, place the burgers on the tray in the Air fryer basket, making sure they don't overlap or touch. Cook on for 15 minutes
5. flipping halfway through.
- **Nutrition Info:** Calories 183, Total Fat 3g, Total Carbs 11g, Protein 28g

169.Tomato Frittata

Servings: 2
Cooking Time: 30 Minutes
Ingredients:
- 4 eggs
- ¼ cup onion, chopped
- ½ cup tomatoes, chopped
- ½ cup milk
- 1 cup Gouda cheese, shredded
- Salt, as required

Directions:
1. In a small baking pan, add all the ingredients and mix well.
2. Press "Power Button" of Air Fry Oven and turn the dial to select the "Air Fry" mode.
3. Press the Time button and again turn the dial to set the cooking time to 30 minutes.
4. Now push the Temp button and rotate the dial to set the temperature at 340 degrees F.
5. Press "Start/Pause" button to start.
6. When the unit beeps to show that it is preheated, open the lid.
7. Arrange the baking pan over the "Wire Rack" and insert in the oven.
8. Cut into 2 wedges and serve.
- **Nutrition Info:** Calories: 247 Cal Total Fat: 16.1 g Saturated Fat: 7.5 g Cholesterol: 332 mg Sodium: 417 mg Total Carbs: 7.30 g Fiber: 0.9 g Sugar: 5.2 g Protein: 18.6 g

170.Squash And Zucchini Mini Pizza

Servings: 4
Cooking Time: 15 Minutes
Ingredients:
- 1 pizza crust
- 1/2 cup parmesan cheese
- 4 tablespoons oregano
- 1 zucchini
- 1 yellow summer squash
- Olive oil
- Salt and pepper

Directions:

1. Start by preheating toaster oven to 350°F.
2. If you are using homemade crust, roll out 8 mini portions; if crust is store-bought, use a cookie cutter to cut out the portions.
3. Sprinkle parmesan and oregano equally on each piece. Layer the zucchini and squash in a circle – one on top of the other – around the entire circle.
4. Brush with olive oil and sprinkle salt and pepper to taste.
5. Bake for 15 minutes and serve.
- **Nutrition Info:** Calories: 151, Sodium: 327 mg, Dietary Fiber: 3.1 g, Total Fat: 8.6 g, Total Carbs: 10.3 g, Protein: 11.4 g.

171. Philly Cheesesteak Egg Rolls

Servings: 4-5
Cooking Time: 20 Minutes
Ingredients:
- 1 egg
- 1 tablespoon milk
- 2 tablespoons olive oil
- 1 small red onion
- 1 small red bell pepper
- 1 small green bell pepper
- 1 pound thinly slice roast beef
- 8 ounces shredded pepper jack cheese
- 8 ounces shredded provolone cheese
- 8-10 egg roll skins
- Salt and pepper

Directions:
1. Start by preheating toaster oven to 425°F.
2. Mix together egg and milk in a shallow bowl and set aside for later use.
3. Chop onions and bell peppers into small pieces.
4. Heat the oil in a medium sauce pan and add the onions and peppers.
5. Cook onions and peppers for 2–3 minutes until softened.
6. Add roast beef to the pan and sauté for another 5 minutes.
7. Add salt and pepper to taste.
8. Add cheese and mix together until melted.
9. Remove from heat and drain liquid from pan.
10. Roll the egg roll skins flat.
11. Add equal parts of the mix to each egg roll and roll them up per the instructions on the package.
12. Brush each egg roll with the egg mixture.
13. Line a pan with parchment paper and lay egg rolls seam-side down with a gap between each roll.
14. Bake for 20–25 minutes, depending on your preference of egg roll crispness.
- **Nutrition Info:** Calories: 769, Sodium: 1114 mg, Dietary Fiber: 2.1 g, Total Fat: 39.9 g, Total Carbs: 41.4 g, Protein: 58.4 g.

DINNER RECIPES

172.Sautéed Green Beans

Servings: 2
Cooking Time: 10 Minutes
Ingredients:

- 8 ounces fresh green beans, trimmed and cut in half
- 1 teaspoon sesame oil
- 1 tablespoon soy sauce

Directions:

1. Preheat the Air fryer to 390 °F and grease an Air fryer basket.
2. Mix green beans, soy sauce, and sesame oil in a bowl and toss to coat well.
3. Arrange green beans into the Air fryer basket and cook for about 10 minutes, tossing once in between.
4. Dish out onto serving plates and serve hot.
- **Nutrition Info:** Calories: 59, Fats: 2.4g, Carbohydrates: 59g, Sugar: 1.7g, Proteins: 2.6g, Sodium: 458mg

173.Pepper Pork Chops

Servings: 2
Cooking Time: 6 Minutes
Ingredients:

- 2 pork chops
- 1 egg white
- ¾ cup xanthum gum
- ½ teaspoon sea salt
- ¼ teaspoon freshly ground black pepper
- 1 oil mister

Directions:

1. Preheat the Air fryer to 400 degree F and grease an Air fryer basket.
2. Whisk egg white with salt and black pepper in a bowl and dip the pork chops in it.
3. Cover the bowl and marinate for about 20 minutes.
4. Pour the xanthum gum over both sides of the chops and spray with oil mister.
5. Arrange the chops in the Air fryer basket and cook for about 6 minutes.
6. Dish out in a bowl and serve warm.
- **Nutrition Info:** Calories: 541, Fat: 34g, Carbohydrates: 3.4g, Sugar: 1g, Protein: 20.3g, Sodium: 547mg

174.Scallops With Spinach

Servings: 2
Cooking Time: 10 Minutes
Ingredients:

- 1: 12-ouncespackage frozen spinach, thawed and drained
- 8 jumbo sea scallops
- Olive oil cooking spray
- 1 tablespoon fresh basil, chopped
- Salt and ground black pepper, as required
- ¾ cup heavy whipping cream
- 1 tablespoon tomato paste
- 1 teaspoon garlic, minced

Directions:

1. Preheat the Air fryer to 350 degree F and grease an Air fryer pan.
2. Season the scallops evenly with salt and black pepper.
3. Mix cream, tomato paste, garlic, basil, salt, and black pepper in a bowl.
4. Place spinach at the bottom of the Air fryer pan, followed by seasoned scallops and top with the cream mixture.
5. Transfer into the Air fryer and cook for about 10 minutes.
6. Dish out in a platter and serve hot.
- **Nutrition Info:** Calories: 203, Fat: 18.3g, Carbohydrates: 12.3g, Sugar: 1.7g, Protein: 26.4g, Sodium: 101mg

175.Broccoli And Tomato Sauce

Servings: 4
Cooking Time: 7 Minutes
Ingredients:

- 1 broccoli head, florets separated
- ¼ cup scallions; chopped
- ½ cup tomato sauce
- 1 tbsp. olive oil
- 1 tbsp. sweet paprika
- Salt and black pepper to taste.

Directions:

1. In a pan that fits the air fryer, combine the broccoli with the rest of the Ingredients: toss.
2. Put the pan in the fryer and cook at 380°F for 15 minutes
3. Divide between plates and serve.
- **Nutrition Info:** Calories: 163; Fat: 5g; Fiber: 2g; Carbs: 4g; Protein: 8g

176.Fennel & Tomato Chicken Paillard

Servings: 1
Cooking Time: 12 Minutes
Ingredients:

- 1/4 cup olive oil
- 1 boneless skinless chicken breast
- Salt and pepper
- 1 garlic clove, thinly sliced
- 1 small diced Roma tomato
- 1/2 fennel bulb, shaved
- 1/4 cup sliced mushrooms
- 2 tablespoons sliced black olives
- 1-1/2 teaspoons capers
- 2 sprigs fresh thyme
- 1 tablespoon chopped fresh parsley

Directions:

1. Start by pounding the chicken until it is about 1/2-inch thick.

2. Preheat the toaster oven to 400°F and brush the bottom of a baking pan with olive oil.
3. Sprinkle salt and pepper on both sides of the chicken and place it in the baking pan.
4. In a bowl, mix together all other ingredients, including the remaining olive oil.
5. Spoon mixture over chicken and bake for 12 minutes.
- **Nutrition Info:** Calories: 797, Sodium: 471 mg, Dietary Fiber: 6.0 g, Total Fat: 63.7 g, Total Carbs: 16.4 g, Protein: 45.8 g.

177.Chinese-style Spicy And Herby Beef

Servings: 4
Cooking Time: 20 Minutes
Ingredients:
- 1 pound flank steak, cut into small pieces
- 1 teaspoon fresh sage leaves, minced
- 1/3 cup olive oil
- 3 teaspoons sesame oil
- 3 tablespoons Shaoxing wine
- 2 tablespoons tamari
- 1 teaspoon hot sauce
- 1/8 teaspoon xanthum gum
- 1 teaspoon seasoned salt
- 3 cloves garlic,minced
- 1 teaspoon fresh rosemary leaves, finely minced
- 1/2 teaspoon freshly cracked black pepper

Directions:
1. Warm the oil in a sauté pan over a moderate heat. Now, sauté the garlic until just tender and fragrant.
2. Now, add the remaining ingredients. Toss to coat well.
3. Then, roast for about 18 minutes at 345 degrees F. Check doneness and serve warm.
- **Nutrition Info:** 354 Calories; 24g Fat; 8g Carbs; 21g Protein; 3g Sugars; 3g Fiber

178.Indian Meatballs With Lamb

Servings: 8
Cooking Time: 14 Minutes
Ingredients:
- 1 garlic clove
- 1 tablespoon butter
- 4 oz chive stems
- ¼ tablespoon turmeric
- 1/3 teaspoon cayenne pepper
- 1 teaspoon ground coriander
- ¼ teaspoon bay leaf
- 1 teaspoon salt
- 1-pound ground lamb
- 1 egg
- 1 teaspoon ground black pepper

Directions:
1. Peel the garlic clove and mince it

2. Combine the minced garlic with the ground lamb.
3. Then sprinkle the meat mixture with the turmeric, cayenne pepper, ground coriander, bay leaf, salt, and ground black pepper.
4. Beat the egg in the forcemeat.
5. Then grate the chives and add them in the lamb forcemeat too.
6. Mix it up to make the smooth mass.
7. Then preheat the air fryer to 400 F.
8. Put the butter in the air fryer basket tray and melt it.
9. Then make the meatballs from the lamb mixture and place them in the air fryer basket tray.
10. Cook the dish for 14 minutes.
11. Stir the meatballs twice during the cooking.
12. Serve the cooked meatballs immediately.
13. Enjoy!
- **Nutrition Info:** calories 134, fat 6.2, fiber 0.4, carbs 1.8, protein 16.9

179.Creamy Lemon Turkey

Servings: 4
Cooking Time: 20 Minutes
Ingredients:
- 1/3 cup sour cream
- 2 cloves garlic, finely minced 1/3 tsp. lemon zest
- 2 small-sized turkey breasts, skinless and cubed 1/3 cup thickened cream
- 2 tablespoons lemon juice
- 1 tsp. fresh marjoram, chopped
- Salt and freshly cracked mixed peppercorns, to taste 1/2 cup scallion, chopped
- 1/2 can tomatoes, diced
- 1½ tablespoons canola oil

Directions:
1. Firstly, pat dry the turkey breast. Mix the remaining items; marinate the turkey for 2 hours.
2. Set the air fryer to cook at 355 °F. Brush the turkey with a nonstick spray; cook for 23 minutes, turning once. Serve with naan and enjoy!
- **Nutrition Info:** 260 Calories; 15.3g Fat; 8.9g Carbs; 28.6g Protein; 1.9g Sugars

180.Summer Fish Packets

Servings: 2
Cooking Time: 20 Minutes
Ingredients:
- 2 snapper fillets
- 1 shallot, peeled and sliced
- 2 garlic cloves, halved
- 1 bell pepper, sliced
- 1 small-sized serrano pepper, sliced
- 1 tomato, sliced

- 1 tablespoon olive oil
- 1/4 teaspoon freshly ground black pepper
- 1/2 teaspoon paprika
- Sea salt, to taste
- 2 bay leaves

Directions:
1. Place two parchment sheets on a working surface. Place the fish in the center of one side of the parchment paper.
2. Top with the shallot, garlic, peppers, and tomato. Drizzle olive oil over the fish and vegetables. Season with black pepper, paprika, and salt. Add the bay leaves.
3. Fold over the other half of the parchment. Now, fold the paper around the edges tightly and create a half moon shape, sealing the fish inside.
4. Cook in the preheated Air Fryer at 390 degrees F for 15 minutes. Serve warm.
- **Nutrition Info:** 329 Calories; 8g Fat; 17g Carbs; 47g Protein; 4g Sugars; 8g Fiber

181.Broccoli Crust Pizza

Servings: 4
Cooking Time: 20 Minutes
Ingredients:
- 3 cups riced broccoli, steamed and drained well
- ½ cup shredded mozzarella cheese
- ½ cup grated vegetarian Parmesan cheese.
- 1 large egg.
- 3 tbsp. low-carb Alfredo sauce

Directions:
1. Take a large bowl, mix broccoli, egg and Parmesan.
2. Cut a piece of parchment to fit your air fryer basket. Press out the pizza mixture to fit on the parchment, working in two batches if necessary. Place into the air fryer basket. Adjust the temperature to 370 Degrees F and set the timer for 5 minutes.
3. When the timer beeps, the crust should be firm enough to flip. If not, add 2 additional minutes. Flip crust.
4. Top with Alfredo sauce and mozzarella. Return to the air fryer basket and cook an additional 7 minutes or until cheese is golden and bubbling. Serve warm.
- **Nutrition Info:** Calories: 136; Protein: 9g; Fiber: 3g; Fat: 6g; Carbs:7g

182.Traditional English Fish And Chips

Servings: 4
Cooking Time: 17 Minutes
Ingredients:
- 1 3/4 pounds potatoes
- 4 tablespoons olive oil
- 1-1/4 teaspoons kosher salt
- 1-1/4 teaspoons black pepper

- 8 sprigs fresh thyme
- 4 (6-ounce) pieces cod
- 1 lemon
- 1 clove garlic
- 2 tablespoons capers

Directions:
1. Start by preheating toaster oven to 450°F.
2. Cut potatoes into 1-inch chunks.
3. Place potatoes, 2 tablespoons oil, salt, and thyme in a baking tray and toss to combine.
4. Spread in a flat layer and bake for 30 minutes.
5. Wrap mixture in foil to keep warm.
6. Wipe tray with a paper towel and then lay cod in the tray.
7. Slice the lemon and top cod with lemon, salt, pepper, and thyme.
8. Drizzle rest of the oil over the cod and bake for 12 minutes.
9. Place cod and potatoes on separate pans and bake together for an additional 5 minutes.
10. Combine and serve.
- **Nutrition Info:** Calories: 442, Sodium: 1002 mg, Dietary Fiber: 5.4 g, Total Fat: 15.8 g, Total Carbs: 32.7 g, Protein: 42.5 g.

183.Cheese Zucchini Boats

Servings: 2
Cooking Time: 20 Minutes
Ingredients:
- 2 medium zucchinis
- ¼ cup full-fat ricotta cheese
- ¼ cup shredded mozzarella cheese
- ¼ cup low-carb, no-sugar-added pasta sauce.
- 2 tbsp. grated vegetarian Parmesan cheese
- 1 tbsp. avocado oil
- ¼ tsp. garlic powder.
- ½ tsp. dried parsley.
- ¼ tsp. dried oregano.

Directions:
1. Cut off 1-inch from the top and bottom of each zucchini.
2. Slice zucchini in half lengthwise and use a spoon to scoop out a bit of the inside, making room for filling. Brush with oil and spoon 2 tbsp. pasta sauce into each shell
3. Take a medium bowl, mix ricotta, mozzarella, oregano, garlic powder and parsley
4. Spoon the mixture into each zucchini shell. Place stuffed zucchini shells into the air fryer basket.
5. Adjust the temperature to 350 Degrees F and set the timer for 20 minutes
6. To remove from the fryer basket, use tongs or a spatula and carefully lift out. Top with Parmesan. Serve immediately.

- **Nutrition Info:** Calories: 215; Protein: 15g; Fiber: 7g; Fat: 19g; Carbs: 3g

184.Delicious Beef Roast With Red Potatoes

Servings: 3
Cooking Time: 25 Minutes
Ingredients:
- 2 tbsp olive oil
- 4 pound top round roast beef
- 1 tsp salt
- ¼ tsp fresh ground black pepper
- 1 tsp dried thyme
- ½ tsp fresh rosemary, chopped
- 3 pounds red potatoes, halved
- Olive oil, black pepper and salt for garnish

Directions:
1. Preheat your Air Fryer to 360 F. In a small bowl, mix rosemary, salt, pepper and thyme; rub oil onto beef. Season with the spice mixture. Place the prepared meat in your Air Fryer's cooking basket and cook for 20 minutes.
2. Give the meat a turn and add potatoes, more pepper and oil. Cook for 20 minutes more. Take the steak out and set aside to cool for 10 minutes. Cook the potatoes in your Air Fryer for 10 more minutes at 400 F. Serve hot.
- **Nutrition Info:** 346 Calories; 11g Fat; 4g Carbs; 32g Protein; 1g Sugars; 1g Fiber

185.Chargrilled Halibut Niçoise With Vegetables

Servings: 6
Cooking Time: 15 Minutes
Ingredients:
- 1 ½ pounds halibut fillets
- Salt and pepper to taste
- 2 tablespoons olive oil
- 2 pounds mixed vegetables
- 4 cups torn lettuce leaves
- 1 cup cherry tomatoes, halved
- 4 large hard-boiled eggs, peeled and sliced

Directions:
1. Place the instant pot air fryer lid on and preheat the instant pot at 390 degrees F.
2. Place the grill pan accessory in the instant pot.
3. Rub the halibut with salt and pepper. Brush the fish with oil.
4. Place on the grill.
5. Surround the fish fillet with the mixed vegetables, close the air fryer lid and grill for 15 minutes.
6. Assemble the salad by serving the fish fillet with mixed grilled vegetables, lettuce, cherry tomatoes, and hard-boiled eggs.

- **Nutrition Info:** Calories: 312; Carbs:16.8 g; Protein: 19.8g; Fat: 18.3g

186.Beef Pieces With Tender Broccoli

Servings: 4
Cooking Time: 13 Minutes
Ingredients:
- 6 oz. broccoli
- 10 oz. beef brisket
- 4 oz chive stems
- 1 teaspoon paprika
- 1/3 cup water
- 1 teaspoon olive oil
- 1 teaspoon butter
- 1 tablespoon flax seeds
- ½ teaspoon chili flakes

Directions:
1. Cut the beef brisket into the medium/convenient pieces.
2. Sprinkle the beef pieces with the paprika and chili flakes.
3. Mix the meat up with the help of the hands.
4. Then preheat the air fryer to 360 F.
5. Spray the air fryer basket tray with the olive oil.
6. Put the beef pieces in the air fryer basket tray and cook the meat for 7 minutes.
7. Stir it once during the cooking.
8. Meanwhile, separate the broccoli into the florets.
9. When the time is over – add the broccoli florets in the air fryer basket tray.
10. Sprinkle the ingredients with the flax seeds and butter.
11. Add water.
12. Dice the chives and add them in the air fryer basket tray too.
13. Stir it gently using the wooden spatula.
14. Then cook the dish at 265 F for 6 minutes more.
15. When the broccoli is tender – the dish is cooked.
16. Serve the dish little bit chilled.
17. Enjoy!
- **Nutrition Info:** calories 187, fat 7.3, fiber 2.4, carbs 6.2, protein 23.4

187.Spicy Sesame-honey Chicken

Servings: 4
Cooking Time: 30 Minutes
Ingredients:
- 1 package of chicken thighs/wings
- 1 tablespoon sugar
- 1-1/3 tablespoons chili garlic sauce
- 1/4 cup soy sauce
- 1 tablespoon sesame oil
- 1 tablespoon ketchup
- 1 tablespoon honey
- 1 tablespoon soy sauce

- 1 teaspoon sugar or brown sugar
- 1 teaspoon cornstarch

Directions:
1. Create marinade by combining 1 tablespoon chili sauce, soy sauce, and sesame oil.
2. Toss chicken in marinade and refrigerate for at least 30 minutes, but up to a day.
3. Preheat toaster oven to 375°F. Place chicken on a baking sheet with a little space between each piece and bake for 30 minutes.
4. While the chicken bakes, create the sauce by combining all the leftover ingredients, including the 1/3 tablespoon of chili sauce.
5. Mix well and microwave in 30-second intervals until the sauce starts to thicken.
6. Toss chicken in sauce and serve.
- **Nutrition Info:** Calories: 401, Sodium: 1439 mg, Dietary Fiber: 0 g, Total Fat: 16.0 g, Total Carbs: 11.2 g, Protein: 50.6 g.

188.Roasted Garlic Zucchini Rolls

Servings: 4
Cooking Time: 20 Minutes
Ingredients:
- 2 medium zucchinis
- ½ cup full-fat ricotta cheese
- ¼ white onion; peeled. And diced
- 2 cups spinach; chopped
- ¼ cup heavy cream
- ½ cup sliced baby portobello mushrooms
- ¾ cup shredded mozzarella cheese, divided.
- 2 tbsp. unsalted butter.
- 2 tbsp. vegetable broth.
- ½ tsp. finely minced roasted garlic
- ¼ tsp. dried oregano.
- ⅛ tsp. xanthan gum
- ¼ tsp. salt
- ½ tsp. garlic powder.

Directions:
1. Using a mandoline or sharp knife, slice zucchini into long strips lengthwise. Place strips between paper towels to absorb moisture. Set aside
2. In a medium saucepan over medium heat, melt butter. Add onion and sauté until fragrant. Add garlic and sauté 30 seconds.
3. Pour in heavy cream, broth and xanthan gum. Turn off heat and whisk mixture until it begins to thicken, about 3 minutes.
4. Take a medium bowl, add ricotta, salt, garlic powder and oregano and mix well. Fold in spinach, mushrooms and ½ cup mozzarella
5. Pour half of the sauce into a 6-inch round baking pan. To assemble the rolls, place two strips of zucchini on a work surface. Spoon 2 tbsp. of ricotta mixture onto the slices and roll up. Place seam side down on top of sauce. Repeat with remaining ingredients

6. Pour remaining sauce over the rolls and sprinkle with remaining mozzarella. Cover with foil and place into the air fryer basket. Adjust the temperature to 350 Degrees F and set the timer for 20 minutes. In the last 5 minutes, remove the foil to brown the cheese. Serve immediately.
- **Nutrition Info:** Calories: 245; Protein: 15g; Fiber: 8g; Fat: 19g; Carbs: 1g

189.Hot Pork Skewers

Servings: 3 To 4
Cooking Time: 1 Hour 20 Minutes
Ingredients:
- 1 lb pork steak, cut in cubes
- ¼ cup soy sauce
- 2 tsp smoked paprika
- 1 tsp powdered chili
- 1 tsp garlic salt
- 1 tsp red chili flakes
- 1 tbsp white wine vinegar
- 3 tbsp steak sauce
- Skewing:
- 1 green pepper, cut in cubes
- 1 red pepper, cut in cubes
- 1 yellow squash, seeded and cut in cubes
- 1 green squash, seeded and cut in cubes
- Salt and black pepper to taste to season

Directions:
1. In a mixing bowl, add the pork cubes, soy sauce, smoked paprika, powdered chili, garlic salt, red chili flakes, white wine vinegar, and steak sauce. Mix them using a ladle. Refrigerate to marinate them for 1 hour.
2. After one hour, remove the marinated pork from the fridge and preheat the Air Fryer to 370 F.
3. On each skewer, stick the pork cubes and vegetables in the order that you prefer. Have fun doing this. Once the pork cubes and vegetables are finished, arrange the skewers in the fryer basket and grill them for 8 minutes. You can do them in batches. Once ready, remove them onto the serving platter and serve with salad.
- **Nutrition Info:** 456 Calories; 37g Fat; 1g Carbs; 21g Protein; 5g Sugars; 6g Fiber

190.Pork Chops With Keto Gravy

Servings: 4
Cooking Time: 17 Minutes
Ingredients:
- 1-pound pork chops
- 1 teaspoon kosher salt
- ½ teaspoon ground cinnamon
- 1 teaspoon ground white pepper
- 1 cup heavy cream
- 6 oz. white mushrooms

- 1 tablespoon butter
- ½ teaspoon ground ginger
- 1 teaspoon ground turmeric
- 4 oz chive stems
- 1 garlic clove, chopped

Directions:
1. Sprinkle the pork chops with the kosher salt, ground cinnamon, ground white pepper, and ground turmeric.
2. Preheat the air fryer to 375 F.
3. Pour the heavy cream in the air fryer basket tray.
4. Then slice the white mushrooms and add them in the heavy cream.
5. After this, add butter, ground ginger, chopped chives, and chopped garlic.
6. Cook the gravy for 5 minutes.
7. Then stir the cream gravy and add the pork chops.
8. Cook the pork chops at 400 F for 12 minutes.
9. When the time is over stir the pork chops gently and transfer them to the serving plates.
10. Enjoy!
- **Nutrition Info:** calories 518, fat 42.4, fiber 1.5, carbs 6.2, protein 28

191.Roasted Tuna On Linguine

Servings: 2
Cooking Time: 20 Minutes
Ingredients:
- 1pound fresh tuna fillets
- Salt and pepper to taste
- 1 tablespoon olive oil
- 12 ounces linguine, cooked according to package Directions:
- 2 cups parsley leaves, chopped
- 1 tablespoon capers, chopped
- Juice from 1 lemon

Directions:
1. Place the instant pot air fryer lid on and preheat the instant pot at 390 degrees F.
2. Place the grill pan accessory in the instant pot.
3. Season the tuna with salt and pepper. Brush with oil.
4. Place on the grill pan, close the air fryer lid and grill for 20 minutes.
5. Once the tuna is cooked, shred using forks and place on top of cooked linguine. Add parsley and capers. Season with salt and pepper and add lemon juice.
- **Nutrition Info:** Calories: 520; Carbs: 60.6g; Protein: 47.7g; Fat: 9.6g

192.Flank Steak Beef

Servings: 4
Cooking Time: 20 Minutes

Ingredients:
- 1 pound flank steaks, sliced
- ¼ cup xanthum gum
- 2 teaspoon vegetable oil
- ½ teaspoon ginger
- ½ cup soy sauce
- 1 tablespoon garlic, minced
- ½ cup water
- ¾ cup swerve, packed

Directions:
1. Preheat the Air fryer to 390 degree F and grease an Air fryer basket.
2. Coat the steaks with xanthum gum on both the sides and transfer into the Air fryer basket.
3. Cook for about 10 minutes and dish out in a platter.
4. Meanwhile, cook rest of the ingredients for the sauce in a saucepan.
5. Bring to a boil and pour over the steak slices to serve.
- **Nutrition Info:** Calories: 372, Fat: 11.8g, Carbohydrates: 1.8g, Sugar: 27.3g, Protein: 34g, Sodium: 871mg

193.Cheese And Garlic Stuffed Chicken Breasts

Servings: 2
Cooking Time: 20 Minutes
Ingredients:
- 1/2 cup Cottage cheese 2 eggs, beaten
- 2 medium-sized chicken breasts, halved
- 2 tablespoons fresh coriander, chopped 1tsp. fine sea salt
- Seasoned breadcrumbs
- 1/3 tsp. freshly ground black pepper, to savor 3 cloves garlic, finely minced

Directions:
1. Firstly, flatten out the chicken breast using a meat tenderizer.
2. In a medium-sized mixing dish, combine the Cottage cheese with the garlic, coriander, salt, and black pepper.
3. Spread 1/3 of the mixture over the first chicken breast. Repeat with the remaining ingredients. Roll the chicken around the filling; make sure to secure with toothpicks.
4. Now, whisk the egg in a shallow bowl. In another shallow bowl, combine the salt, ground black pepper, and seasoned breadcrumbs.
5. Coat the chicken breasts with the whisked egg; now, roll them in the breadcrumbs.
6. Cook in the air fryer cooking basket at 365 °F for 22 minutes. Serve immediately.
- **Nutrition Info:** 424 Calories; 24.5g Fat; 7.5g Carbs; 43.4g Protein; 5.3g Sugars

194.Spiced Salmon Kebabs

Servings: 3
Cooking Time: 15 Minutes
Ingredients:
- 2 tablespoons chopped fresh oregano
- 2 teaspoons sesame seeds
- 1 teaspoon ground cumin
- Salt and pepper to taste
- 1 ½ pounds salmon fillets
- 2 tablespoons olive oil
- 2 lemons, sliced into rounds

Directions:
1. Place the instant pot air fryer lid on and preheat the instant pot at 390 degrees F.
2. Place the grill pan accessory in the instant pot.
3. Create dry rub by combining the oregano, sesame seeds, cumin, salt, and pepper.
4. Rub the salmon fillets with the dry rub and brush with oil.
5. Place on the grill pan, close the air fryer lid and grill the salmon for 15 minutes.
6. Serve with lemon slices once cooked.
- **Nutrition Info:** Calories per serving 447 ; Carbs: 4.1g; Protein:47.6 g; Fat:26.6 g

195.Chat Masala Grilled Snapper

Servings: 5
Cooking Time: 25 Minutes
Ingredients:
- 2 ½ pounds whole fish
- Salt to taste
- 1/3 cup chat masala
- 3 tablespoons fresh lime juice
- 5 tablespoons olive oil

Directions:
1. Place the instant pot air fryer lid on and preheat the instant pot at 390 degrees F.
2. Place the grill pan accessory in the instant pot.
3. Season the fish with salt, chat masala and lime juice.
4. Brush with oil.
5. Place the fish on a foil basket and place it inside the grill.
6. Close the air fryer lid and cook for 25 minutes.
- **Nutrition Info:** Calories:308; Carbs: 0.7g; Protein: 35.2g; Fat: 17.4g

196.Keto Lamb Kleftiko

Servings: 6
Cooking Time: 30 Minutes
Ingredients:
- 2 oz. garlic clove, peeled
- 1 tablespoon dried oregano
- ½ lemon
- ¼ tablespoon ground cinnamon
- 3 tablespoon butter, frozen
- 18 oz. leg of lamb
- 1 cup heavy cream
- 1 teaspoon bay leaf
- 1 teaspoon dried mint
- 1 tablespoon olive oil

Directions:
1. Crush the garlic cloves and combine them with the dried oregano, and ground cinnamon. Mix it.
2. Then chop the lemon.
3. Sprinkle the leg of lamb with the crushed garlic mixture.
4. Then rub it with the chopped lemon.
5. Combine the heavy cream, bay leaf, and dried mint together.
6. Whisk the mixture well.
7. After this, add the olive oil and whisk it one more time more.
8. Then pour the cream mixture on the leg of lamb and stir it carefully.
9. Leave the leg of lamb for 10 minutes to marinate.
10. Preheat the air fryer to 380 F.
11. Chop the butter and sprinkle the marinated lamb.
12. Then place the leg of lamb in the air fryer basket tray and sprinkle it with the remaining cream mixture.
13. Then sprinkle the meat with the chopped butter.
14. Cook the meat for 30 minutes.
15. When the time is over – remove the meat from the air fryer and sprinkle it gently with the remaining cream mixture.
16. Serve it!
- **Nutrition Info:** calories 318, fat 21.9, fiber 0.9, carbs 4.9, protein 25.1

197.Buttered Scallops

Servings: 2
Cooking Time: 4 Minutes
Ingredients:
- ¾ pound sea scallops, cleaned and patted very dry
- 1 tablespoon butter, melted
- ½ tablespoon fresh thyme, minced
- Salt and black pepper, as required

Directions:
1. Preheat the Air fryer to 390 degree F and grease an Air fryer basket.
2. Mix scallops, butter, thyme, salt, and black pepper in a bowl.
3. Arrange scallops in the Air fryer basket and cook for about 4 minutes.
4. Dish out the scallops in a platter and serve hot.
- **Nutrition Info:** Calories: 202, Fat: 7.1g, Carbohydrates: 4.4g, Sugar: 0g, Protein: 28.7g, Sodium: 393mg

198.Salmon Casserole

Servings: 8
Cooking Time: 12 Minutes
Ingredients:

- 7 oz Cheddar cheese, shredded
- ½ cup cream
- 1-pound salmon fillet
- 1 tablespoon dried dill
- 1 teaspoon dried parsley
- 1 teaspoon salt
- 1 teaspoon ground coriander
- ½ teaspoon ground black pepper
- 2 green pepper, chopped
- 4 oz chive stems, diced
- 7 oz bok choy, chopped
- 1 tablespoon olive oil

Directions:

1. Sprinkle the salmon fillet with the dried dill, dried parsley, ground coriander, and ground black pepper.
2. Massage the salmon fillet gently and leave it for 5 minutes to make the fish soaks the spices.
3. Meanwhile, sprinkle the air fryer casserole tray with the olive oil inside.
4. After this, cut the salmon fillet into the cubes.
5. Separate the salmon cubes into 2 parts.
6. Then place the first part of the salmon cubes in the casserole tray.
7. Sprinkle the fish with the chopped bok choy, diced chives, and chopped green pepper.
8. After this, place the second part of the salmon cubes over the vegetables.
9. Then sprinkle the casserole with the shredded cheese and heavy cream.
10. Preheat the air fryer to 380 F.
11. Cook the salmon casserole for 12 minutes.
12. When the dish is cooked – it will have acrunchy light brown crust.
13. Serve it and enjoy!
- **Nutrition Info:** calories 216, fat 14.4, fiber 1.1, carbs 4.3, protein 18.2

199.Sweet Chicken Breast

Servings: 4
Cooking Time: 12 Minutes
Ingredients:

- 1-pound chicken breast, boneless, skinless
- 3 tablespoon Stevia extract
- 1 teaspoon ground white pepper
- ½ teaspoon paprika
- 1 teaspoon cayenne pepper
- 1 teaspoon lemongrass
- 1 teaspoon lemon zest
- 1 tablespoon apple cider vinegar
- 1 tablespoon butter

Directions:

1. Sprinkle the chicken breast with the apple cider vinegar.
2. After this, rub the chicken breast with the ground white pepper, paprika, cayenne pepper, lemongrass, and lemon zest.
3. Leave the chicken breast for 5 minutes to marinate.
4. After this, rub the chicken breast with the stevia extract and leave it for 5 minutes more.
5. Preheat the air fryer to 380 F.
6. Rub the prepared chicken breast with the butter and place it in the air fryer basket tray.
7. Cook the chicken breast for 12 minutes.
8. Turn the chicken breast into another side after 6 minutes of cooking.
9. Serve the dish hot!
10. Enjoy!
- **Nutrition Info:** calories 160, fat 5.9, fiber 0.4, carbs 1, protein 24.2

200.Cheese Breaded Pork

Servings: 6
Cooking Time: 15 Minutes
Ingredients:

- 6 pork chops
- 6 tbsp seasoned breadcrumbs
- 2 tbsp parmesan cheese, grated
- 1 tbsp melted butter
- ½ cup mozzarella cheese, shredded
- 1 tbsp marinara sauce

Directions:

1. Preheat your air fryer to 390 f. Grease the cooking basket with cooking spray. In a small bowl, mix breadcrumbs and parmesan cheese. In another microwave proof bowl, add butter and melt in the microwave.
2. Brush the pork with butter and dredge into the breadcrumbs. Add pork to the cooking basket and cook for 6 minutes. Turnover and top with marinara sauce and shredded mozzarella; cook for 3 more minutes
- **Nutrition Info:** Calories: 431 Cal Total Fat: 0 g Saturated Fat: 0 g Cholesterol: 0 mg Sodium: 0 mg Total Carbs: 0 g Fiber: 0 g Sugar: 0 g Protein: 0 g

201.Sage Beef

Servings: 4
Cooking Time: 30 Minutes
Ingredients:

- 2pounds beef stew meat, cubed
- 1tablespoon sage, chopped
- 2tablespoons butter, melted
- ½ teaspoon coriander, ground
- ½ tablespoon garlic powder
- 1teaspoon Italian seasoning

- Salt and black pepper to the taste

Directions:
1. In the air fryer's pan, mix the beef with the sage, melted butter and the other ingredients, introduce the pan in the fryer and cook at 360 degrees F for 30 minutes.
2. Divide everything between plates and serve.
- **Nutrition Info:** Calories 290, Fat 11, Fiber 6, Carbs 20, Protein 29

202.Marinated Cajun Beef

Servings: 2
Cooking Time: 20 Minutes
Ingredients:
- 1/3 cup beef broth
- 2 tablespoons Cajun seasoning, crushed
- 1/2 teaspoon garlic powder
- 3/4 pound beef tenderloins
- ½ tablespoon pear cider vinegar
- 1/3 teaspoon cayenne pepper
- 1 ½ tablespoon olive oil
- 1/2 teaspoon freshly ground black pepper
- 1 teaspoon salt

Directions:
1. Firstly, coat the beef tenderloins with salt, cayenne pepper, and black pepper.
2. Mix the remaining items in a medium-sized bowl; let the meat marinate for 40 minutes in this mixture.
3. Roast the beef for about 22 minutes at 385 degrees F, turning it halfway through the cooking time.
- **Nutrition Info:** 483 Calories; 23g Fat; 5g Carbs; 53g Protein; 6g Sugars; 4g Fiber

203.Broiled Tilapia With Parmesan And Herbs

Servings: 4
Cooking Time: 8 Minutes
Ingredients:
- 4 (6- to 8-ounce) farm-raised tilapia filets
- 1/2 cup freshly grated parmesan cheese
- 2 tablespoons low-fat mayonnaise
- 2 tablespoons light sour cream
- 2 tablespoons melted unsalted butter
- 2 tablespoons lemon juice
- 1/2 teaspoon dried basil
- 1/2 teaspoon dried tarragon
- 1/8 teaspoon onion powder
- Salt and pepper to taste

Directions:
1. Mix together 1/4 cup parmesan and all other ingredients, except tilapia.
2. Place mixture in a plastic zipper bag, add fish and toss.
3. Pour fish mixture into a shallow pan and set aside to marinate for 20 minutes.

4. Place the fish in a broiler pan, top with a few spoonful of marinade, and sprinkle the rest of the parmesan over the fish.
5. Broil until lightly browned, around 8 minutes.
- **Nutrition Info:** Calories: 369, Sodium: 459 mg, Dietary Fiber: 0 g, Total Fat: 17.7 g, Total Carbs: 2.0 g, Protein: 51.6 g.

204.Garlic Parmesan Shrimp

Servings: 2
Cooking Time: 10 Minutes
Ingredients:
- 1 pound shrimp, deveined and peeled
- ½ cup parmesan cheese, grated
- ¼ cup cilantro, diced
- 1 tablespoon olive oil
- 1 teaspoon salt
- 1 teaspoon fresh cracked pepper
- 1 tablespoon lemon juice
- 6 garlic cloves, diced

Directions:
1. Preheat the Air fryer to 350 degree F and grease an Air fryer basket.
2. Drizzle shrimp with olive oil and lemon juice and season with garlic, salt and cracked pepper.
3. Cover the bowl with plastic wrap and refrigerate for about 3 hours.
4. Stir in the parmesan cheese and cilantro to the bowl and transfer to the Air fryer basket.
5. Cook for about 10 minutes and serve immediately.
- **Nutrition Info:** Calories: 602, Fat: 23.9g, Carbohydrates: 46.5g, Sugar: 2.9g, Protein: 11.3g, Sodium: 886mg

205.Pork Belly With Honey

Servings: 8
Cooking Time: 35 Minutes
Ingredients:
- 2 pounds pork belly
- ½ tsp pepper
- 1 tbsp olive oil
- 1 tbsp salt
- 3 tbsp honey

Directions:
1. Preheat your air fryer to 400 f. Season the pork belly with salt and pepper. Grease the basket with oil. Add seasoned meat and cook for 15 minutes. Add honey and cook for 10 minutes more. Serve with green salad.
- **Nutrition Info:** Calories: 274 Cal Total Fat: 18 g Saturated Fat: 0 g Cholesterol: 0 mg Sodium: 0 mg Total Carbs: 8 g Fiber: 0 g Sugar: 0 g Protein: 18 g

206. Sirloin Steak With Cremini Mushroom Sauce

Servings: 5
Cooking Time: 20 Minutes
Ingredients:
- 2 tablespoons butter
- 2 pounds sirloin, cut into four pieces
- Salt and cracked black pepper, to taste
- 1 teaspoon cayenne pepper
- 1/2 teaspoon dried rosemary
- 1/2 teaspoon dried dill
- 1/4 teaspoon dried thyme
- 1 pound Cremini mushrooms, sliced
- 1 cup sour cream
- 1 teaspoon mustard
- 1/2 teaspoon curry powder

Directions:
1. Start by preheating your Air Fryer to 396 degrees F. Grease a baking pan with butter.
2. Add the sirloin, salt, black pepper, cayenne pepper, rosemary, dill, and thyme to the baking pan. Cook for 9 minutes.
3. Next, stir in the mushrooms, sour cream, mustard, and curry powder. Continue to cook another 5 minutes or until everything is heated through.
4. Spoon onto individual serving plates.
- **Nutrition Info:** 349 Calories; 12g Fat; 4g Carbs; 49g Protein; 6g Sugars; 4g Fiber

207. Baked Veggie Egg Rolls

Servings: 2
Cooking Time: 20 Minutes
Ingredients:
- 1/2 tablespoon olive or vegetable oil
- 2 cups thinly-sliced chard
- 1/4 cup grated carrot
- 1/2 cup chopped pea pods
- 3 shiitake mushrooms
- 2 scallions
- 2 medium cloves garlic
- 1/2 tablespoon fresh ginger
- 1/2 tablespoon soy sauce
- 6 egg roll wrappers
- Olive oil spray for cookie sheet and egg rolls

Directions:
1. Start by mincing mushrooms, garlic, and ginger and slicing scallions.
2. Heat oil on medium heat in a medium skillet and char peas, carrots, scallions, and mushrooms.
3. Cook 3 minutes, then add ginger. Stir in soy sauce and remove from heat.
4. Preheat toaster oven to 400°F and spray cookie sheet. Spoon even portions of vegetable mix over each egg roll wrapper, and wrap them up.
5. Place egg rolls on cookie sheet and spray with olive oil. Bake for 20 minutes until egg roll shells are browned.
- **Nutrition Info:** Calories: 421, Sodium: 1166 mg, Dietary Fiber: 8.2 g, Total Fat: 7.7 g, Total Carbs: 76.9 g, Protein: 13.7 g.

208. Rice Flour Coated Shrimp

Servings: 3
Cooking Time: 20 Minutes
Ingredients:
- 3 tablespoons rice flour
- 1 pound shrimp, peeled and deveined
- 2 tablespoons olive oil
- 1 teaspoon powdered sugar
- Salt and black pepper, as required

Directions:
1. Preheat the Air fryer to 325 °F and grease an Air fryer basket.
2. Mix rice flour, olive oil, sugar, salt, and black pepper in a bowl.
3. Stir in the shrimp and transfer half of the shrimp to the Air fryer basket.
4. Cook for about 10 minutes, flipping once in between.
5. Dish out the mixture onto serving plates and repeat with the remaining mixture.
- **Nutrition Info:** Calories: 299, Fat: 12g, Carbohydrates: 11.1g, Sugar: 0.8g, Protein: 35g, Sodium: 419mg

209. Prawn Burgers

Servings: 2
Cooking Time: 6 Minutes
Ingredients:
- ½ cup prawns, peeled, deveined and finely chopped
- ½ cup breadcrumbs
- 2-3 tablespoons onion, finely chopped
- 3 cups fresh baby greens
- ½ teaspoon ginger, minced
- ½ teaspoon garlic, minced
- ½ teaspoon red chili powder
- ½ teaspoon ground cumin
- ¼ teaspoon ground turmeric
- Salt and ground black pepper, as required

Directions:
1. Preheat the Air fryer to 390 degree F and grease an Air fryer basket.
2. Mix the prawns, breadcrumbs, onion, ginger, garlic, and spices in a bowl.
3. Make small-sized patties from the mixture and transfer to the Air fryer basket.
4. Cook for about 6 minutes and dish out in a platter.
5. Serve immediately warm alongside the baby greens.

- **Nutrition Info:** Calories: 240, Fat: 2.7g, Carbohydrates: 37.4g, Sugar: 4g, Protein: 18g, Sodium: 371mg

210.Tasty Grilled Red Mullet

Servings: 8
Cooking Time: 15 Minutes
Ingredients:
- 8 whole red mullets, gutted and scales removed
- Salt and pepper to taste
- Juice from 1 lemon
- 1 tablespoon olive oil

Directions:
1. Place the instant pot air fryer lid on and preheat the instant pot at 390 degrees F.
2. Place the grill pan accessory in the instant pot.
3. Season the red mullet with salt, pepper, and lemon juice.
4. Place red mullets on the grill pan and brush with olive oil.
5. Close the air fryer lid and grill for 15 minutes.
- **Nutrition Info:** Calories: 152; Carbs: 0.9g; Protein: 23.1g; Fat: 6.2g

211.Party Stuffed Pork Chops

Servings: 4
Cooking Time: 40 Minutes
Ingredients:
- 8 pork chops
- ¼ tsp pepper
- 4 cups stuffing mix
- ½ tsp salt
- 2 tbsp olive oil
- 4 garlic cloves, minced
- 2 tbsp sage leaves

Directions:
1. Preheat your air fryer to 350 f. cut a hole in pork chops and fill chops with stuffing mix. In a bowl, mix sage leaves, garlic cloves, oil, salt and pepper. Cover chops with marinade and let marinate for 10 minutes. Place the chops in your air fryer's cooking basket and cook for 25 minutes. Serve and enjoy!
- **Nutrition Info:** Calories: 364 Cal Total Fat: 13 g Saturated Fat: 4 g Cholesterol: 119 mg Sodium: 349 mg Total Carbs: 19 g Fiber: 3 g Sugar: 6 g Protein: 40 g

212.Red Wine Infused Mushrooms

Servings: 6
Cooking Time: 30 Minutes
Ingredients:
- 1 tablespoon butter
- 2 pounds fresh mushrooms, quartered
- 2 teaspoons Herbs de Provence
- ½ teaspoon garlic powder

- 2 tablespoons red wine

Directions:
1. Preheat the Air fryer to 325 °F and grease an Air fryer pan.
2. Mix the butter, Herbs de Provence, and garlic powder in the Air fryer pan and toss to coat well.
3. Cook for about 2 minutes and stir in the mushrooms and red wine.
4. Cook for about 28 minutes and dish out in a platter to serve hot.
- **Nutrition Info:** Calories: 54, Fat: 2.4g, Carbohydrates: 5.3g, Sugar: 2.7g, Protein: 4.8g, Sodium: 23mg

213.Chicken Lasagna With Eggplants

Servings: 10
Cooking Time: 17 Minutes
Ingredients:
- 6 oz Cheddar cheese, shredded
- 7 oz Parmesan cheese, shredded
- 2 eggplants
- 1-pound ground chicken
- 1 teaspoon paprika
- 1 teaspoon salt
- ½ teaspoon cayenne pepper
- ½ cup heavy cream
- 2 teaspoon butter
- 4 oz chive stems, diced

Directions:
1. Take the air fryer basket tray and spread it with the butter.
2. Then peel the eggplants and slice them.
3. Separate the sliced eggplants into 3 parts.
4. Combine the ground chicken with the paprika, salt, cayenne pepper, and diced chives.
5. Mix the mixture up.
6. Separate the ground chicken mixture into 2 parts.
7. Make the layer of the first part of the sliced eggplant in the air fryer basket tray.
8. Then make the layer of the ground chicken mixture.
9. After this, sprinkle the ground chicken layer with the half of the shredded Cheddar cheese,
10. Then cover the cheese with the second part of the sliced eggplant.
11. The next step is to make the layer of the ground chicken and all shredded Cheddar cheese,
12. Cover the cheese layer with the last part of the sliced eggplants.
13. Then sprinkle the eggplants with shredded Parmesan cheese.
14. Pour the heavy cream and add butter.
15. Preheat the air fryer to 365 F.
16. Cook the lasagna for 17 minutes.

17. When the time is over – let the lasagna chill gently.
18. Serve it!
- **Nutrition Info:** calories 291, fat 17.6, fiber 4.6, carbs 7.8, protein 27.4

214. Baked Egg And Veggies

Servings: 2
Cooking Time: 20 Minutes
Ingredients:
- 1 cup fresh spinach; chopped
- 1 small zucchini, sliced lengthwise and quartered
- 1 medium Roma tomato; diced
- ½ medium green bell pepper; seeded and diced
- 2 large eggs.
- 2 tbsp. salted butter
- ¼ tsp. garlic powder.
- ¼ tsp. onion powder.
- ½ tsp. dried basil
- ¼ tsp. dried oregano.

Directions:
1. Grease two (4-inchramekins with 1 tbsp. butter each.
2. Take a large bowl, toss zucchini, bell pepper, spinach and tomatoes. Divide the mixture in two and place half in each ramekin.
3. Crack an egg on top of each ramekin and sprinkle with onion powder, garlic powder, basil and oregano. Place into the air fryer basket. Adjust the temperature to 330 Degrees F and set the timer for 10 minutes. Serve immediately.
- **Nutrition Info:** Calories: 150; Protein: 3g; Fiber: 2g; Fat: 10g; Carbs: 6g

215. Tex-mex Chicken Quesadillas

Servings: 4
Cooking Time: 10 Minutes
Ingredients:
- 2 green onions
- 2 cups shredded skinless rotisserie chicken meat
- 1-1/2 cups shredded Monterey Jack cheese
- 1 pickled jalapeño
- 1/4 cup fresh cilantro leaves
- 4 burrito-size flour tortillas
- 1/2 cup reduced-fat sour cream

Directions:
1. Start by preheating toaster oven to 425°F.
2. Thinly slice the green onions and break apart.
3. Mix together chicken, cheese, jalapeño, and onions in a bowl, then evenly divide mixture onto one half of each tortilla.
4. Fold opposite half over mixture and place quesadillas onto a baking sheet.
5. Bake for 10 minutes.

6. Cut in halves or quarters and serve with sour cream.
- **Nutrition Info:** Calories: 830, Sodium: 921 mg, Dietary Fiber: 1.8 g, Total Fat: 59.0 g, Total Carbs: 13.8 g, Protein: 60.8 g.

216. Creamy Breaded Shrimp

Servings: 3
Cooking Time: 20 Minutes
Ingredients:
- ¼ cup all-purpose flour
- 1 cup panko breadcrumbs
- 1 pound shrimp, peeled and deveined
- ½ cup mayonnaise
- ¼ cup sweet chili sauce
- 1 tablespoon Sriracha sauce

Directions:
1. Preheat the Air fryer to 400-degree F and grease an Air fryer basket.
2. Place flour in a shallow bowl and mix the mayonnaise, chili sauce, and Sriracha sauce in another bowl.
3. Place the breadcrumbs in a third bowl.
4. Coat each shrimp with the flour, dip into mayonnaise mixture and finally, dredge in the breadcrumbs.
5. Arrange half of the coated shrimps into the Air fryer basket and cook for about 10 minutes.
6. Dish out the coated shrimps onto serving plates and repeat with the remaining mixture.
- **Nutrition Info:** Calories: 540, Fat: 18.2g, Carbohydrates: 33.1g, Sugar: 10.6g, Protein: 36.8g, Sodium: 813mg

217. Spicy Paprika Steak

Servings: 2
Cooking Time: 20 Minutes
Ingredients:
- 1/2 Ancho chili pepper, soaked in hot water before using
- 1 tablespoon brandy
- 2 teaspoons smoked paprika
- 1 1/2 tablespoons olive oil
- 2 beef steaks
- Kosher salt, to taste
- 1 teaspoon ground allspice
- 3 cloves garlic, sliced

Directions:
1. Sprinkle the beef steaks with salt, paprika, and allspice. Add the steak to a baking dish that fits your fryer. Scatter the sliced garlic over the top.
2. Now, drizzle it with brandy and olive oil; spread minced Ancho chili pepper over the top.
3. Bake at 385 degrees F for 14 minutes, turning halfway through. Serve warm.

- **Nutrition Info:** 450 Calories; 26g Fat; 4g Carbs; 58g Protein; 3g Sugars; 3g Fiber

218.Lemongrass Pork Chops

Servings: 3
Cooking Time: 2 Hrs 20 Minutes
Ingredients:
- 3 slices pork chops
- 2 garlic cloves, minced
- 1 ½ tbsp sugar
- 4 stalks lemongrass, trimmed and chopped
- 2 shallots, chopped
- 2 tbsp olive oil
- 1 ¼ tsp soy sauce
- 1 ¼ tsp fish sauce
- 1 ½ tsp black pepper

Directions:
1. In a bowl, add the garlic, sugar, lemongrass, shallots, olive oil, soy sauce, fish sauce, and black pepper; mix well. Add the pork chops, coat them with the mixture and allow to marinate for around 2 hours to get nice and savory.
2. Preheat the Air Fryer to 400 F. Cooking in 2 to 3 batches, remove and shake each pork chop from the marinade and place it in the fryer basket. Cook it for 7 minutes. Turn the pork chops with kitchen tongs and cook further for 5 minutes. Remove the chops and serve with a side of sautéed asparagus.
- **Nutrition Info:** 346 Calories; 11g Fat; 4g Carbs; 32g Protein; 1g Sugars; 1g Fiber

219.Curried Eggplant

Servings: 2
Cooking Time: 10 Minutes
Ingredients:
- 1 large eggplant, cut into ½-inch thick slices
- 1 garlic clove, minced
- ½ fresh red chili, chopped
- 1 tablespoon vegetable oil
- ¼ teaspoon curry powder
- Salt, to taste

Directions:
1. Preheat the Air fryer to 300 degree F and grease an Air fryer basket.
2. Mix all the ingredients in a bowl and toss to coat well.
3. Arrange the eggplant slices in the Air fryer basket and cook for about 10 minutes, tossing once in between.
4. Dish out onto serving plates and serve hot.
- **Nutrition Info:** Calories: 121, Fat: 7.3g, Carbohydrates: 14.2g, Sugar: 7g, Protein: 2.4g, Sodium: 83mg

220.Lemon Garlic Shrimps

Servings: 2
Cooking Time: 8 Minutes

Ingredients:
- ¾ pound medium shrimp, peeled and deveined
- 1½ tablespoons fresh lemon juice
- 1 tablespoon olive oil
- 1 teaspoon lemon pepper
- ¼ teaspoon paprika
- ¼ teaspoon garlic powder

Directions:
1. Preheat the Air fryer to 400 degree F and grease an Air fryer basket.
2. Mix lemon juice, olive oil, lemon pepper, paprika and garlic powder in a large bowl.
3. Stir in the shrimp and toss until well combined.
4. Arrange shrimp into the Air fryer basket in a single layer and cook for about 8 minutes.
5. Dish out the shrimp in serving plates and serve warm.
- **Nutrition Info:** Calories: 260, Fat: 12.4g, Carbohydrates: 0.3g, Sugar: 0.1g, Protein: 35.6g, Sodium: 619mg

221.Coconut-crusted Haddock With Curried Pumpkin Seeds

Servings: 4
Cooking Time: 10 Minutes
Ingredients:
- 2 teaspoons canola oil
- 2 teaspoons honey
- 1 teaspoon curry powder
- 1/4 teaspoon ground cinnamon
- 1 teaspoon salt
- 1 cup pumpkin seeds
- 1-1/2 pounds haddock or cod filets
- 1/2 cup roughly grated unsweetened coconut
- 3/4 cups panko-style bread crumbs
- 2 tablespoons butter, melted
- 3 tablespoons apricot fruit spread
- 1 tablespoon lime juice

Directions:
1. Start by preheating toaster oven to 350°F.
2. In a medium bowl, mix honey, oil, curry powder, 1/2 teaspoon salt, and cinnamon.
3. Add pumpkin seeds to the bowl and toss to coat, then lay flat on a baking sheet.
4. Toast for 14 minutes, then transfer to a bowl to cool.
5. Increase the oven temperature to 450°F.
6. Brush a baking sheet with oil and lay filets flat.
7. In another medium mixing bowl, mix together bread crumbs, butter, and remaining salt.
8. In a small bowl mash together apricot spread and lime juice.
9. Brush each filet with apricot mixture, then press bread crumb mixture onto each piece.

10. Bake for 10 minutes.
11. Transfer to a plate and top with pumpkin seeds to serve.
- **Nutrition Info:** Calories: 273, Sodium: 491 mg, Dietary Fiber: 6.1 g, Total Fat: 8.4 g, Total Carbs: 47.3 g, Protein: 7.0 g.

222.Stuffed Potatoes

Servings: 4
Cooking Time: 31 Minutes
Ingredients:
- 4 potatoes, peeled
- 1 tablespoon butter
- ½ of brown onion, chopped
- 2 tablespoons chives, chopped
- ½ cup Parmesan cheese, grated
- 3 tablespoons canola oil

Directions:
1. Preheat the Air fryer to 390 °F and grease an Air fryer basket.
2. Coat the potatoes with canola oil and arrange into the Air fryer basket.
3. Cook for about 20 minutes and transfer into a platter.
4. Cut each potato in half and scoop out the flesh from each half.
5. Heat butter in a frying pan over medium heat and add onions.
6. Sauté for about 5 minutes and dish out in a bowl.
7. Mix the onions with the potato flesh, chives, and half of cheese.
8. Stir well and stuff the potato halves evenly with the onion potato mixture.
9. Top with the remaining cheese and arrange the potato halves into the Air fryer basket.
10. Cook for about 6 minutes and dish out to serve warm.
- **Nutrition Info:** Calories: 328, Fat: 11.3g, Carbohydrates: 34.8g, Sugar: 3.1g, Protein: 5.8g, Sodium: 77mg

223.Morning Ham And Cheese Sandwich

Servings: 4
Cooking Time: 15 Minutes
Ingredients:
- 8 slices whole wheat bread
- 4 slices lean pork ham
- 4 slices cheese
- 8 slices tomato

Directions:
1. Preheat your air fryer to 360 f. Lay four slices of bread on a flat surface. Spread the slices with cheese, tomato, turkey and ham. Cover with the remaining slices to form sandwiches. Add the sandwiches to the air fryer cooking basket and cook for 10 minutes.

- **Nutrition Info:** Calories: 361 Cal Total Fat: 16.7 g Saturated Fat: 0 g Cholesterol: 0 mg Sodium: 1320 mg Total Carbs: 32.5 g Fiber: 2.3 g Sugar: 5.13 g Protein: 19.3 g

224.Beef With Apples And Plums

Servings: 4
Cooking Time: 30 Minutes
Ingredients:
- 2pounds beef stew meat, cubed
- 1cup apples, cored and cubed
- 1cup plums, pitted and halved
- 2tablespoons butter, melted
- Salt and black pepper to the taste
- ½ cup red wine
- 1tablespoon chives, chopped

Directions:
1. In the air fryer's pan, mix the beef with the apples and the other ingredients, toss, put the pan in the machine and cook at 390 degrees F for 30 minutes.
2. Divide the mix between plates and serve right away.
- **Nutrition Info:** Calories 290, Fat 12, Fiber 5, Carbs 19, Protein 28

225.Basil Tomatoes

Servings: 2
Cooking Time: 10 Minutes
Ingredients:
- 2 tomatoes, halved
- 1 tablespoon fresh basil, chopped
- Olive oil cooking spray
- Salt and black pepper, as required

Directions:
1. Preheat the Air fryer to 320 degree F and grease an Air fryer basket.
2. Spray the tomato halves evenly with olive oil cooking spray and season with salt, black pepper and basil.
3. Arrange the tomato halves into the Air fryer basket, cut sides up.
4. Cook for about 10 minutes and dish out onto serving plates.
- **Nutrition Info:** Calories: 22, Fat: 4.8g, Carbohydrates: 4.8g, Sugar: 3.2g, Protein: 1.1g, Sodium: 84mg

226.Air Fryer Veggie Quesdillas

Servings: 4
Cooking Time: 40 Minutes
Ingredients:
- 4 sprouted whole-grain flour tortillas (6-in.)
- 1 cup sliced red bell pepper
- 4 ounces reduced-fat Cheddar cheese, shredded
- 1 cup sliced zucchini
- 1 cup canned black beans, drained and rinsed (no salt)

- Cooking spray
- 2 ounces plain 2% reduced-fat Greek yogurt
- 1 teaspoon lime zest
- 1 Tbsp. fresh juice (from 1 lime)
- ¼ tsp. ground cumin
- 2 tablespoons chopped fresh cilantro
- 1/2 cup drained refrigerated pico de gallo

Directions:
1. Place tortillas on work surface, sprinkle 2 tablespoons shredded cheese over half of each tortilla and top with cheese on each tortilla with 1/4 cup each red pepper slices, zucchini slices, and black beans. Sprinkle evenly with remaining 1/2 cup cheese.
2. Fold tortillas over to form half-moon shaped quesadillas, lightly coat with cooking spray, and secure with toothpicks.
3. Lightly spray air fryer basket with cooking spray. Place 2 quesadillas in the basket, and cook at 400°F for 10 minutes until tortillas are golden brown and slightly crispy, cheese is melted, and vegetables are slightly softened. Turn quesadillas over halfway through cooking.
4. Repeat with remaining quesadillas.
5. Meanwhile, stir yogurt, lime juice, lime zest and cumin in a small bowl.
6. Cut each quesadilla into wedges and sprinkle with cilantro.
7. Serve with 1 tablespoon cumin cream and 2 tablespoons pico de gallo each.
- **Nutrition Info:** Calories 291 Fat 8g Saturated fat 4g Unsaturated fat 3g Protein 17g Carbohydrate 36g Fiber 8g Sugars 3g Sodium 518mg Calcium 30% DV Potassium 6% DV

227.Turkey Wontons With Garlic-parmesan Sauce

Servings: 8
Cooking Time: 20 Minutes
Ingredients:
- 8 ounces cooked turkey breasts, shredded 16 wonton wrappers
- 1½ tablespoons margarine, melted
- 1/3 cup cream cheese, room temperature 8 ounces Asiago cheese, shredded
- 3 tablespoons Parmesan cheese, grated
- 1 tsp. garlic powder
- Fine sea salt and freshly ground black pepper, to taste

Directions:
1. In a small-sized bowl, mix the margarine, Parmesan, garlic powder, salt, and black pepper; give it a good stir.
2. Lightly grease a mini muffin pan; lay 1 wonton wrapper in each mini muffin cup. Fill each cup with the cream cheese and turkey mixture.
3. Air-fry for 8 minutes at 335 °F. Immediately top with Asiago cheese and serve warm.
- **Nutrition Info:** 362 Calories; 13.5g Fat; 40.4g Carbs; 18.5g Protein; 1.2g Sugars

228.Award Winning Breaded Chicken

Servings: 4
Cooking Time: 20 Minutes
Ingredients:
- 1 1/2 tsp.s olive oil
- 1 tsp. red pepper flakes, crushed 1/3 tsp. chicken bouillon granules 1/3 tsp. shallot powder
- 1 1/2 tablespoons tamari soy sauce 1/3 tsp. cumin powder
- 1½ tablespoons mayo 1 tsp. kosher salt
- For the chicken:
- 2 beaten eggs Breadcrumbs
- 1½ chicken breasts, boneless and skinless 1 ½ tablespoons plain flour

Directions:
1. Margarine fly the chicken breasts, and then, marinate them for at least 55 minutes. Coat the chicken with plain flour; then, coat with the beaten eggs; finally, roll them in the breadcrumbs.
2. Lightly grease the cooking basket. Air-fry the breaded chicken at 345 °F for 12 minutes, flipping them halfway.
- **Nutrition Info:** 262 Calories; 14.9g Fat; 2.7g Carbs; 27.5g Protein; 0.3g Sugars

MEAT RECIPES

229.Strawberry-glazed Turkey

Servings:2
Cooking Time: 37 Minutes
Ingredients:
- 2 pounds (907 g) turkey breast
- 1 tablespoon olive oil
- Salt and ground black pepper, to taste
- 1 cup fresh strawberries

Directions:
1. Rub the turkey bread with olive oil on a clean work surface, then sprinkle with salt and ground black pepper.
2. Transfer the turkey in the air fryer basket and spritz with cooking spray.
3. Put the air fryer basket on the baking pan and slide into Rack Position 2, select Air Fry, set temperature to 375ºF (190ºC) and set time to 30 minutes.
4. Flip the turkey breast halfway through.
5. Meanwhile, put the strawberries in a food processor and pulse until smooth.
6. When cooking is complete, spread the puréed strawberries over the turkey and fry for 7 more minutes.
7. Serve immediately.

230.Easy Lamb Chops With Asparagus

Servings:4
Cooking Time: 15 Minutes
Ingredients:
- 4 asparagus spears, trimmed
- 2 tablespoons olive oil, divided
- 1 pound (454 g) lamb chops
- 1 garlic clove, minced
- 2 teaspoons chopped fresh thyme, for serving
- Salt and ground black pepper, to taste

Directions:
1. Spritz the air fryer basket with cooking spray.
2. On a large plate, brush the asparagus with 1 tablespoon olive oil, then sprinkle with salt. Set aside.
3. On a separate plate, brush the lamb chops with remaining olive oil and sprinkle with salt and ground black pepper.
4. Arrange the lamb chops in the pan.
5. Put the air fryer basket on the baking pan and slide into Rack Position 2, select Air Fry, set temperature to 400ºF (205ºC) and set time to 15 minutes.
6. Flip the lamb chops and add the asparagus and garlic halfway through.
7. When cooking is complete, the lamb should be well browned and the asparagus should be tender.
8. Serve them on a plate with thyme on top.

231.Meatballs(14)

Servings: 4
Cooking Time: 25 Minutes
Ingredients:
- 1 lb ground beef
- 1 tsp fresh rosemary, chopped
- 1 tbsp garlic, chopped
- 1/2 tsp pepper
- 1 tsp garlic powder
- 1 tsp onion powder
- 1/4 cup breadcrumbs
- 2 eggs
- 1 lb ground pork
- 1/2 tsp pepper
- 1 tsp sea salt

Directions:
1. Fit the oven with the rack in position
2. Add all ingredients into the mixing bowl and mix until well combined.
3. Make small balls from the meat mixture and place it into the parchment-lined baking pan.
4. Set to bake at 400 F for 30 minutes. After 5 minutes place the baking pan in the preheated oven.
5. Serve and enjoy.
- **Nutrition Info:** Calories: 441 Fat 13.7 g Carbohydrates 7.2 g Sugar 1 g Protein 68.1 g Cholesterol 266 mg

232.Easy Cocktail Franks Rolls

Servings:4
Cooking Time: 20 Minutes
Ingredients:
- 12 oz cocktail franks
- 8 oz can crescent rolls

Directions:
1. Cut the dough in 1 by 5-inch rectangles with a knife. Gently roll the franks in the strips, making sure the ends are visible Place in freezer for 5 minutes.
2. Preheat oven to 330 F on AirFry function. Take the franks out of the freezer and place them in the frying basket. Press Start and cook for 8-10 minutes. Increase temperature to 390 F, and cook for another 3 minutes until a fine golden texture appears.

233.Garlic Kangaroo

Servings:x
Cooking Time:x
Ingredients:
- 1 lb. boneless kangaroo
- 2 cup dry breadcrumbs
- 2 tsp. oregano
- 2 tsp. red chili flakes

- 2 tsp. garlic paste
- 1 ½ tbsp. ginger-garlic paste
- 4 tbsp. lemon juice
- 2 tsp. salt
- 1 tsp. red chili powder
- 6 tbsp. corn flour
- 4 eggs

Directions:
1. Mix all the ingredients for the marinade and put the kangaroo Oregano Fingers inside and let it rest overnight. Mix the breadcrumbs, oregano and red chili flakes well and place the marinated Oregano Fingers on this mixture. Cover it with plastic wrap and leave it till right before you serve to cook. Pre heat the oven at 160 degrees Fahrenheit for 5 minutes.
2. Place the Oregano Fingers in the fry basket and close it. Let them cook at the same temperature for another 15 minutes or so. Toss the Oregano Fingers well so that they are cooked uniformly. Drizzle the garlic paste and serve.

234.Beer Corned Beef With Carrots

Servings:4
Cooking Time: 35 Minutes
Ingredients:
- 1 tbsp beef spice
- 1 white onion, chopped
- 2 carrots, chopped
- 12 oz bottle beer
- 1 ½ cups chicken broth
- 4 pounds corned beef

Directions:
1. Cover beef with beer and let sit in the fridge for 30 minutes. Transfer to a pot over medium heat and add in chicken broth, carrots, and onion. Bring to a boil and simmer for 10 minutes. Drain boiled meat and veggies and place them in a baking dish. Sprinkle with beef spice. Select Bake function, adjust the temperature to 400 F, and press Start. Cook for 30 minutes.

235.Chicken Grandma's Easy To Cook Wontons

Servings:x
Cooking Time:x
Ingredients:
- 1 ½ cup all-purpose flour
- 2 tsp. ginger-garlic paste
- 2 tsp. soya sauce
- ½ tsp. salt
- 5 tbsp. water
- 2 cups minced chicken
- 2 tbsp. oil
- 2 tsp. vinegar

Directions:

1. Squeeze the dough and cover it with plastic wrap and set aside. Next, cook the ingredients for the filling and try to ensure that the chicken is covered well with the sauce.
2. Roll the dough and place the filling in the center. Now, wrap the dough to cover the filling and pinch the edges together.
3. Pre heat the oven at 200° F for 5 minutes. Place the wontons in the fry basket and close it. Let them cook at the same temperature for another 20 minutes. Recommended sides are chili sauce or ketchup.

236.Garlic Venison With Red Chili Flakes

Servings:x
Cooking Time:x
Ingredients:
- 1 lb. boneless venison cut into Oregano Fingers
- 2 cup dry breadcrumbs
- 6 tbsp. corn flour
- 4 eggs
- 2 tsp. oregano
- 2 tsp. red chili flakes
- 2 tsp. garlic paste
- 1 ½ tbsp. ginger-garlic paste
- 4 tbsp. lemon juice
- 2 tsp. salt
- 1 tsp. red chili powder

Directions:
1. Mix all the ingredients for the marinade and put the venison Oregano Fingers inside and let it rest overnight.
2. Mix the breadcrumbs, oregano and red chili flakes well and place the marinated Oregano Fingers on this mixture. Cover it with plastic wrap and leave it till right before you serve to cook.
3. Pre heat the oven at 160 degrees Fahrenheit for 5 minutes. Place the Oregano Fingers in the fry basket and close it. Let them cook at the same temperature for another 15 minutes or so. Toss the Oregano Fingers well so that they are cooked uniformly. Drizzle the garlic paste and serve.

237.Pork, Bell Pepper, And Pineapple Skewers

Servings:4
Cooking Time: 12 Minutes
Ingredients:
- ¼ teaspoon kosher salt or ⅛ teaspoon fine salt
- 1 medium pork tenderloin (about 1 pound / 454 g), cut into 1½-inch chunks
- 1 green bell pepper, seeded and cut into 1-inch pieces

- 1 red bell pepper, seeded and cut into 1-inch pieces
- 2 cups fresh pineapple chunks
- ¾ cup Teriyaki Sauce or store-bought variety, divided
- Special Equipment:
- 12 (9- to 12-inch) wooden skewers, soaked in water for about 30 minutes

Directions:
1. Sprinkle the pork cubes with the salt.
2. Thread the pork, bell peppers, and pineapple onto a skewer. Repeat until all skewers are complete. Brush the skewers generously with about half of the Teriyaki Sauce. Place them in the air fryer basket.
3. Put the air fryer basket on the baking pan and slide into Rack Position 2, select Roast, set temperature to 375ºF (190ºC), and set time to 10 minutes.
4. After about 5 minutes, remove from the oven. Turn over the skewers and brush with the remaining half of Teriyaki Sauce. Return to the oven and continue cooking until the vegetables are tender and browned in places and the pork is browned and cooked through.
5. Remove from the oven and serve.

238.Peach And Cherry Chicken

Servings:4
Cooking Time: 15 Minutes
Ingredients:
- $^1/_3$ cup peach preserves
- 1 teaspoon ground rosemary
- ½ teaspoon black pepper
- ½ teaspoon salt
- ½ teaspoon marjoram
- 1 teaspoon light olive oil
- 1 pound (454 g) boneless chicken breasts, cut in 1½-inch chunks
- 1 (10-ounce / 284-g) package frozen dark cherries, thawed and drained
- Cooking spray

Directions:
1. In a medium bowl, mix peach preserves, rosemary, pepper, salt, marjoram, and olive oil.
2. Stir in chicken chunks and toss to coat well with the preserve mixture.
3. Spritz the baking pan with cooking spray and lay chicken chunks in the pan.
4. Slide the baking pan into Rack Position 1, select Convection Bake, set the temperature to 400ºF (205ºC) and set the time to 15 minutes.
5. After 7 minutes, remove from the oven and flip the chicken chunks. Return the pan to the oven and continue cooking.

6. When cooking is complete, the chicken should no longer pink and the juices should run clear.
7. Scatter the cherries over and cook for an additional minute to heat cherries.
8. Serve immediately.

239.Chicken With Vegetables

Servings: 4
Cooking Time: 35 Minutes
Ingredients:
- 1 lb chicken breasts, skinless, boneless and cut into pieces
- 3 cups potatoes cut into pieces
- 4 cups Brussels sprouts, trimmed and quartered
- 1 lemon juice
- 1/3 cup vinaigrette dressing
- 1 onion, diced
- 1/4 cup olives, quartered
- 1 tsp oregano
- 1 1/2 tsp Dijon mustard
- 1/4 tsp pepper
- 1/4 tsp salt

Directions:
1. Fit the oven with the rack in position
2. Place chicken in the center of the baking pan.
3. Place potatoes, sprouts, and onions around the chicken.
4. In a small bowl, mix vinaigrette, oregano, mustard, lemon juice, and salt and pour over chicken and vegetables.
5. Sprinkle olives and season with pepper.
6. Set to bake at 400 F for 40 minutes. After 5 minutes place the baking pan in the preheated oven.
7. Serve and enjoy.
- **Nutrition Info:** Calories: 397 Fat 13 g Carbohydrates 31.4 g Sugar 6.7 g Protein 38.3 g Cholesterol 101 mg

240.Flank Steak Fajitas

Servings:x
Cooking Time:x
Ingredients:
- 3 cloves garlic
- ½ cup soy sauce
- ½ cup honey
- 3 sprigs rosemary
- Salt and pepper, to taste
- 2 limes, juiced
- 3 bell peppers of various colors, washed, seeded and sliced
- 2 medium onions, peeled and sliced into rings
- 10 Portobello mushrooms, washed and sliced
- 4 flour tortillas

Directions:

1. Combine garlic, soy sauce, honey, rosemary, salt, pepper and lime juice in a Ziploc bag. Add steak and marinate for 1-2 hours in the refrigerator.
2. Remove meat from marinade and shake off excess liquid.
3. Place oven on the grill and heat until smoking. At this point, you can sear the meat in the pot or directly on the grill. If you cook meat directly on the grill, sear for 3-4 minutes on each side.
4. While meat cooks on the grill, add 1 Tbsp oil to the oven a add peppers, onions, mushrooms, salt and pepper. Allow vegetables to sear. Stir frequently for about 6 minutes.
5. Meat and vegetables should be ready about the same time. Transfer both to a platter and place tortillas in oven to toast, about 30 seconds. Allow meat to rest. Slice against the grain and serve along with vegetables.

241.Veal Club Classic Sandwich

Servings:x
Cooking Time:x
Ingredients:

- 2 slices of white bread
- 1 tbsp. softened butter
- ½ tsp. olive oil
- ½ flake garlic crushed
- ¼ cup chopped onion
- ¼ tsp. mustard powder
- ½ tbsp. sugar
- ¼ tbsp. red chili sauce
- ½ lb. cubed veal
- 1 small capsicum
- ¼ tbsp. Worcestershire sauce
- ½ cup water

Directions:

1. Take the slices of bread and remove the edges. Now cut the slices horizontally. Cook the ingredients for the sauce and wait till it thickens. Now, add the veal to the sauce and stir till it obtains the flavors. Roast the capsicum and peel the skin off. Cut the capsicum into slices. Mix the ingredients together and apply it to the bread slices.
2. Pre-heat the oven for 5 minutes at 300 Fahrenheit. Open the basket of the Fryer and place the prepared Classic Sandwiches in it such that no two Classic Sandwiches are touching each other. Now keep the fryer at 250 degrees for around 15 minutes. Turn the Classic Sandwiches in between the cooking process to cook both slices. Serve the Classic Sandwiches with tomato ketchup or mint sauce.

242.Flavorful Lemon Pepper Chicken

Servings: 4
Cooking Time: 25 Minutes
Ingredients:

- 4 chicken breasts, boneless & skinless
- 3 tbsp fresh lemon juice
- 2 tsp ground black pepper
- 5 tbsp olive oil
- 1/2 tsp sea salt

Directions:

1. Fit the oven with the rack in position
2. Heat 2 tablespoons of oil in a pan over medium-high heat. Brown chicken in a pan.
3. In a small bowl, mix lemon juice, remaining oil, pepper, and salt.
4. Place browned chicken into the baking dish. Pour lemon juice mixture over chicken.
5. Set to bake at 425 F for 30 minutes. After 5 minutes place the baking dish in the preheated oven.
6. Serve and enjoy.

- **Nutrition Info:** Calories: 433 Fat 28.4 g Carbohydrates 0.9 g Sugar 0.3 g Protein 42.4 g Cholesterol 130 mg

243.Herb Turkey Tenderloin

Servings: 4
Cooking Time: 40 Minutes
Ingredients:

- 24 oz turkey tenderloin
- 1 tbsp dried rosemary
- 1 tbsp dried sage
- Pepper
- Salt

Directions:

1. Fit the oven with the rack in position
2. Rub turkey tenderloin with rosemary, sage, pepper, and salt.
3. Place turkey tenderloin into the baking pan.
4. Set to bake at 350 F for 45 minutes. After 5 minutes place the baking pan in the preheated oven.
5. Slice and serve.

- **Nutrition Info:** Calories: 185 Fat 2.4 g Carbohydrates 0.9 g Sugar 0 g Protein 42.3 g Cholesterol 68 mg

244.Guacamole Stuffed Chicken

Servings: 4
Cooking Time: 10 Minutes
Ingredients:

- Nonstick cooking spray
- 2 chicken breasts, boneless & skinless
- ½ cup guacamole
- 2/3 cup cheddar cheese, grated
- 1 cup panko bread crumbs
- ½ tsp Adobo seasoning

Directions:

1. Place baking pan in position 2. Spray the fryer basket with cooking spray.
2. Cut the chicken breasts in half, similar to butterflying them but cut all the way through. Place the chicken between two sheets of plastic wrap and pound really thin.
3. Spread 2 tablespoons guacamole over each piece of chicken. Sprinkle with the cheese. Fold the chicken pieces in half covering the filling.
4. In a shallow dish, combine bread crumbs and seasoning. Coat each side of chicken with mixture and place in the fryer basket.
5. Place the basket in the oven and set to air fry on 375°F for 10 minutes. Turn chicken over halfway through cooking time. Serve immediately.

Nutrition Info: Calories:363, Total Fat: 15g, Saturated Fat: 5g, Total Carbs: 22g, Net Carbs: 19g, Protein: 35g, Sugar: 2g, Fiber: 3g, Sodium: 441mg, Potassium: 604mg, Phosphorus: 400mg

245.Tasty Chicken Tenders

Servings: 4
Cooking Time: 30 Minutes
Ingredients:
- 2 lbs frozen chicken tenders
- 1 tbsp dried oregano
- 1 cup parmesan cheese, grated
- 1/2 cup butter, melted
- 1 tsp garlic powder
- 1 tbsp paprika
- Pepper
- Salt

Directions:
1. Fit the oven with the rack in position
2. In a shallow dish, mix parmesan cheese, oregano, paprika, garlic powder, pepper, and salt.
3. Place melted butter in a separate shallow dish.
4. Dip each chicken tender in melted butter then coat with parmesan cheese mixture.
5. Place coated chicken tenders in a baking pan.
6. Set to bake at 350 F for 35 minutes. After 5 minutes place the baking pan in the preheated oven.
7. Serve and enjoy.
- **Nutrition Info:** Calories: 833 Fat 50.7 g Carbohydrates 54.5 g Sugar 0.4 g Protein 43.3 g Cholesterol 157 mg

246.Canadian Ham & Cheese Breakfast Toasts

Servings:4
Cooking Time: 15 Minutes
Ingredients:
- 8 whole-wheat bread, slices
- 4 Canadian ham slices
- 4 cheddar cheese slices
- 8 tomato slices

Directions:
1. Lay 4 slices of bread on a flat surface. Top with cheddar cheese, tomato, and ham slices. Cover with the remaining bread slices to form sandwiches. Add the sandwiches to the cooking basket. Select Toast function, adjust the temperature to 360 F, and press Start. Toast for 10 minutes.

247.Copycat Chicken Sandwich

Servings: 4
Cooking Time: 15 Minutes
Ingredients:
- 2 chicken breasts, boneless & skinless
- 1 cup buttermilk
- 1 tbsp. + 2 tsp paprika, divided
- 1 tbsp. + 1 ½ tsp garlic powder, divided
- 2 tsp salt, divided
- 2 tsp pepper, divided
- 4 brioche buns
- 1 cup flour
- ½ cup corn starch
- 1 tbsp. onion powder
- 1 tbsp. cayenne pepper
- ½ cup mayonnaise
- 1 tsp hot sauce
- Sliced pickles

Directions:
1. Place chicken between two sheets of plastic wrap and pound to ½-inch thick. Cut crosswise to get 4 cutlets.
2. In a large bowl, whisk together buttermilk and one teaspoon each paprika, garlic powder, salt, and pepper. Add chicken, cover, and refrigerate overnight.
3. Place the buns on the baking pan and place in position 2 of the oven. Set to toast for about 2-5 minutes depending how toasted you want them. Set aside.
4. In a medium shallow dish, combine flour, cornstarch, onion powder, cayenne pepper, and remaining paprika, garlic powder, salt, and pepper.
5. Whisk in 2-3 tablespoons of the buttermilk batter chicken was marinating in until smooth.
6. Lightly spray fryer basket with cooking spray.
7. Dredge chicken in the flour mixture forming a thick coating of the batter. Place in fryer basket.
8. Place basket in the oven. Set oven to air fryer on 375°F for 10 minutes. Cook until crispy and golden brown, turning chicken over halfway through cooking time.

9. In a small bowl, whisk together mayonnaise, hot sauce, 1 teaspoon paprika, and ½ teaspoon garlic powder.
10. To serve, spread top of buns with mayonnaise mixture. Place chicken on bottom buns and top with pickles then top bun.
- **Nutrition Info:** Calories: 689, Total Fat 27g, Saturated Fat 5g, Total Carbs 71g, Net Carbs 67g, Protein 38g, Sugar 7g, Fiber 4g, Sodium 1734mg, Potassium 779mg, Phosphorus 435mg

248.Chicken-fried Steak Supreme

Servings: 8
Cooking Time: 30 Minutes
Ingredients:
- ½ pound beef-bottom round, sliced into strips
- 1 cup of breadcrumbs (Panko brand works well)
- 2 medium-sized eggs
- Pinch of salt and pepper
- ½ tablespoon of ground thyme

Directions:
1. Preparing the Ingredients. Cover the basket of the air fryer oven with a lining of tin foil, leaving the edges uncovered to allow air to circulate through the basket. Preheat the air fryer oven to 350 degrees. In a mixing bowl, beat the eggs until fluffy and until the yolks and whites are fully combined, and set aside. In a separate mixing bowl, combine the breadcrumbs, thyme, salt and pepper, and set aside. One by one, dip each piece of raw steak into the bowl with dry ingredients, coating all sides; then submerge into the bowl with wet ingredients, then dip again into the dry ingredients. This double coating will ensure an extra crisp air fry. Lay the coated steak pieces on the foil covering the air-fryer basket, in a single flat layer.
2. Air Frying. Set the air fryer oven timer for 15 minutes. After 15 minutes, the air fryer will turn off and the steak should be mid-way cooked and the breaded coating starting to brown. Using tongs, turn each piece of steak over to ensure a full all-over fry. Reset the air fryer oven to 320 degrees for 15 minutes. After 15 minutes, when the air fryer shuts off, remove the fried steak strips using tongs and set on a serving plate. Eat as soon as cool enough to handle and enjoy!

249.Simple & Healthy Baked Chicken Breasts

Servings: 6
Cooking Time: 20 Minutes

Ingredients:
- 6 chicken breasts, skinless & boneless
- 1/4 tsp paprika
- 1 tsp Italian seasoning
- 2 tbsp olive oil
- 1/4 tsp pepper
- 1/2 tsp seasoning salt

Directions:
1. Fit the oven with the rack in position
2. Brush chicken with oil and season with paprika, Italian seasoning, pepper, and salt.
3. Place chicken breasts into the baking dish.
4. Set to bake at 400 F for 25 minutes. After 5 minutes place the baking dish in the preheated oven.
5. Serve and enjoy.
- **Nutrition Info:** Calories: 320 Fat 15.7 g Carbohydrates 0.2 g Sugar 0.1 g Protein 42.3 g Cholesterol 130 mg

250.Italian Steak And Spinach Rolls

Servings:4
Cooking Time: 9 Minutes
Ingredients:
- 2 teaspoons dried Italian seasoning
- 2 cloves garlic, minced
- 1 tablespoon vegetable oil
- 1 teaspoon kosher salt
- 1 teaspoon ground black pepper
- 1 pound (454 g) flank steak, ¼ to ½ inch thick
- 1 (10-ounce / 284-g) package frozen spinach, thawed and squeezed dry
- ½ cup diced jarred roasted red pepper
- 1 cup shredded Mozzarella cheese
- Cooking spray

Directions:
1. Combine the Italian seasoning, garlic, vegetable oil, salt, and ground black pepper in a large bowl. Stir to mix well.
2. Dunk the steak in the seasoning mixture and toss to coat well. Wrap the bowl in plastic and marinate under room temperature for at least 30 minutes.
3. Spritz the air fryer basket with cooking spray.
4. Remove the marinated steak from the bowl and unfold on a clean work surface, then spread the top of the steak with a layer of spinach, a layer of red pepper and a layer of cheese. Leave a ¼-inch edge uncovered.
5. Roll the steak up to wrap the filling, then secure with 3 toothpicks. Cut the roll in half and transfer the rolls in the prepared basket, seam side down.
6. Put the air fryer basket on the baking pan and slide into Rack Position 2, select Air Fry, set temperature to 400ºF (205ºC) and set time to 9 minutes.

7. Flip the rolls halfway through the cooking.
8. When cooking is complete, the steak should be lightly browned and the internal temperature reaches at least 145ºF (63ºC).
9. Remove the rolls from the oven and slice to serve.

251.Chicken Wings With Honey & Cashew Cream

Servings:4
Cooking Time: 25 Minutes
Ingredients:
- 2 lb chicken wings
- 1 tbsp fresh cilantro, chopped
- Salt and black pepper to taste
- 1 tbsp cashews cream
- 1 garlic clove, minced
- 1 tbsp plain yogurt
- 2 tbsp honey
- ½ tbsp white wine vinegar
- ½ tbsp ginger, minced
- ½ tbsp garlic chili sauce

Directions:
1. Preheat on AirFry function to 360 F. Season the wings with salt and black pepper, place them in a baking dish. Press Start and cook for 15 minutes. In a bowl, mix the remaining ingredients. Top the chicken with sauce and cook for 5 more minutes. Serve warm.

252.Herb Beef Tips

Servings: 6
Cooking Time: 20 Minutes
Ingredients:
- 2 lbs sirloin steak, cut into 1-inch cubes
- 1/4 tsp red chili flakes
- 1/2 tsp pepper
- 1/2 tsp dried thyme
- 1 tsp onion powder
- 1 tsp dried oregano
- 2 tbsp lemon juice
- 2 tbsp water
- 1/4 cup olive oil
- 1 cup parsley, chopped
- 1 tsp garlic, minced
- 1/2 tsp salt

Directions:
1. Fit the oven with the rack in position
2. Add all ingredients into the zip-lock bag, seal bag shake well and place in the refrigerator for 1 hour.
3. Place marinated steak cubes into the parchment-lined baking pan.
4. Set to bake at 400 F for 25 minutes. After 5 minutes place the baking pan in the preheated oven.
5. Serve and enjoy.

- **Nutrition Info:** Calories: 361 Fat 18 g Carbohydrates 1.6 g Sugar 0.4 g Protein 46.3 g Cholesterol 135 mg

253.Pesto Chicken

Servings: 4
Cooking Time: 30 Minutes
Ingredients:
- 4 chicken breasts, boneless & skinless
- 2 tbsp fresh basil
- 8 oz mozzarella cheese, sliced
- 2 tomatoes, sliced
- 1/2 cup pesto
- 1 tbsp garlic, minced

Directions:
1. Fit the oven with the rack in position
2. Place chicken into the baking dish and sprinkle with basil and garlic.
3. Pour pesto over chicken. Arrange sliced tomatoes and cheese on top of chicken.
4. Set to bake at 400 F for 35 minutes. After 5 minutes place the baking dish in the preheated oven.
5. Serve and enjoy.
- **Nutrition Info:** Calories: 587 Fat 34 g Carbohydrates 7.1 g Sugar 3.6 g Protein 62 g Cholesterol 167 mg

254.Mustard Chicken Tenders

Servings: 4
Cooking Time: 20 Minutes
Ingredients:
- ½ C. coconut flour
- 1 tbsp. spicy brown mustard
- 2 beaten eggs
- 1 pound of chicken tenders

Directions:
1. Preparing the Ingredients. Season tenders with pepper and salt.
2. Place a thin layer of mustard onto tenders and then dredge in flour and dip in egg.
3. Air Frying. Add to the air fryer oven, set temperature to 390°F, and set time to 20 minutes.
- **Nutrition Info:** CALORIES: 403; FAT: 20G; PROTEIN:22G; SUGAR:4G

255.Seafood Grandma's Easy To Cook Wontons

Servings:x
Cooking Time:x
Ingredients:
- 1 ½ cup all-purpose flour
- ½ tsp. salt
- 5 tbsp. water
- For filling:
- 2 cups minced seafood (prawns, shrimp, oysters, scallops)
- 2 tbsp. oil

- 2 tsp. ginger-garlic paste
- 2 tsp. soya sauce
- 2 tsp. vinegar

Directions:
1. Squeeze the dough and cover it with plastic wrap and set aside. Next, cook the ingredients for the filling and try to ensure that the seafood is covered well with the sauce. Roll the dough and place the filling in the center. Now, wrap the dough to cover the filling and pinch the edges together. Pre heat the oven at 200° F for 5 minutes.
2. Place the wontons in the fry basket and close it. Let them cook at the same temperature for another 20 minutes. Recommended sides are chili sauce or ketchup.

256.Country Fried Steak

Servings: 2
Cooking Time: 12 Minutes
Ingredients:
- 1 tsp. pepper
- 2 C. almond milk
- 2 tbsp. almond flour
- 6 ounces ground sausage meat
- 1 tsp. pepper
- 1 tsp. salt
- 1 tsp. garlic powder
- 1 tsp. onion powder
- 1 C. panko breadcrumbs
- 1 C. almond flour
- 3 beaten eggs
- 6 ounces sirloin steak, pounded till thin

Directions:
1. Preparing the Ingredients.Season panko breadcrumbs with spices.
2. Dredge steak in flour, then egg, and then seasoned panko mixture.
3. Place into air fryer rack/basket.
4. Air Frying. Set temperature to 370°F, and set time to 12 minutes.
5. To make sausage gravy, cook sausage and drain off fat, but reserve 2 tablespoons.
6. Add flour to sausage and mix until incorporated. Gradually mix in milk over medium to high heat till it becomes thick.
7. Season mixture with pepper and cook 3 minutes longer.
8. Serve steak topped with gravy and enjoy!
- **Nutrition Info:** CALORIES: 395; FAT: 11G; PROTEIN:39G; SUGAR:5G

257.Honey Glazed Chicken Breasts

Servings:4
Cooking Time: 10 Minutes
Ingredients:
- 4 (4-ounce / 113-g) boneless, skinless chicken breasts
- Chicken seasoning or rub, to taste
- Salt and ground black pepper, to taste
- ¼ cup honey
- 2 tablespoons soy sauce
- 2 teaspoons grated fresh ginger
- 2 garlic cloves, minced
- Cooking spray

Directions:
1. Spritz the air fryer basket with cooking spray.
2. Rub the chicken breasts with chicken seasoning, salt, and black pepper on a clean work surface.
3. Arrange the chicken breasts in the basket and spritz with cooking spray.
4. Put the air fryer basket on the baking pan and slide into Rack Position 2, select Air Fry, set temperature to 400ºF (205ºC) and set time to 10 minutes.
5. Flip the chicken breasts halfway through.
6. When cooking is complete, the internal temperature of the thickest part of the chicken should reach at least 165ºF (74ºC).
7. Meanwhile, combine the honey, soy sauce, ginger, and garlic in a saucepan and heat over medium-high heat for 3 minutes or until thickened. Stir constantly.
8. Remove the chicken from the oven and serve with the honey glaze.

258.Swiss Cheese Ham Muffins

Servings: 8
Cooking Time: 25 Minutes
Ingredients:
- 4 whole eggs, beaten
- 3 oz ham
- 1 cup milk
- 1 ½ cups Swiss cheese, grated
- Salt and black pepper to taste
- ¼ cup green onion, chopped

Directions:
1. Preheat your to 350 F on Air Fry. In a bowl, mix eggs, onion, salt, cheese, pepper, and milk. Prepare baking forms and place ham slices in each one. Top with the egg mixture.
2. Place the muffin forms in the baking tray and cook for 15 minutes. Let cool for 10 minutes. Serve.

259.Pesto Pork Chops

Servings: 6
Cooking Time: 25 Minutes
Ingredients:
- 6 pork chops
- 1/2 cup pesto
- 2 lbs cherry tomatoes
- 2 tbsp olive oil
- Pepper
- Salt

Directions:

1. Fit the oven with the rack in position
2. Brush pork chops with oil and season with pepper and salt.
3. Place pork chops into the baking dish. Add cherry tomatoes around the pork chops.
4. Pour pesto over pork chops.
5. Set to bake at 425 F for 30 minutes. After 5 minutes place the baking dish in the preheated oven.
6. Serve and enjoy.
- **Nutrition Info:** Calories: 413 Fat 33.5 g Carbohydrates 7.2 g Sugar 5.3 g Protein 21.3 g Cholesterol 74 mg

260. Quick Baked Pork Patties

Servings: 4
Cooking Time: 10 Minutes
Ingredients:

- 1 1/4 lbs ground pork
- 2 tsp honey
- 1 small onion, chopped
- 1 tsp pork seasoning
- 1 tsp garlic paste
- Pepper
- Salt

Directions:

1. Fit the oven with the rack in position 2.
2. Line the air fryer basket with parchment paper.
3. Add all ingredients into the mixing bowl and mix until well combined.
4. Make the equal shape of patties from meat mixture and place in the air fryer basket then place an air fryer basket in the baking pan.
5. Place a baking pan on the oven rack. Set to air fry at 360 F for 10 minutes.
6. Serve and enjoy.
- **Nutrition Info:** Calories: 228 Fat 5 g Carbohydrates 5.7 g Sugar 4.5 g Protein 37.3 g Cholesterol 103 mg

261. Turkey And Cauliflower Meatloaf

Servings: 6
Cooking Time: 50 Minutes
Ingredients:

- 2 pounds (907 g) lean ground turkey
- $1^1/_3$ cups riced cauliflower
- 2 large eggs, lightly beaten
- ¼ cup almond flour
- $^2/_3$ cup chopped yellow or white onion
- 1 teaspoon ground dried turmeric
- 1 teaspoon ground cumin
- 1 teaspoon ground coriander
- 1 tablespoon minced garlic
- 1 teaspoon salt
- 1 teaspoon ground black pepper
- Cooking spray

Directions:

1. Spritz the baking pan with cooking spray.
2. Combine all the ingredients in a large bowl. Stir to mix well. Pour half of the mixture in the prepared pan and press with a spatula to coat the bottom evenly. Spritz the mixture with cooking spray.
3. Slide the baking pan into Rack Position 1, select Convection Bake, set temperature to 350ºF (180ºC) and set time to 25 minutes.
4. When cooking is complete, the meat should be well browned and the internal temperature should reach at least 165ºF (74ºC).
5. Remove the pan from the oven and serve immediately.

262. Pesto & Spinach Beef Rolls

Servings: 4
Cooking Time: 30 Minutes
Ingredients:

- 2 lb beef steak, thinly sliced
- Salt and black pepper to taste
- 3 tbsp pesto
- ½ cup mozzarella cheese, shredded
- 1 cup spinach, chopped
- 1 bell pepper, deseeded and sliced

Directions:

1. Preheat oven to 400 F on Bake function. Place the beef slices between 2 baking paper sheets and flatten them with a rolling pin to about a fifth of an inch thick. Lay the slices on a clean surface and spread them with the pesto. Top with mozzarella, spinach, and bell pepper.
2. Roll up the slices and secure using a toothpick. Season with salt and pepper. Place the slices in the greased basket and Bake for 15 minutes. Serve immediately!

263. Teriyaki Pork Ribs In Tomato Sauce

Servings: 4
Cooking Time: 20 Minutes
Ingredients:

- 1 pound pork ribs
- Salt and black pepper to taste
- 1 tbsp sugar
- 1 tsp ginger juice
- 1 tsp five-spice powder
- 1 tbsp teriyaki sauce
- 1 tbsp soy sauce
- 1 garlic clove, minced
- 2 tbsp honey
- 1 tbsp water
- 1 tbsp tomato sauce

Directions:

1. In a bowl, mix pepper, sugar, five-spice powder, salt, ginger juice, and teriyaki sauce.

Add in the pork ribs and let marinate for 2 hours.

2. Preheat on Bake function to 380 F. Put the marinated pork ribs in a baking tray and place in the oven. Press Start and cook for 8 minutes.
3. In a pan over medium heat, mix soy sauce, garlic, honey, water, and tomato sauce. Stir and cook for 2-3 minutes until the sauce thickens. Pour the sauce over the pork ribs and serve.

264.Ricotta And Parsley Stuffed Turkey Breasts

Servings: 4
Cooking Time: 25 Minutes
Ingredients:
- 1 turkey breast, quartered
- 1 cup Ricotta cheese
- 1/4 cup fresh Italian parsley, chopped
- 1 teaspoon garlic powder
- 1/2 teaspoon cumin powder
- 1 egg, beaten
- 1 teaspoon paprika
- Salt and ground black pepper, to taste
- Crushed tortilla chips
- 1 ½ tablespoons extra-virgin olive oil

Directions:
1. Preparing the Ingredients. Firstly, flatten out each piece of turkey breast with a rolling pin. Prepare three mixing bowls.
2. In a shallow bowl, combine Ricotta cheese with the parsley, garlic powder, and cumin powder.
3. Place the Ricotta/parsley mixture in the middle of each piece. Repeat with the remaining pieces of the turkey breast and roll them up.
4. In another shallow bowl, whisk the egg together with paprika. In the third shallow bowl, combine the salt, pepper, and crushed tortilla chips.
5. Dip each roll in the whisked egg, then, roll them over the tortilla chips mixture.
6. Transfer prepared rolls to the Oven rack/basket. Drizzle olive oil over all. Place the Rack on the middle-shelf of the air fryer oven.
7. Air Frying. Cook at 350 degrees F for 25 minutes, working in batches. Serve warm, garnished with some extra parsley, if desired.

265.Parmesan Coated Chicken Cutlets

Servings:4
Cooking Time: 30 Minutes
Ingredients:
- ¼ cup Parmesan cheese, grated
- 4 chicken cutlets
- ⅛ tbsp paprika
- ¼ tsp pepper
- 2 tbsp panko breadcrumbs
- 1 tbsp parsley
- ½ tbsp garlic powder
- 2 large eggs, beaten

Directions:
1. In a bowl, mix Parmesan cheese, breadcrumbs, garlic powder, pepper, and paprika. Add eggs to another bowl. Dip the chicken cutlets in the eggs, dredge them in cheese/panko mixture and place them in the basket. Press Start and cook for 20-25 minutes on AirFry function at 400 F until crispy.

266.Sirloin Steak And Pepper Fajitas

Servings:4
Cooking Time: 15 Minutes
Ingredients:
- 8 (6-inch) flour tortillas
- 1 pound (454 g) top sirloin steak, sliced ¼-inch thick
- 1 red bell pepper, deseeded and sliced ½-inch thick
- 1 green bell pepper, deseeded and sliced ½-inch thick
- 1 jalapeño, deseeded and sliced thin
- 1 medium onion, sliced ½-inch thick
- 2 tablespoons vegetable oil
- 2 tablespoons Mexican seasoning
- 1 teaspoon kosher salt
- 2 tablespoons salsa
- 1 small avocado, sliced

Directions:
1. Line the baking pan with aluminum foil. Place the tortillas on the foil in two stacks and wrap in the foil.
2. Slide the baking pan into Rack Position 2, select Roast, set temperature to 325ºF (163ºC), and set time to 6 minutes.
3. After 3 minutes, remove from the oven and flip the packet of tortillas over. Return to the oven and continue cooking.
4. While the tortillas warm, place the steak, bell peppers, jalapeño, and onion in a large bowl and drizzle the oil over. Sprinkle with the Mexican seasoning and salt, and toss to coat.
5. When cooking is complete, remove from the oven and place the packet of tortillas on top of the oven to keep warm. Place the beef and peppers mixture in the baking pan, spreading out into a single layer as much as possible.
6. Select Roast, set temperature to 375ºF (190ºC), and set time to 9 minutes.

7. After about 5 minutes, remove from the oven and stir the ingredients. Return to the oven and continue cooking.
8. When cooking is complete, the vegetables will be soft and browned in places, and the beef will be browned on the outside and barely pink inside. Remove from the oven. Unwrap the tortillas and spoon the fajita mixture into the tortillas. Serve with salsa and avocado slices.

267.Spicy Chicken Nuggets

Servings: 6
Cooking Time: 10 Minutes
Ingredients:
- Nonstick cooking spray
- ¼ cup mayonnaise
- 2 tbsp. sweet chili sauce
- 1 tbsp. honey
- 1 tbsp. + 2 tsp hot sauce, divided
- 1 cup buttermilk
- ¾ cup flour
- ½ cup cornstarch
- 1 egg
- ½ tsp salt
- ¼ tsp pepper
- 1 cup panko bread crumbs
- 1 lb. chicken breasts, boneless, skinless & cut in 1-inch pieces

Directions:
1. Place the baking pan in position 2 of the oven. Lightly spray the fryer basket with cooking spray.
2. In a small bowl, whisk together mayonnaise, chili sauce, honey and 2 teaspoons hot sauce. Cover until ready to use.
3. In a large bowl, whisk together buttermilk, flour, cornstarch, egg, remaining hot sauce, salt, and pepper.
4. Place bread crumbs in a shallow dish.
5. One at a time, dip the chicken into buttermilk mixture then roll in bread crumbs to coat. Place in fryer basket in a single layer, these will need to be cooked in batches. Lightly spray the nuggets with cooking spray.
6. Place basket in the oven and set to air fry on 375°F for 10 minutes. Cook chicken until gold brown outside and no longer pink inside, turning over halfway through cooking time. Repeat with remaining chicken pieces.
7. Serve drizzled with reserved sauce.
- **Nutrition Info:** Calories: 459, Total Fat 11g, Saturated Fat 2g, Total Carbs 41g, Net Carbs 39g, Protein 24g, Sugar 7g, Fiber 2g, Sodium 615mg, Potassium 409mg, Phosphorus 268mg

268.Drumsticks With Barbecue-honey Sauce

Servings:5
Cooking Time: 18 Minutes
Ingredients:
- 1 tablespoon olive oil
- 10 chicken drumsticks
- Chicken seasoning or rub, to taste
- Salt and ground black pepper, to taste
- 1 cup barbecue sauce
- ¼ cup honey

Directions:
1. Grease the basket with olive oil.
2. Rub the chicken drumsticks with chicken seasoning or rub, salt and ground black pepper on a clean work surface.
3. Arrange the chicken drumsticks in the basket.
4. Put the air fryer basket on the baking pan and slide into Rack Position 2, select Air Fry, set temperature to 390ºF (199ºC) and set time to 18 minutes.
5. Flip the drumsticks halfway through.
6. When cooking is complete, the drumsticks should be lightly browned.
7. Meanwhile, combine the barbecue sauce and honey in a small bowl. Stir to mix well.
8. Remove the drumsticks from the oven and baste with the sauce mixture to serve.

269.Pork Cutlet Rolls

Servings: 4
Cooking Time: 15 Minutes
Ingredients:
- 4 Pork Cutlets
- 4 Sundried Tomatoes in oil
- 2 Tbsps Parsley, finely chopped
- 1 Green Onion, finely chopped
- Black Pepper to taste
- 2 Tsps Paprika
- 1/2 Tbsp Olive Oil
- * String for Rolled Meat

Directions:
1. Preparing the Ingredients. Preheat the air fryer oven to 390 degrees
2. Finely chop the tomatoes and mix with the parsley and green onion. Add salt and pepper to taste
3. Spread out the cutlets and coat them with the tomato mixture. Roll up the cutlets and secure intact with the string
4. Rub the rolls with salt, pepper, and paprika powder and thinly coat them with olive oil
5. Air Frying. Put the cutlet rolls in the air fryer oven tray and cook for 15 minutes. Roast until nicely brown and done.
6. Serve with tomato sauce.

270.Garlic Lemony Chicken Breast

Servings:2
Cooking Time: 20 Minutes
Ingredients:
- 1 chicken breast
- 2 lemon, juiced and rind reserved
- 1 tbsp chicken seasoning
- 1 tbsp garlic puree
- A handful of peppercorns
- Salt and black pepper to taste

Directions:
1. Place a silver foil sheet on a flat surface. Add all seasonings alongside the lemon rind. Lay the chicken breast onto a chopping board and trim any fat and little bones; season.
2. Rub the chicken seasoning on both sides. Place on the foil sheet and seal tightly; flatten with a rolling pin. Place the breast in the basket and cook for 15 minutes at 350 F on AirFry function.

271.Chicken Mexican Burritos

Servings:x
Cooking Time:x
Ingredients:
- ½ lb. chicken (You will need to cut the chicken into small pieces)
- 2 carrots (Cut in to long thin slices)
- 1-2 lettuce leaves shredded.
- 1 or 2 spring onions chopped finely. Also cut the greens.
- Take one tomato. Remove the seeds and chop it into small pieces.
- 1 green chili chopped.
- 1 tbsp. Olive oil
- 1 medium onion finely sliced
- 3 flakes garlic crushed
- 1 tsp. white wine
- A pinch of salt to taste
- ½ tsp. red chili flakes
- 1 cup of cheddar cheese grated.
- 1 cup boiled rice (not necessary).
- A few flour tortillas to put the filing in.
- ½ small onion chopped
- 1 tbsp. olive oil
- 2 tbsp. tomato puree
- ¼ tsp. red chili powder
- 1 tsp. of salt to taste
- 4-5 flour tortillas

Directions:
1. Cook the chicken, onions and garlic in two cups of water. You will need to cook till the chicken pieces have turned very soft. Now, mash the beans very fine.
2. In a pan, add oil and a few more onions to the pan and cook till the onions have turned translucent. Add the tomato puree and the cooked chicken and stir. Add the chili

powder and salt to the pan and continue to cook till you get a thick paste. Set it aside.
3. For the filling, you will need to sauté the onions and garlic in oil. Add the French beans and the chopped carrots. You will need to stir-fry for a few minutes and add the remaining ingredients for the filling. Cook for another ten minutes and take the pan off the flame.
4. Mix it well and add the jalapenos. To make the salad, toss the ingredients together. Place a tortilla and add a layer of the French beans to it.
5. Cover the edges using the chicken paste. Put the filling in the center of the tortilla along with the salad and some boiled rice. Roll up the tortilla using the chicken sauce to help you hold it together. Pre-heat the oven for around 5 minutes at 200 Fahrenheit. Open the fry basket and keep the burritos inside. Close the basket properly.
6. Let the oven remain at 200 Fahrenheit for another 15 minutes or so. Halfway through, remove the basket and turn all the burritos over in order to get a uniform cook. You can either serve the burritos as they are or you can cut them into pieces so that they are easier to eat. Recommended sides are salsa or some salad.

272.Festive Stuffed Pork Chops

Servings:4
Cooking Time: 40 Minutes
Ingredients:
- 4 pork chops
- Salt and black pepper to taste
- 4 cups stuffing mix
- 2 tbsp olive oil
- 4 garlic cloves, minced
- 2 tbsp fresh sage leaves, chopped

Directions:
1. Cut a hole in pork chops and fill chops with stuffing mix. In a bowl, mix sage, garlic, oil, salt, and pepper. Rub the chops with the marinade and let sit for 10 minutes.
2. Preheat on Bake function to 380 F. Put the chops in a baking tray and place in the oven. Press Start and cook for 25 minutes. Serve and enjoy!

273.Savory Honey & Garlic Chicken

Servings: 2
Cooking Time: 20 Minutes + Marinating Time
Ingredients:
- 2 chicken drumsticks, skin removed
- 2 tbsp olive oil
- 2 tbsp honey
- ½ tbsp garlic, minced

Directions:

1. Add garlic, olive oil, and honey to a sealable zip bag. Add chicken and toss to coat; set aside for 30 minutes. Add the coated chicken to the basket and fit in the baking sheet; cook for 15 minutes at 400 F on Air Fry function, flipping once. Serve and enjoy!

274.Quail Fried Baked Pastry

Servings:x
Cooking Time:x
Ingredients:
- 2 tbsp. unsalted butter
- 1 ½ cup all-purpose flour
- 1 tsp. coarsely crushed coriander
- 1 dry red chili broken into pieces
- A small amount of salt (to taste)
- ½ tsp. dried mango powder
- ½ tsp. red chili power.
- A pinch of salt to taste
- Add as much water as required to make the dough stiff and firm
- 1 lb. quail
- ¼ cup boiled peas
- 1 tsp. powdered ginger
- 1 or 2 green chilies that are finely chopped or mashed
- ½ tsp. cumin
- 1-2 tbsp. coriander.

Directions:
1. You will first need to make the outer covering. In a large bowl, add the flour, butter and enough water to knead it into dough that is stiff. Transfer this to a container and leave it to rest for five minutes. Place a pan on medium flame and add the oil. Roast the mustard seeds and once roasted, add the coriander seeds and the chopped dry red chilies. Add all the dry ingredients for the filling and mix the ingredients well. Add a little water and continue to stir the ingredients.
2. Make small balls out of the dough and roll them out. Cut the rolled-out dough into halves and apply a little water on the edges to help you fold the halves into a cone. Add the filling to the cone and close up the samosa.
3. Pre-heat the oven for around 5 to 6 minutes at 300 Fahrenheit. Place all the samosas in the fry basket and close the basket properly. Keep the oven at 200 degrees for another 20 to 25 minutes. Around the halfway point, open the basket and turn the samosas over for uniform cooking. After this, fry at 250 degrees for around 10 minutes in order to give them the desired golden-brown color. Serve hot. Recommended sides are tamarind or mint sauce.

275.Stuffed Pork Loin

Servings: 8
Cooking Time: 35 Minutes
Ingredients:
- 3 tbsp. butter
- 2 onions, sliced thin
- ½ cup beef broth
- 3 lb. pork loin, center cut
- 2 tbsp. extra virgin olive oil
- 1 tsp salt
- 1/4 tsp pepper
- 1 tsp Italian seasoning
- 2 cups gruyere cheese, grated
- Nonstick cooking spray

Directions:
1. Melt butter in a large skillet over med-high heat. Add onions and broth and cook until onions are brown and tender, about 15 minutes. Transfer to bowl and keep warm.
2. Butterfly the pork making sure you do not cut all the way through. Open up the tenderloin, cover with plastic wrap and pound to 1/3-inch thick.
3. In a small bowl, combine salt, pepper, and Italian seasoning. Rub both sides of pork with mixture.
4. Spread half the cooked onions on one side of pork and top with half the cheese. Tightly roll up pork and tie with butcher string.
5. Heat oil in skillet. Add the tenderloin and brown on all sides.
6. Set the oven to convection bake on 425°F for 35 minutes.
7. Lightly spray the baking pan with cooking spray and place pork on it. After the oven has preheated for 5 minutes, place the baking pan in position 1 and cook 30 minutes. Basting occasionally with juice from the pan.
8. Top pork with remaining onions and cheese. Increase heat to broil and cook another 5 minutes, or until cheese is melted and golden brown. Let rest 5 minutes before slicing and serving.
- **Nutrition Info:** Calories: 448, Total Fat 24g, Saturated Fat 11g, Total Carbs 3g, Net Carbs 0g, Protein 55g, Sugar 1g, Fiber 0g, Sodium 715mg, Potassium 795mg, Phosphorus 665mg

276.Balsamic Chicken Breast Roast

Servings:2
Cooking Time: 40 Minutes
Ingredients:
- ¼ cup balsamic vinegar
- 2 teaspoons dried oregano
- 2 garlic cloves, minced
- 1 tablespoon olive oil
- ⅛ teaspoon salt

- ½ teaspoon freshly ground black pepper
- 2 (4-ounce / 113-g) boneless, skinless, chicken-breast halves
- Cooking spray

Directions:
1. In a small bowl, add the vinegar, oregano, garlic, olive oil, salt, and pepper. Mix to combine.
2. Put the chicken in a resealable plastic bag. Pour the vinegar mixture in the bag with the chicken, seal the bag, and shake to coat the chicken. Refrigerate for 30 minutes to marinate.
3. Spritz the baking pan with cooking spray. Put the chicken in the prepared baking pan and pour the marinade over the chicken.
4. Slide the baking pan into Rack Position 1, select Convection Bake, set temperature to 400ºF (205ºC) and set time to 40 minutes.
5. After 20 minutes, remove the pan from the oven. Flip the chicken. Return the pan to the oven and continue cooking.
6. When cooking is complete, the internal temperature of the chicken should registers at least 165ºF (74ºC).
7. Let sit for 5 minutes, then serve.

277.Squab Cutlet

Servings:x
Cooking Time:x
Ingredients:
- 2 lb. boneless squab cut into slices
- 1st Marinade:
- 3 tbsp. vinegar or lemon juice
- 2 or 3 tsp. paprika
- 1 tsp. black pepper
- 1 tsp. salt
- 3 tsp. ginger-garlic paste
- 2nd Marinade:
- 1 cup yogurt
- 4 tsp. tandoori masala
- 2 tbsp. dry fenugreek leaves
- 1 tsp. black salt
- 1 tsp. chat masala
- 1 tsp. garam masala powder
- 1 tsp. red chili powder
- 1 tsp. salt
- 3 drops of red color

Directions:
1. Make the first marinade and soak the cut squab in it for four hours. While this is happening, make the second marinade and soak the squab in it overnight to let the flavors blend. Pre heat the oven at 160 degrees Fahrenheit for 5 minutes.
2. Place the Oregano Fingers in the fry basket and close it. Let them cook at the same temperature for another 15 minutes or so. Toss the Oregano Fingers well so that they

are cooked uniformly. Serve them with mint sauce.

278.Lamb Loin Chops With Horseradish Cream Sauce

Servings:4
Cooking Time: 13 Minutes
Ingredients:
- For the Lamb:
- 4 lamb loin chops
- 2 tablespoons vegetable oil
- 1 clove garlic, minced
- ½ teaspoon kosher salt
- ½ teaspoon black pepper
- For the Horseradish Cream Sauce:
- 1 to 1½ tablespoons prepared horseradish
- 1 tablespoon Dijon mustard
- ½ cup mayonnaise
- 2 teaspoons sugar
- Cooking spray

Directions:
1. Spritz the air fryer basket with cooking spray.
2. Place the lamb chops on a plate. Rub with the oil and sprinkle with the garlic, salt and black pepper. Let sit to marinate for 30 minutes at room temperature.
3. Make the horseradish cream sauce: Mix the horseradish, mustard, mayonnaise, and sugar in a bowl until well combined. Set half of the sauce aside until ready to serve.
4. Arrange the marinated chops in the basket.
5. Put the air fryer basket on the baking pan and slide into Rack Position 2, select Air Fry, set temperature to 325ºF (163ºC) and set time to 10 minutes.
6. Flip the lamb chops halfway through.
7. When cooking is complete, the lamb should be lightly browned.
8. Transfer the chops from the oven to the bowl of the horseradish sauce. Roll to coat well.
9. Put the coated chops back in the basket.
10. Set the temperature to 400ºF (205ºC) and the time to 3 minutes.
11. When cooking is complete, the internal temperature should reach 145ºF (63ºC) on a meat thermometer (for medium-rare). Flip the lamb halfway through.
12. Serve hot with the horseradish cream sauce.

279.Garlic Chicken

Servings: 6
Cooking Time: 40 Minutes
Ingredients:
- 2 lbs chicken thighs, skinless and boneless
- 10 garlic cloves, sliced
- 2 tbsp olive oil
- 2 tbsp fresh parsley, chopped

- 1 fresh lemon juice
- Pepper
- Salt

Directions:
1. Fit the oven with the rack in position
2. Place chicken in baking pan and season with pepper and salt.
3. Sprinkle parsley and garlic over the chicken. Drizzle with oil and lemon juice.
4. Set to bake at 450 F for 45 minutes. After 5 minutes place the baking pan in the preheated oven.
5. Serve and enjoy.
- **Nutrition Info:** Calories: 337 Fat 16 g Carbohydrates 1.9 g Sugar 0.2 g Protein 44.2 g Cholesterol 135 mg

280.Cheesy Bacon Chicken

Servings: 4
Cooking Time: 30 Minutes
Ingredients:
- 4 chicken breasts, sliced in half
- 1 cup cheddar cheese, shredded
- 8 bacon slices, cooked & chopped
- 6 oz cream cheese
- Pepper
- Salt

Directions:
1. Fit the oven with the rack in position
2. Place season chicken with pepper and salt and place it into the greased baking dish.
3. Add cream cheese and bacon on top of chicken.
4. Sprinkle shredded cheddar cheese on top of chicken.
5. Set to bake at 400 F for 35 minutes. After 5 minutes place the baking dish in the preheated oven.
6. Serve and enjoy.
- **Nutrition Info:** Calories: 745 Fat 50.9 g Carbohydrates 2.1 g Sugar 0.2 g Protein 66.6 g Cholesterol 248 mg

281.Pineapple Chicken

Servings:6
Cooking Time: 10 Minutes
Ingredients:
- 1½ pounds (680 g) boneless, skinless chicken breasts, cut into 1-inch chunks
- ¾ cup soy sauce
- 2 tablespoons ketchup
- 2 tablespoons brown sugar
- 2 tablespoons rice vinegar
- 1 red bell pepper, cut into 1-inch chunks
- 1 green bell pepper, cut into 1-inch chunks
- 6 scallions, cut into 1-inch pieces
- 1 cup (¾-inch chunks) fresh pineapple, rinsed and drained
- Cooking spray

Directions:
1. Place the chicken in a large bowl. Add the soy sauce, ketchup, brown sugar, vinegar, red and green peppers, and scallions. Toss to coat.
2. Spritz the baking pan with cooking spray and place the chicken and vegetables on the pan.
3. Slide the baking pan into Rack Position 2, select Roast, set temperature to 375ºF (190ºC), and set time to 10 minutes.
4. After 6 minutes, remove from the oven. Add the pineapple chunks to the pan and stir. Return the pan to the oven and continue cooking.
5. When cooking is complete, remove from the oven. Serve with steamed rice, if desired.

282.Veal Marinade Cutlet

Servings:x
Cooking Time:x
Ingredients:
- 2 cups sliced veal
- 1 big capsicum (Cut this capsicum into big cubes)
- 1 onion (Cut it into quarters. Now separate the layers carefully.)
- 5 tbsp. gram flour
- A pinch of salt to taste
- For the filling:
- 2 cup fresh green coriander
- ½ cup mint leaves
- 4 tsp. fennel
- 2 tbsp. ginger-garlic paste
- 1 small onion
- Salt to taste
- 3 tbsp. lemon juice

Directions:
1. You will first need to make the sauce. Add the ingredients to a blender and make a thick paste. Slit the pieces of veal and stuff half the paste into the cavity obtained. Take the remaining paste and add it to the gram flour and salt. Toss the pieces of veal in this mixture and set aside. Apply a little bit of the mixture on the capsicum and onion.
2. Place these on a stick along with the veal pieces. Pre heat the oven at 290 Fahrenheit for around 5 minutes. Open the basket.
3. Arrange the satay sticks properly. Close the basket. Keep the sticks with the veal at 180 degrees for around half an hour while the sticks with the vegetables are to be kept at the same temperature for only 7 minutes. Turn the sticks in between so that one side does not get burnt and also to provide a uniform cook.

283.Cheesy Pepperoni And Chicken Pizza

Servings:6
Cooking Time: 15 Minutes
Ingredients:

- 2 cups cooked chicken, cubed
- 1 cup pizza sauce
- 20 slices pepperoni
- ¼ cup grated Parmesan cheese
- 1 cup shredded Mozzarella cheese
- Cooking spray

Directions:

1. Spritz the baking pan with cooking spray.
2. Arrange the chicken cubes in the prepared baking pan, then top the cubes with pizza sauce and pepperoni. Stir to coat the cubes and pepperoni with sauce. Scatter the cheeses on top.
3. Put the air fryer basket on the baking pan and slide into Rack Position 2, select Air Fry, set temperature to 375ºF (190ºC) and set time to 15 minutes.
4. When cooking is complete, the pizza should be frothy and the cheeses should be melted.
5. Serve immediately.

284.Italian-style Pork Chops

Servings: 4
Cooking Time: 30 Minutes + Marinating Time
Ingredients:

- 4 pork chops, sliced
- 2 tbsp olive oil
- Salt and black pepper to taste
- 1 whole egg, beaten
- 1 tbsp flour
- 1 cup breadcrumbs
- 1 tsp Italian herbs

Directions:

1. In a bowl, place olive oil, salt, and pepper and mix well. Stir in the pork, cover, and let it marinate for 15 minutes. Place the beaten egg in a plate. In a separate plate, add the breadcrumbs
2. Preheat on Air Fry function to 400 F. Dip the pork in the egg and then into the breadcrumbs. Place in the cooking basket and fit in the baking tray; cook for 20 minutes, shaking once. Serve warm.

285.Duck Liver Fries

Servings:x
Cooking Time:x
Ingredients:

- A pinch of salt to taste
- 1 tbsp. lemon juice
- For the garnish:
- 1 cup melted cheddar cheese
- 1 lb. duck liver (Cut in to long Oregano Fingers)
- ingredients for the marinade:
- 1 tbsp. olive oil
- 1 tsp. mixed herbs
- ½ tsp. red chili flakes

Directions:

1. Take all the ingredients mentioned under the heading "For the marinade" and mix them well.
2. Cook the duck liver Oregano Fingers and soak them in the marinade.
3. Pre heat the oven for around 5 minutes at 300 Fahrenheit. Take out the basket of the fryer and place the chicken Oregano Fingers in them. Close the basket.
4. Now keep the fryer at 220 Fahrenheit for 20 or 25 minutes. In between the process, toss the fries twice or thrice so that they get cooked properly.
5. Towards the end of the cooking process (the last 2 minutes or so), sprinkle the cut coriander leaves on the fries. Add the melted cheddar cheese over the fries and serve hot.

FISH & SEAFOOD RECIPES

286.Coconut Chili Fish Curry

Servings:4
Cooking Time: 22 Minutes
Ingredients:
- 2 tablespoons sunflower oil, divided
- 1 pound (454 g) fish, chopped
- 1 ripe tomato, pureéd
- 2 red chilies, chopped
- 1 shallot, minced
- 1 garlic clove, minced
- 1 cup coconut milk
- 1 tablespoon coriander powder
- 1 teaspoon red curry paste
- ½ teaspoon fenugreek seeds
- Salt and white pepper, to taste

Directions:
1. Coat the air fryer basket with 1 tablespoon of sunflower oil. Place the fish in the basket.
2. Put the air fryer basket on the baking pan and slide into Rack Position 2, select Air Fry, set temperature to 380ºF (193ºC), and set time to 10 minutes.
3. Flip the fish halfway through the cooking time.
4. When cooking is complete, transfer the cooked fish to the baking pan greased with the remaining 1 tablespoon of sunflower oil. Stir in the remaining ingredients.
5. Put the air fryer basket on the baking pan and slide into Rack Position 2, select Air Fry, set temperature to 350ºF (180ºC), and set time to 12 minutes.
6. When cooking is complete, they should be heated through. Cool for 5 to 8 minutes before serving.

287.Mediterranean Sole

Servings: 6
Cooking Time: 20 Minutes
Ingredients:
- Nonstick cooking spray
- 2 tbsp. olive oil
- 8 scallions, sliced thin
- 2 cloves garlic, diced fine
- 4 tomatoes, chopped
- ½ cup dry white wine
- 2 tbsp. fresh parsley, chopped fine
- 1 tsp oregano
- 1 tsp pepper
- 2 lbs. sole, cut in 6 pieces
- 4 oz. feta cheese, crumbled

Directions:
1. Place the rack in position 1 of the oven. Spray an 8x11-inch baking dish with cooking spray.
2. Heat the oil in a medium skillet over medium heat. Add scallions and garlic and cook until tender, stirring frequently.
3. Add the tomatoes, wine, parsley, oregano, and pepper. Stir to mix. Simmer for 5 minutes, or until sauce thickens. Remove from heat.
4. Pour half the sauce on the bottom of the prepared dish. Lay fish on top then pour remaining sauce over the top. Sprinkle with feta.
5. Set the oven to bake on 400°F for 25 minutes. After 5 minutes, place the baking dish on the rack and cook 15-18 minutes or until fish flakes easily with a fork. Serve immediately.
- **Nutrition Info:** Calories: 220, Total Fat 12g, Saturated Fat 4g, Total Carbs 6g, Net Carbs 4g, Protein 22g, Sugar 4g, Fiber 2g, Sodium 631mg, Potassium 540mg, Phosphorus 478mg

288.Spicy Grilled Halibut

Servings: 4
Cooking Time: 10 Minutes
Ingredients:
- ½ cup fresh lemon juice
- 2 jalapeno peppers, seeded & chopped fine
- 4 6 oz. halibut fillets
- Nonstick cooking spray
- ¼ cup cilantro, chopped

Directions:
1. In a small bowl, combine lemon juice and chilies, mix well.
2. Place fish in a large Ziploc bag and add marinade. Toss to coat. Refrigerate 30 minutes.
3. Lightly spray the baking pan with cooking spray. Set oven to broil on 400°F for 15 minutes.
4. After 5 minutes, lay fish on the pan and place in position 2 of the oven. Cook 10 minutes, or until fish flakes easily with a fork. Turn fish over and brush with marinade halfway through cooking time.
5. Sprinkle with cilantro before serving.
- **Nutrition Info:** Calories: 328, Total Fat 24g, Saturated Fat 4g, Total Carbs 3g, Net Carbs 3g, Protein 25g, Sugar 1g, Fiber 0g, Sodium 137mg, Potassium 510mg, Phosphorus 284mg

289.Smoked Paprika Tiger Shrimp

Servings:4
Cooking Time: 10 Minutes
Ingredients:
- 1 lb tiger shrimp
- 2 tbsp olive oil

- ¼ tbsp garlic powder
- 1 tbsp smoked paprika
- 2 tbsp fresh parsley, chopped
- Sea salt to taste

Directions:
1. Preheat on AirFry function to 380 F. Mix garlic powder, smoked paprika, salt, parsley, and olive oil in a large bowl. Add in the shrimp and toss to coat. Place the shrimp in the frying basket press Start. Fry for 6-7 minutes. Serve with salad.

290.Honey Glazed Salmon

Servings: 4
Cooking Time: 8 Minutes
Ingredients:
- 4 salmon fillets
- 2 tsp soy sauce
- 1 tbsp honey
- Pepper
- Salt

Directions:
1. Fit the oven with the rack in position 2.
2. Brush salmon with soy sauce and season with pepper and salt.
3. Place salmon in the air fryer basket then place an air fryer basket in the baking pan.
4. Place a baking pan on the oven rack. Set to air fry at 375 F for 8 minutes.
5. Brush salmon with honey and serve.
- **Nutrition Info:** Calories: 253 Fat 11 g Carbohydrates 4.6 g Sugar 4.4 g Protein 34.7 g Cholesterol 78 mg

291.Prawn Momo's Recipe

Servings:x
Cooking Time:x
Ingredients:
- 1 ½ cup all-purpose flour
- ½ tsp. salt
- 5 tbsp. water
- For filling:
- 2 cups minced prawn
- 2 tbsp. oil
- 2 tsp. ginger-garlic paste
- 2 tsp. soya sauce
- 2 tsp. vinegar

Directions:
1. Squeeze the dough and cover it with plastic wrap and set aside. Next, cook the ingredients for the filling and try to ensure that the prawn is covered well with the sauce. Roll the dough and cut it into a square.
2. Place the filling in the center. Now, wrap the dough to cover the filling and pinch the edges together. Pre heat the oven at 200° F for 5 minutes. Place the wontons in the fry basket and close it. Let them cook at the

same temperature for another 20 minutes. Recommended sides are chili sauce or ketchup.

292.Sticky Hoisin Tuna

Servings:4
Cooking Time: 5 Minutes
Ingredients:
- ½ cup hoisin sauce
- 2 tablespoons rice wine vinegar
- 2 teaspoons sesame oil
- 2 teaspoons dried lemongrass
- 1 teaspoon garlic powder
- ¼ teaspoon red pepper flakes
- ½ small onion, quartered and thinly sliced
- 8 ounces (227 g) fresh tuna, cut into 1-inch cubes
- Cooking spray
- 3 cups cooked jasmine rice

Directions:
1. In a small bowl, whisk together the hoisin sauce, vinegar, sesame oil, lemongrass, garlic powder, and red pepper flakes.
2. Add the sliced onion and tuna cubes and gently toss until the fish is evenly coated.
3. Arrange the coated tuna cubes in the air fryer basket in a single layer.
4. Put the air fryer basket on the baking pan and slide into Rack Position 2, select Air Fry, set temperature to 390ºF (199ºC), and set time to 5 minutes.
5. Flip the fish halfway through the cooking time.
6. When cooking is complete, the fish should begin to flake. Continue cooking for 1 minute, if necessary. Remove from the oven and serve over hot jasmine rice.

293.Golden Beer-battered Cod

Servings:4
Cooking Time: 15 Minutes
Ingredients:
- 2 eggs
- 1 cup malty beer
- 1 cup all-purpose flour
- ½ cup cornstarch
- 1 teaspoon garlic powder
- Salt and pepper, to taste
- 4 (4-ounce / 113-g) cod fillets
- Cooking spray

Directions:
1. In a shallow bowl, beat together the eggs with the beer. In another shallow bowl, thoroughly combine the flour and cornstarch. Sprinkle with the garlic powder, salt, and pepper.
2. Dredge each cod fillet in the flour mixture, then in the egg mixture. Dip each piece of fish in the flour mixture a second time.

3. Spritz the air fryer basket with cooking spray. Arrange the cod fillets in the pan in a single layer.
4. Put the air fryer basket on the baking pan and slide into Rack Position 2, select Air Fry, set temperature to 400ºF (205ºC), and set time to 15 minutes.
5. Flip the fillets halfway through the cooking time.
6. When cooking is complete, the cod should reach an internal temperature of 145ºF (63ºC) on a meat thermometer and the outside should be crispy. Let the fish cool for 5 minutes and serve.

294.Maryland Crab Cakes

Servings: 6
Cooking Time: 10 Minutes
Ingredients:
- Nonstick cooking spray
- 2 eggs
- 1 cup Panko bread crumbs
- 1 stalk celery, chopped
- 3 tbsp. mayonnaise
- 1 tsp Worcestershire sauce
- ¼ cup mozzarella cheese, grated
- 1 tsp Italian seasoning
- 1 tbsp. fresh parsley, chopped
- 1 tsp pepper
- ¾ lb. lump crabmeat, drained

Directions:
1. Place baking pan in position 2 of the oven. Lightly spray the fryer basket with cooking spray.
2. In a large bowl, combine all ingredients except crab meat, mix well.
3. Fold in crab carefully so it retains some chunks. Form mixture into 12 patties.
4. Place patties in a single layer in the fryer basket. Place the basket on the baking pan.
5. Set oven to air fryer on 350°F for 10 minutes. Cook until golden brown, turning over halfway through cooking time. Serve immediately.
- **Nutrition Info:** Calories: 172, Total Fat 8g, Saturated Fat 2g, Total Carbs 14g, Net Carbs 13g, Protein 16g, Sugar 1g, Fiber 1g, Sodium 527mg, Potassium 290mg, Phosphorus 201mg

295.Easy Salmon Cakes

Servings: 2
Cooking Time: 15 Minutes + Cooling Time
Ingredients:
- 8 oz salmon, cooked
- 1 ½ oz potatoes, mashed
- A handful of capers
- A handful of parsley, chopped
- Zest of 1 lemon

- 1 ¾ oz plain flour

Directions:
1. Carefully flake the salmon in a bowl. Stir in zest, capers, dill, and mashed potatoes. Shape the mixture into cakes and dust them with flour. Place in the fridge for 60 minutes.
2. Preheat your to 350 F on Air Fry function. Remove the cakes from the fridges and arrange them on the greased basket. Fit in the baking tray and cook for 10 minutes, shaing once halfway through. Serve chilled.

296.Rosemary Buttered Prawns

Servings: 2
Cooking Time: 15 Minutes + Marinating Time
Ingredients:
- 8 large prawns
- 1 rosemary sprig, chopped
- ½ tbsp melted butter
- Salt and black pepper to taste

Directions:
1. Combine butter, rosemary, salt, and pepper in a bowl. Add in the prawns and mix to coat. Cover the bowl and refrigerate for 1 hour.
2. Preheat on Air Fry function to 350 F Remove the prawns from the fridge and place them in the basket. Fit in the baking tray and cook for 10 minutes, flipping once. Serve.

297.Squab Oregano Fingers

Servings:x
Cooking Time:x
Ingredients:
- ½ lb. squab Oregano Fingers
- 2 cups of dry breadcrumbs
- 1 cup oil for frying
- 1 ½ tbsp. ginger-garlic paste
- 3 tbsp. lemon juice
- 2 tsp salt
- 1 ½ tsp pepper powder
- 1 tsp red chili flakes or to taste
- 3 eggs
- 5 tbsp. corn flour
- 2 tsp tomato ketchup

Directions:
1. Make the marinade and transfer the Oregano Fingers into the marinade. Leave them on a plate to dry for fifteen minutes. Now cover the Oregano Fingers with the crumbs and set aside to dry for fifteen minutes.
2. Pre heat the oven at 160 degrees Fahrenheit for 5 minutes or so. Keep the fish in the fry basket now and close it properly. Let the Oregano Fingers cook at the same temperature for another 25 minutes. In between the cooking process,

toss the fish once in a while to avoid burning the food. Serve either with tomato ketchup or chili sauce. Mint sauce also works well with the fish.

298.Paprika Cod

Servings: 4
Cooking Time: 15 Minutes
Ingredients:
- 4 cod fillets
- 1 tsp smoked paprika
- 1/2 cup parmesan cheese, grated
- 1/2 tbsp olive oil
- 1 tsp parsley
- Pepper
- Salt

Directions:
1. Fit the oven with the rack in position
2. Brush fish fillets with oil and season with pepper and salt.
3. In a shallow dish, mix parmesan cheese, paprika, and parsley.
4. Coat fish fillets with cheese mixture and place into the baking dish.
5. Set to bake at 400 F for 20 minutes. After 5 minutes place the baking dish in the preheated oven.
6. Serve and enjoy.
- **Nutrition Info:** Calories: 125 Fat 5 g Carbohydrates 0.7 g Sugar 0.1 g Protein 19.8 g Cholesterol 52 mg

299.Healthy Haddock

Servings: 2
Cooking Time: 25 Minutes
Ingredients:
- 1 lb haddock fillets
- 1/4 cup parsley, chopped
- 1 lemon juice
- 1/4 cup brown sugar
- 1/4 cup onion, diced
- 1 tsp ginger, grated
- 3/4 cup soy sauce
- Pepper
- Salt

Directions:
1. Fit the oven with the rack in position
2. Add fish fillets and remaining ingredients into the large bowl and coat well and place in the refrigerator for 1 hour.
3. Place marinated fish fillets into the baking dish.
4. Set to bake at 325 F for 30 minutes. After 5 minutes place the baking dish in the preheated oven.
5. Serve and enjoy.
- **Nutrition Info:** Calories: 391 Fat 2.5 g Carbohydrates 28 g Sugar 20.4 g Protein 61.7 g Cholesterol 168 mg

300.Seafood Pizza

Servings:x
Cooking Time:x
Ingredients:
- One pizza base
- Grated pizza cheese (mozzarella cheese preferably) for topping
- Some pizza topping sauce
- Use cooking oil for brushing and topping purposes
- ingredients for topping:
- 2 onions chopped
- 2 cups mixed seafood
- 2 capsicums chopped
- 2 tomatoes that have been deseeded and chopped
- 1 tbsp. (optional) mushrooms/corns
- 2 tsp. pizza seasoning
- Some cottage cheese that has been cut into small cubes (optional)

Directions:
1. Put the pizza base in a pre-heated oven for around 5 minutes. (Pre heated to 340 Fahrenheit). Take out the base. Pour some pizza sauce on top of the base at the center. Using a spoon spread the sauce over the base making sure that you leave some gap around the circumference. Grate some mozzarella cheese and sprinkle it over the sauce layer. Take all the vegetables and the seafood and mix them in a bowl. Add some oil and seasoning.
2. Also add some salt and pepper according to taste. Mix them properly. Put this topping over the layer of cheese on the pizza. Now sprinkle some more grated cheese and pizza seasoning on top of this layer. Pre heat the oven at 250 Fahrenheit for around 5 minutes.
3. Open the fry basket and place the pizza inside. Close the basket and keep the fryer at 170 degrees for another 10 minutes. If you feel that it is undercooked you may put it at the same temperature for another 2 minutes or so.

301.Blackened Mahi Mahi

Servings: 4
Cooking Time: 12 Minutes
Ingredients:
- 4 mahi-mahi fillets
- 1 tsp cumin
- 1 tsp paprika
- 1/2 tsp cayenne pepper
- 1 tsp oregano
- 1 tsp garlic powder
- 1 tsp onion powder
- 1/2 tsp pepper
- 3 tbsp olive oil

- 1/2 tsp salt

Directions:
1. Fit the oven with the rack in position
2. Brush fish fillets with oil and place them into the baking dish.
3. Mix together the remaining ingredients and sprinkle over fish fillets.
4. Set to bake at 450 F for 17 minutes. After 5 minutes place the baking dish in the preheated oven.
5. Serve and enjoy.
- **Nutrition Info:** Calories: 189 Fat 11.7 g Carbohydrates 2.1 g Sugar 0.5 g Protein 19.4 g Cholesterol 86 mg

302.Roasted Nicoise Salad

Servings:4
Cooking Time: 15 Minutes
Ingredients:
- 10 ounces (283 g) small red potatoes, quartered
- 8 tablespoons extra-virgin olive oil, divided
- 1 teaspoon kosher salt, divided
- ½ pound (227 g) green beans, trimmed
- 1 pint cherry tomatoes
- 1 teaspoon Dijon mustard
- 3 tablespoons red wine vinegar
- Freshly ground black pepper, to taste
- 1 (9-ounce / 255-g) bag spring greens, washed and dried if needed
- 2 (5-ounce / 142-g) cans oil-packed tuna, drained
- 2 hard-cooked eggs, peeled and quartered
- $^1/_3$ cup kalamata olives, pitted

Directions:
1. In a large bowl, drizzle the potatoes with 1 tablespoon of olive oil and season with ¼ teaspoon of kosher salt. Transfer to the baking pan.
2. Slide the baking pan into Rack Position 2, select Roast, set temperature to 375ºF (190ºC), and set time to 15 minutes.
3. Meanwhile, in a mixing bowl, toss the green beans and cherry tomatoes with 1 tablespoon of olive oil and ¼ teaspoon of kosher salt until evenly coated.
4. After 10 minutes, remove the pan and fold in the green beans and cherry tomatoes. Return the pan to the oven and continue cooking.
5. Meanwhile, make the vinaigrette by whisking together the remaining 6 tablespoons of olive oil, mustard, vinegar, the remaining ½ teaspoon of kosher salt, and black pepper in a small bowl. Set aside.
6. When done, remove from the oven. Allow the vegetables to cool for 5 minutes.
7. Spread out the spring greens on a plate and spoon the tuna into the center of the greens.

Arrange the potatoes, green beans, cheery tomatoes, and eggs around the tuna. Serve drizzled with the vinaigrette and scattered with the olives.

303.Bacon-wrapped Scallops

Servings:4
Cooking Time: 10 Minutes
Ingredients:
- 8 slices bacon, cut in half
- 16 sea scallops, patted dry
- Cooking spray
- Salt and freshly ground black pepper, to taste
- 16 toothpicks, soaked in water for at least 30 minutes

Directions:
1. On a clean work surface, wrap half of a slice of bacon around each scallop and secure with a toothpick.
2. Lay the bacon-wrapped scallops in the air fryer basket in a single layer.
3. Spritz the scallops with cooking spray and sprinkle the salt and pepper to season.
4. Put the air fryer basket on the baking pan and slide into Rack Position 2, select Air Fry, set temperature to 370ºF (188ºC), and set time to 10 minutes.
5. Flip the scallops halfway through the cooking time.
6. When cooking is complete, the bacon should be cooked through and the scallops should be firm. Remove the scallops from the oven to a plate Serve warm.

304.Marinated Salmon

Servings: 2
Cooking Time: 10 Minutes
Ingredients:
- 2 salmon fillets, skinless and boneless
- For marinade:
- 2 tbsp scallions, minced
- 1 tbsp ginger, grated
- 2 garlic cloves, minced
- 2 tbsp mirin
- 2 tbsp soy sauce
- 1 tbsp olive oil

Directions:
1. Fit the oven with the rack in position 2.
2. Add all marinade ingredients into the zip-lock bag and mix well.
3. Add salmon in the bag. The sealed bag shakes well and places it in the fridge for 30 minutes.
4. Arrange marinated salmon fillets in an air fryer basket then place an air fryer basket in the baking pan.
5. Place a baking pan on the oven rack. Set to air fry at 360 F for 10 minutes.

6. Serve and enjoy.
- **Nutrition Info:** Calories: 345 Fat 18.2 g Carbohydrates 11.6 g Sugar 4.5 g Protein 36.1 g Cholesterol 78 mg

305.Rosemary Garlic Shrimp

Servings: 4
Cooking Time: 10 Minutes
Ingredients:
- 1 lb shrimp, peeled and deveined
- 2 garlic cloves, minced
- 1/2 tbsp fresh rosemary, chopped
- 1 tbsp olive oil
- Pepper
- Salt

Directions:
1. Fit the oven with the rack in position
2. Add shrimp and remaining ingredients in a large bowl and toss well.
3. Pour shrimp mixture into the baking dish.
4. Set to bake at 400 F for 15 minutes. After 5 minutes place the baking dish in the preheated oven.
5. Serve and enjoy.
- **Nutrition Info:** Calories: 168 Fat 5.5 g Carbohydrates 2.5 g Sugar 0 g Protein 26 g Cholesterol 239 mg

306.Quick Paella

Servings: 4
Cooking Time: 15 Minutes
Ingredients:
- 1 (10-ounce) package frozen cooked rice, thawed
- 1 (6-ounce) jar artichoke hearts, drained and chopped
- ¼ cup vegetable broth
- ½ teaspoon turmeric
- ½ teaspoon dried thyme
- 1 cup frozen cooked small shrimp
- ½ cup frozen baby peas
- 1 tomato, diced

Directions:
1. Preparing the Ingredients. In a 6-by-6-by-2-inch pan, combine the rice, artichoke hearts, vegetable broth, turmeric, and thyme, and stir gently.
2. Air Frying. Place in the air fryer oven and bake for 8 to 9 minutes or until the rice is hot. Remove from the air fryer oven and gently stir in the shrimp, peas, and tomato. Cook for 5 to 8 minutes or until the shrimp and peas are hot and the paella is bubbling.
- **Nutrition Info:** CALORIES: 345; FAT: 1G; PROTEIN:18G; FIBER:4G

307.Mustard-crusted Sole Fillets

Servings:4
Cooking Time: 10 Minutes

Ingredients:
- 5 teaspoons low-sodium yellow mustard
- 1 tablespoon freshly squeezed lemon juice
- 4 (3.5-ounce / 99-g) sole fillets
- 2 teaspoons olive oil
- ½ teaspoon dried marjoram
- ½ teaspoon dried thyme
- ⅛ teaspoon freshly ground black pepper
- 1 slice low-sodium whole-wheat bread, crumbled

Directions:
1. Whisk together the mustard and lemon juice in a small bowl until thoroughly mixed and smooth. Spread the mixture evenly over the sole fillets, then transfer the fillets to the baking pan.
2. In a separate bowl, combine the olive oil, marjoram, thyme, black pepper, and bread crumbs and stir to mix well. Gently but firmly press the mixture onto the top of fillets, coating them completely.
3. Slide the baking pan into Rack Position 1, select Convection Bake, set temperature to 320ºF (160ºC), and set time to 10 minutes.
4. When cooking is complete, the fish should reach an internal temperature of 145ºF (63ºC) on a meat thermometer. Remove from the oven and serve on a plate.

308.Tuna Sandwich

Servings:x
Cooking Time:x
Ingredients:
- 2 slices of white bread
- 1 tbsp. softened butter
- 1 tin tuna
- 1 small capsicum
- For Barbeque Sauce:
- ¼ tbsp. Worcestershire sauce
- ½ tsp. olive oil
- ¼ tsp. mustard powder
- ½ flake garlic crushed
- ¼ cup chopped onion
- ½ tbsp. sugar
- 1 tbsp. tomato ketchup
- ½ cup water.
- ¼ tbsp. red chili sauce
- A pinch of salt and black pepper to taste

Directions:
1. Take the slices of bread and remove the edges. Now cut the slices horizontally. Cook the ingredients for the sauce and wait till it thickens. Now, add the lamb to the sauce and stir till it obtains the flavors. Roast the capsicum and peel the skin off. Cut the capsicum into slices. Mix the ingredients together and apply it to the bread slices.
2. Pre-heat the oven for 5 minutes at 300 Fahrenheit. Open the basket of the Fryer

and place the prepared Classic Sandwiches in it such that no two Classic Sandwiches are touching each other. Now keep the fryer at 250 degrees for around 15 minutes. Turn the Classic Sandwiches in between the cooking process to cook both slices. Serve the Classic Sandwiches with tomato ketchup or mint sauce.

309.Garlic-butter Catfish

Servings: 2
Cooking Time: 20 Minutes
Ingredients:
- 2 catfish fillets
- 2 tsp blackening seasoning
- Juice of 1 lime
- 2 tbsp butter, melted
- 1 garlic clove, mashed
- 2 tbsp cilantro

Directions:
1. In a bowl, blend in garlic, lime juice, cilantro, and butter. Pour half of the mixture over the fillets and sprinkle with blackening seasoning. Place the fillets in the basket and fit in the baking tray; cook for 15 minutes at 360 F on Air Fry function. Serve the fish with remaining sauce.

310.Spicy Orange Shrimp

Servings:4
Cooking Time: 12 Minutes
Ingredients:
- $^1/_3$ cup orange juice
- 3 teaspoons minced garlic
- 1 teaspoon Old Bay seasoning
- ¼ to ½ teaspoon cayenne pepper
- 1 pound (454 g) medium shrimp, thawed, deveined, peeled, with tails off, and patted dry
- Cooking spray

Directions:
1. Stir together the orange juice, garlic, Old Bay seasoning, and cayenne pepper in a medium bowl. Add the shrimp to the bowl and toss to coat well.
2. Cover the bowl with plastic wrap and marinate in the refrigerator for 30 minutes.
3. Spritz the air fryer basket with cooking spray. Place the shrimp in the pan and spray with cooking spray.
4. Put the air fryer basket on the baking pan and slide into Rack Position 2, select Air Fry, set temperature to 400ºF (205ºC), and set time to 12 minutes.
5. Flip the shrimp halfway through the cooking time.
6. When cooked, the shrimp should be opaque and crisp. Remove from the oven and serve hot.

311.Cajun Catfish Cakes With Cheese

Servings:4
Cooking Time: 15 Minutes
Ingredients:
- 2 catfish fillets
- 3 ounces (85 g) butter
- 1 cup shredded Parmesan cheese
- 1 cup shredded Swiss cheese
- ½ cup buttermilk
- 1 teaspoon baking powder
- 1 teaspoon baking soda
- 1 teaspoon Cajun seasoning

Directions:
1. Bring a pot of salted water to a boil. Add the catfish fillets to the boiling water and let them boil for 5 minutes until they become opaque.
2. Remove the fillets from the pot to a mixing bowl and flake them into small pieces with a fork.
3. Add the remaining ingredients to the bowl of fish and stir until well incorporated.
4. Divide the fish mixture into 12 equal portions and shape each portion into a patty. Place the patties in the air fryer basket.
5. Put the air fryer basket on the baking pan and slide into Rack Position 2, select Air Fry, set temperature to 380ºF (193ºC), and set time to 15 minutes.
6. Flip the patties halfway through the cooking time.
7. When cooking is complete, the patties should be golden brown and cooked through. Remove from the oven. Let the patties sit for 5 minutes and serve.

312.Paprika Basil Baked Basa

Servings: 2
Cooking Time: 30 Minutes
Ingredients:
- 2 basa fish fillets
- 4 lemon slices
- 1/8 tsp lemon juice
- 1/2 tbsp dried basil
- 1/2 tbsp sweet paprika
- 4 tbsp butter, melted
- 1/8 tsp salt

Directions:
1. Fit the oven with the rack in position
2. Place fish fillets into the baking dish.
3. Pour remaining ingredients over fish fillets.
4. Set to bake at 350 F for 30 minutes. After 5 minutes place the baking dish in the preheated oven.
5. Serve and enjoy.
- **Nutrition Info:** Calories: 433 Fat 35.2 g Carbohydrates 6.5 g Sugar 3.4 g Protein 24.4 g Cholesterol 61 mg

313.Cajun Salmon With Lemon

Servings:1
Cooking Time: 10 Minutes
Ingredients:
- 1 salmon fillet
- ¼ tsp brown sugar
- Juice of ½ lemon
- 1 tbsp cajun seasoning
- 2 lemon wedges
- 1 tbsp fresh parsley, chopped

Directions:
1. Preheat on Bake function to 350 F. Combine sugar and lemon and coat in the salmon. Sprinkle with the Cajun seasoning as well. Place a parchment paper on a baking tray and press Start. Cook for 14-16 minutes. Serve with lemon wedges and chopped parsley.

314.Air Fryer Salmon

Servings: 2
Cooking Time: 10 Minutes
Ingredients:
- ½ tsp. salt
- ½ tsp. garlic powder
- ½ tsp. smoked paprika
- Salmon

Directions:
1. Preparing the Ingredients. Mix spices and sprinkle onto salmon.
2. Place seasoned salmon into the air fryer oven.
3. Air Frying. Set temperature to 400°F, and set time to 10 minutes.
- **Nutrition Info:** CALORIES: 185; FAT: 11G; PROTEIN:21G; SUGAR:0G

315.Parmesan Shrimp

Servings: 4
Cooking Time: 10 Minutes
Ingredients:
- 2 tbsp. olive oil
- 1 tsp. onion powder
- 1 tsp. basil
- ½ tsp. oregano
- 1 tsp. pepper
- 2/3 C. grated parmesan cheese
- 4 minced garlic cloves
- pounds of jumbo cooked shrimp (peeled/deveined)

Directions:
1. Preparing the Ingredients. Mix all seasonings together and gently toss shrimp with the mixture.
2. Air Frying. Spray olive oil into the Oven rack/basket and add seasoned shrimp. Place the Rack on the middle-shelf of the air fryer oven. Cook 8-10 minutes at 350 degrees. Squeeze lemon juice over shrimp right before devouring!
- **Nutrition Info:** CALORIES: 351; FAT:11G; PROTEIN:19G; SUGAR:1G

316.Breaded Fish Fillets

Servings:4
Cooking Time: 7 Minutes
Ingredients:
- 1 pound (454 g) fish fillets
- 1 tablespoon coarse brown mustard
- 1 teaspoon Worcestershire sauce
- ½ teaspoon hot sauce
- Salt, to taste
- Cooking spray
- Crumb Coating:
- ¾ cup panko bread crumbs
- ¼ cup stone-ground cornmeal
- ¼ teaspoon salt

Directions:
1. On your cutting board, cut the fish fillets crosswise into slices, about 1 inch wide.
2. In a small bowl, stir together the mustard, Worcestershire sauce, and hot sauce to make a paste and rub this paste on all sides of the fillets. Season with salt to taste.
3. In a shallow bowl, thoroughly combine all the ingredients for the crumb coating and spread them on a sheet of wax paper.
4. Roll the fish fillets in the crumb mixture until thickly coated. Spritz all sides of the fish with cooking spray, then arrange them in the air fryer basket in a single layer.
5. Put the air fryer basket on the baking pan and slide into Rack Position 2, select Air Fry, set temperature to 400ºF (205ºC), and set time to 7 minutes.
6. When cooking is complete, the fish should flake apart with a fork. Remove from the oven and serve warm.

317.Prawn French Cuisine Galette

Servings:x
Cooking Time:x
Ingredients:
- 2 tbsp. garam masala
- 1 lb. minced prawn
- 3 tsp ginger finely chopped
- 1-2 tbsp. fresh coriander leaves
- 2 or 3 green chilies finely chopped
- 1 ½ tbsp. lemon juice
- Salt and pepper to taste

Directions:
1. Mix the ingredients in a clean bowl.
2. Mold this mixture into round and flat French Cuisine Galettes.
3. Wet the French Cuisine Galettes slightly with water.

4. Pre heat the oven at 160 degrees Fahrenheit for 5 minutes. Place the French Cuisine Galettes in the fry basket and let them cook for another 25 minutes at the same temperature. Keep rolling them over to get a uniform cook. Serve either with mint sauce or ketchup.

318.Air Fry Tuna Patties

Servings: 4
Cooking Time: 6 Minutes
Ingredients:
- 1 egg, lightly beaten
- 8 oz can tuna, drained
- 1/4 cup breadcrumbs
- 1 tbsp mustard
- 1/4 tsp garlic powder
- Pepper
- Salt

Directions:
1. Fit the oven with the rack in position 2.
2. Add all ingredients into the large bowl and mix until well combined.
3. Make four equal shapes of patties from the mixture and place in the air fryer basket then place an air fryer basket in the baking pan.
4. Place a baking pan on the oven rack. Set to air fry at 400 F for 6 minutes.
5. Serve and enjoy.
- **Nutrition Info:** Calories: 122 Fat 2.7 g Carbohydrates 6.1 g Sugar 0.7 g Protein 17.5 g Cholesterol 58 mg

319.Cheesy Tuna Patties

Servings:4
Cooking Time: 17 To 18 Minutes
Ingredients:
- Tuna Patties:
- 1 pound (454 g) canned tuna, drained
- 1 egg, whisked
- 2 tablespoons shallots, minced
- 1 garlic clove, minced
- 1 cup grated Romano cheese
- Sea salt and ground black pepper, to taste
- 1 tablespoon sesame oil
- Cheese Sauce:
- 1 tablespoon butter
- 1 cup beer
- 2 tablespoons grated Colby cheese

Directions:
1. Mix together the canned tuna, whisked egg, shallots, garlic, cheese, salt, and pepper in a large bowl and stir to incorporate.
2. Divide the tuna mixture into four equal portions and form each portion into a patty with your hands. Refrigerate the patties for 2 hours.

3. When ready, brush both sides of each patty with sesame oil, then place in the baking pan.
4. Slide the baking pan into Rack Position 1, select Convection Bake, set temperature to 360ºF (182ºC), and set time to 14 minutes.
5. Flip the patties halfway through the cooking time.
6. Meanwhile, melt the butter in a saucepan over medium heat.
7. Pour in the beer and whisk constantly, or until it begins to bubble. Add the grated Colby cheese and mix well. Continue cooking for 3 to 4 minutes, or until the cheese melts. Remove from the heat.
8. When cooking is complete, the patties should be lightly browned and cooked through. Remove the patties from the oven to a plate. Drizzle them with the cheese sauce and serve immediately.

320.Shrimp Momo's Recipe

Servings:x
Cooking Time:x
Ingredients:
- 1 ½ cup all-purpose flour
- ½ tsp. salt
- 5 tbsp. water
- For filling:
- 2 cups minced shrimp
- 2 tbsp. oil
- 2 tsp. ginger-garlic paste
- 2 tsp. soya sauce
- 2 tsp. vinegar

Directions:
1. Squeeze the dough and cover it with plastic wrap and set aside. Next, cook the ingredients for the filling and try to ensure that the shrimp is covered well with the sauce. Roll the dough and cut it into a square. Place the filling in the center.
2. Now, wrap the dough to cover the filling and pinch the edges together. Pre heat the oven at 200° F for 5 minutes. Place the wontons in the fry basket and close it. Let them cook at the same temperature for another 20 minutes. Recommended sides are chili sauce or ketchup.

321.Delicious Baked Basa

Servings: 4
Cooking Time: 10 Minutes
Ingredients:
- 4 basa fish fillets
- 1/4 cup green onion, sliced
- 1/2 tsp garlic powder
- 1/4 tsp lemon pepper seasoning
- 4 tbsp fresh lemon juice
- 8 tsp butter, melted

- Salt

Directions:
1. Fit the oven with the rack in position
2. Place fish fillets into the baking dish.
3. Pour remaining ingredients over fish fillets.
4. Set to bake at 425 F for 15 minutes. After 5 minutes place the baking dish in the preheated oven.
5. Serve and enjoy.
- **Nutrition Info:** Calories: 214 Fat 15.3 g Carbohydrates 3.8 g Sugar 2.3 g Protein 15.4 g Cholesterol 20 mg

322.Old Bay Crab Cakes

Servings: 4
Cooking Time: 20 Minutes
Ingredients:
- 2 slices dried bread, crusts removed
- Small amount of milk
- 1 tablespoon mayonnaise
- 1 tablespoon Worcestershire sauce
- 1 tablespoon baking powder
- 1 tablespoon parsley flakes
- 1 teaspoon Old Bay® Seasoning
- 1/4 teaspoon salt
- 1 egg
- 1 pound lump crabmeat

Directions:
1. Preparing the Ingredients. Crush your bread over a large bowl until it is broken down into small pieces. Add milk and stir until bread crumbs are moistened. Mix in mayo and Worcestershire sauce. Add remaining ingredients and mix well. Shape into 4 patties.
2. Air Frying. Cook at 360 degrees for 20 minutes, flip half way through.
- **Nutrition Info:** CALORIES: 165; CARBS:5.8; FAT: 4.5G; PROTEIN:24G; FIBER:0G

323.Cajun Red Snapper

Servings: 2
Cooking Time: 12 Minutes
Ingredients:
- 8 oz red snapper fillets
- 2 tbsp parmesan cheese, grated
- 1/4 cup breadcrumbs
- 1/2 tsp Cajun seasoning
- 1/4 tsp Worcestershire sauce
- 1 garlic clove, minced
- 1/4 cup butter

Directions:
1. Fit the oven with the rack in position
2. Melt butter in a pan over low heat. Add Cajun seasoning, garlic, and Worcestershire sauce into the melted butter and stir well.
3. Brush fish fillets with melted butter and place into the baking dish.

4. Mix together parmesan cheese and breadcrumbs and sprinkle over fish fillets.
5. Set to bake at 400 F for 17 minutes. After 5 minutes place the baking dish in the preheated oven.
6. Serve and enjoy.
- **Nutrition Info:** Calories: 424 Fat 27 g Carbohydrates 10.6 g Sugar 1 g Protein 33.9 g Cholesterol 119 mg

324.Scallops And Spring Veggies

Servings: 4
Cooking Time: 8 Minutes
Ingredients:
- ½ pound asparagus ends trimmed, cut into 2-inch pieces
- 1 cup sugar snap peas
- 1 pound sea scallops
- 1 tablespoon lemon juice
- 2 teaspoons olive oil
- ½ teaspoon dried thyme
- Pinch salt
- Freshly ground black pepper

Directions:
1. Preparing the Ingredients. Place the asparagus and sugar snap peas in the Oven rack/basket. Place the Rack on the middle-shelf of the air fryer oven.
2. Air Frying. Cook for 2 to 3 minutes or until the vegetables are just starting to get tender.
3. Meanwhile, check the scallops for a small muscle attached to the side, and pull it off and discard.
4. In a medium bowl, toss the scallops with the lemon juice, olive oil, thyme, salt, and pepper. Place into the Oven rack/basket on top of the vegetables. Place the Rack on the middle-shelf of the air fryer oven.
5. Air Frying. Steam for 5 to 7 minutes. Until the scallops are just firm, and the vegetables are tender. Serve immediately.
- **Nutrition Info:** CALORIES: 162; CARBS:10G; FAT: 4G; PROTEIN:22G; FIBER:3G

325.Thyme Rosemary Shrimp

Servings: 4
Cooking Time: 10 Minutes
Ingredients:
- 1 lb shrimp, peeled and deveined
- 1/2 tbsp fresh rosemary, chopped
- 1 tbsp olive oil
- 2 garlic cloves, minced
- 1/2 tbsp fresh thyme, chopped
- Pepper
- Salt

Directions:
1. Fit the oven with the rack in position
2. Add shrimp and remaining ingredients in a large bowl and toss well.

3. Pour shrimp mixture into the baking dish.
4. Set to bake at 400 F for 15 minutes. After 5 minutes place the baking dish in the preheated oven.
5. Serve and enjoy.
- **Nutrition Info:** Calories: 169 Fat 5.5 g Carbohydrates 2.7 g Sugar 0 g Protein 26 g Cholesterol 239 mg

326.Tuna Lettuce Wraps

Servings:4
Cooking Time: 4 To 7 Minutes
Ingredients:
- 1 pound (454 g) fresh tuna steak, cut into 1-inch cubes
- 2 garlic cloves, minced
- 1 tablespoon grated fresh ginger
- ½ teaspoon toasted sesame oil
- 4 low-sodium whole-wheat tortillas
- 2 cups shredded romaine lettuce
- 1 red bell pepper, thinly sliced
- ¼ cup low-fat mayonnaise

Directions:
1. Combine the tuna cubes, garlic, ginger, and sesame oil in a medium bowl and toss until well coated. Allow to sit for 10 minutes.
2. When ready, place the tuna cubes in the air fryer basket.
3. Put the air fryer basket on the baking pan and slide into Rack Position 2, select Air Fry, set temperature to 390ºF (199ºC), and set time to 6 minutes.
4. When cooking is complete, the tuna cubes should be cooked through and golden brown. Remove the tuna cubes from the oven to a plate.
5. Make the wraps: Place the tortillas on a flat work surface and top each tortilla evenly with the cooked tuna, lettuce, bell pepper, and finish with the mayonnaise. Roll them up and serve immediately.

327.Rosemary & Garlic Prawns

Servings:2
Cooking Time: 15 Minutes + Chilling Time
Ingredients:
- 8 large prawns
- 2 garlic cloves, minced
- 1 rosemary sprig, chopped
- 1 tbsp butter, melted
- Salt and black pepper to taste

Directions:
1. Combine garlic, butter, rosemary, salt, and pepper in a bowl. Add in the prawns and mix to coat. Cover the bowl and refrigerate for 1 hour. Preheat on AirFry function to 350 F. Remove the prawns from the fridge and transfer to the frying basket. Cook for 6-8 minutes.

328.Caesar Shrimp Salad

Servings:4
Cooking Time: 15 Minutes
Ingredients:
- ½ baguette, cut into 1-inch cubes (about 2½ cups)
- 4 tablespoons extra-virgin olive oil, divided
- ¼ teaspoon granulated garlic
- ¼ teaspoon kosher salt
- ¾ cup Caesar dressing, divided
- 2 romaine lettuce hearts, cut in half lengthwise and ends trimmed
- 1 pound (454 g) medium shrimp, peeled and deveined
- 2 ounces (57 g) Parmesan cheese, coarsely grated

Directions:
1. Make the croutons: Put the bread cubes in a medium bowl and drizzle 3 tablespoons of olive oil over top. Season with granulated garlic and salt and toss to coat. Transfer to the air fryer basket in a single layer.
2. Put the air fryer basket on the baking pan and slide into Rack Position 2, select Air Fry, set temperature to 400ºF (205ºC), and set time to 4 minutes.
3. Toss the croutons halfway through the cooking time.
4. When done, remove from the oven and set aside.
5. Brush 2 tablespoons of Caesar dressing on the cut side of the lettuce. Set aside.
6. Toss the shrimp with the ¼ cup of Caesar dressing in a large bowl until well coated. Set aside.
7. Coat the baking pan with the remaining 1 tablespoon of olive oil. Arrange the romaine halves on the coated pan, cut side down. Brush the tops with the remaining 2 tablespoons of Caesar dressing.
8. Slide the baking pan into Rack Position 2, select Roast, set temperature to 375ºF (190ºC), and set time to 10 minutes.
9. After 5 minutes, remove from the oven and flip the romaine halves. Spoon the shrimp around the lettuce. Return the pan to the oven and continue cooking.
10. When done, remove from the oven. If they are not quite cooked through, roast for another 1 minute.
11. On each of four plates, put a romaine half. Divide the shrimp among the plates and top with croutons and grated Parmesan cheese. Serve immediately.

329.Delicious Shrimp Casserole

Servings: 10
Cooking Time: 30 Minutes
Ingredients:

- 1 lb shrimp, peeled & tail off
- 2 tsp onion powder
- 2 tsp old bay seasoning
- 2 cups cheddar cheese, shredded
- 10.5 oz can cream of mushroom soup
- 12 oz long-grain rice
- 1 tsp salt

Directions:
1. Fit the oven with the rack in position
2. Cook rice according to the packet instructions.
3. Add shrimp into the boiling water and cook for 4 minutes or until cooked. Drain shrimp.
4. In a bowl, mix rice, shrimp, and remaining ingredients and pour into the greased 13*9-inch casserole dish.
5. Set to bake at 350 F for 35 minutes. After 5 minutes place the casserole dish in the preheated oven.
6. Serve and enjoy.
- **Nutrition Info:** Calories: 286 Fat 9 g Carbohydrates 31 g Sugar 1 g Protein 18.8 g Cholesterol 120 mg

330.Lemon-garlic Butter Lobster

Servings: 2
Cooking Time: 15 Minutes
Ingredients:
- 4 oz lobster tails
- 1 tsp garlic, minced
- 1 tbsp butter
- Salt and black pepper to taste
- ½ tbsp lemon Juice

Directions:
1. Add all the ingredients to a food processor except for lobster and blend well. Wash lobster and halve using a meat knife; clean the skin of the lobster and cover with the marinade.
2. Preheat your to 380 F on Air Fry function. Place the lobster in the cooking basket and fit in the baking tray; cook for 10 minutes. Serve with fresh herbs.

331.Fish And Chips

Servings: 4
Cooking Time: 20 Minutes
Ingredients:
- 4 (4-ounce) fish fillets
- Pinch salt
- Freshly ground black pepper
- ½ teaspoon dried thyme
- 1 egg white
- ¾ cup crushed potato chips
- 2 tablespoons olive oil, divided
- 1 russet potatoes, peeled and cut into strips

Directions:

1. Preparing the Ingredients. Pat the fish fillets dry and sprinkle with salt, pepper, and thyme. Set aside.
2. In a shallow bowl, beat the egg white until foamy. In another bowl, combine the potato chips and 1 tablespoon of olive oil and mix until combined.
3. Dip the fish fillets into the egg white, then into the crushed potato chip mixture to coat.
4. Toss the fresh potato strips with the remaining 1 tablespoon olive oil.
5. Air Frying. Use your separator to divide the Oven rack/basket in half, then fry the chips and fish. The chips will take about 20 minutes; the fish will take about 10 to 12 minutes to cook.
- **Nutrition Info:** CALORIES: 374; FAT:16G; PROTEIN:30G; FIBER:4G

332.Simple Lemon Salmon

Servings: 2
Cooking Time: 20 Minutes
Ingredients:
- 2 salmon fillets
- Salt to taste
- Zest of a lemon

Directions:
1. Spray the fillets with olive oil and rub them with salt and lemon zest. Line baking paper in a baking dish. Cook the fillets in your for 10 minutes at 360 F on Air Fry, turning once.

333.Air Fried Cod Fillets

Servings:4
Cooking Time: 12 Minutes
Ingredients:
- 4 cod fillets
- ¼ teaspoon fine sea salt
- 1 teaspoon cayenne pepper
- ¼ teaspoon ground black pepper, or more to taste
- ½ cup fresh Italian parsley, coarsely chopped
- ½ cup non-dairy milk
- 4 garlic cloves, minced
- 1 Italian pepper, chopped
- 1 teaspoon dried basil
- ½ teaspoon dried oregano
- Cooking spray

Directions:
1. Lightly spritz the air fryer basket with cooking spray.
2. Season the fillets with salt, cayenne pepper, and black pepper.
3. Pulse the remaining ingredients in a food processor, then transfer the mixture to a shallow bowl. Coat the fillets with the mixture. Place the fillets in the basket.

4. Put the air fryer basket on the baking pan and slide into Rack Position 2, select Air Fry, set temperature to 375ºF (190ºC), and set time to 12 minutes.
5. When cooking is complete, the fish will be flaky. Remove from the oven and serve on a plate.

334.Quick Tuna Patties

Servings: 10
Cooking Time: 10 Minutes
Ingredients:
- 15 oz can tuna, drained and flaked
- 3 tbsp parmesan cheese, grated
- 1/2 cup breadcrumbs
- 1 tbsp lemon juice
- 2 eggs, lightly beaten
- 1/2 tsp dried mixed herbs
- 1/2 tsp garlic powder
- 2 tbsp onion, minced
- 1 celery stalk, chopped
- Pepper
- Salt

Directions:
1. Fit the oven with the rack in position 2.
2. Add all ingredients into the mixing bowl and mix until well combined.
3. Make patties from mixture and place in the air fryer basket then place the air fryer basket in the baking pan.
4. Place a baking pan on the oven rack. Set to air fry at 360 F for 10 minutes.
5. Serve and enjoy.
- **Nutrition Info:** Calories: 90 Fat 1.8 g Carbohydrates 4.4 g Sugar 0.6 g Protein 13.2 g Cholesterol 47 mg

335.Cheese Carp Fries

Servings:x
Cooking Time:x
Ingredients:
- 1 lb. carp Oregano Fingers
- ingredients for the marinade:
- 1 tbsp. olive oil
- 1 tsp. mixed herbs
- ½ tsp. red chili flakes
- A pinch of salt to taste
- 1 tbsp. lemon juice
- For the garnish:
- 1 cup melted cheddar cheese

Directions:
1. Take all the ingredients mentioned under the heading "For the marinade" and mix them well. Cook the carp Oregano Fingers and soak them in the marinade.
2. Pre heat the oven for around 5 minutes at 300 Fahrenheit. Take out the basket of the fryer and place the carp in them. Close the

basket. Now keep the fryer at 220 Fahrenheit for 20 or 25 minutes.
3. In between the process, toss the fries twice or thrice so that they get cooked properly. Towards the end of the cooking process (the last 2 minutes or so), sprinkle the melted cheddar cheese over the fries and serve hot.

336.Shrimp And Cherry Tomato Kebabs

Servings:4
Cooking Time: 5 Minutes
Ingredients:
- 1½ pounds (680 g) jumbo shrimp, cleaned, shelled and deveined
- 1 pound (454 g) cherry tomatoes
- 2 tablespoons butter, melted
- 1 tablespoons Sriracha sauce
- Sea salt and ground black pepper, to taste
- 1 teaspoon dried parsley flakes
- ½ teaspoon dried basil
- ½ teaspoon dried oregano
- ½ teaspoon mustard seeds
- ½ teaspoon marjoram
- Special Equipment:
- 4 to 6 wooden skewers, soaked in water for 30 minutes

Directions:
1. Put all the ingredients in a large bowl and toss to coat well.
2. Make the kebabs: Thread, alternating jumbo shrimp and cherry tomatoes, onto the wooden skewers. Place the kebabs in the air fryer basket.
3. Put the air fryer basket on the baking pan and slide into Rack Position 2, select Air Fry, set temperature to 400ºF (205ºC), and set time to 5 minutes.
4. When cooking is complete, the shrimp should be pink and the cherry tomatoes should be softened. Remove from the oven. Let the shrimp and cherry tomato kebabs cool for 5 minutes and serve hot.

337.Coconut-crusted Prawns

Servings:4
Cooking Time: 8 Minutes
Ingredients:
- 12 prawns, cleaned and deveined
- 1 teaspoon fresh lemon juice
- ½ teaspoon cumin powder
- Salt and ground black pepper, to taste
- 1 medium egg
- $^1/_3$ cup beer
- ½ cup flour, divided
- 1 tablespoon curry powder
- 1 teaspoon baking powder
- ½ teaspoon grated fresh ginger
- 1 cup flaked coconut

Directions:

1. In a large bowl, toss the prawns with the lemon juice, cumin powder, salt, and pepper until well coated. Set aside.
2. In a shallow bowl, whisk together the egg, beer, ¼ cup of flour, curry powder, baking powder, and ginger until combined.
3. In a separate shallow bowl, put the remaining ¼ cup of flour, and on a plate, place the flaked coconut.
4. Dip the prawns in the flour, then in the egg mixture, finally roll in the flaked coconut to coat well. Transfer the prawns to a baking sheet.
5. Put the air fryer basket on the baking pan and slide into Rack Position 2, select Air Fry, set temperature to 350ºF (180ºC), and set time to 8 minutes.
6. After 5 minutes, remove from the oven and flip the prawns. Return to the oven and continue cooking for 3 minutes more.
7. When cooking is complete, remove from the oven and serve warm.

338.Lemon Pepper Tilapia Fillets

Servings:4
Cooking Time: 15 Minutes
Ingredients:
- 1 lb tilapia fillets
- 1 tbsp Italian seasoning
- 2 tbsp canola oil
- 2 tbsp lemon pepper
- Salt to taste
- 2-3 butter buds

Directions:

1. Preheat your oven to 400 F on Bake function. Drizzle tilapia fillets with canola oil. In a bowl, mix salt, lemon pepper, butter buds, and Italian seasoning; spread on the fish. Place the fillet on a baking tray and press Start. Cook for 10 minutes until tender and crispy. Serve warm.

339.Simple Salmon Patties

Servings: 2
Cooking Time: 7 Minutes
Ingredients:
- 8 oz salmon fillet, minced
- 1 egg, lightly beaten
- 1/4 tsp garlic powder
- 1/4 tsp onion powder
- 1/8 tsp paprika
- 2 tbsp breadcrumbs
- Pepper
- Salt

Directions:

1. Fit the oven with the rack in position 2.
2. Add all ingredients into the bowl and mix until well combined.

3. Make patties from mixture and place in the air fryer basket then place an air fryer basket in the baking pan.
4. Place a baking pan on the oven rack. Set to air fry at 390 F for 7 minutes.
5. Serve and enjoy.
- **Nutrition Info:** Calories: 211 Fat 9.6 g Carbohydrates 5.6 g Sugar 0.8 g Protein 25.8 g Cholesterol 132 mg

340.Herbed Scallops With Vegetables

Servings:4
Cooking Time: 9 Minutes
Ingredients:
- 1 cup frozen peas
- 1 cup green beans
- 1 cup frozen chopped broccoli
- 2 teaspoons olive oil
- ½ teaspoon dried oregano
- ½ teaspoon dried basil
- 12 ounces (340 g) sea scallops, rinsed and patted dry

Directions:

1. Put the peas, green beans, and broccoli in a large bowl. Drizzle with the olive oil and toss to coat well. Transfer the vegetables to the air fryer basket.
2. Put the air fryer basket on the baking pan and slide into Rack Position 2, select Air Fry, set temperature to 400ºF (205ºC), and set time to 5 minutes.
3. When cooking is complete, the vegetables should be fork-tender. Transfer the vegetables to a serving bowl. Scatter with the oregano and basil and set aside.
4. Place the scallops in the basket.
5. Put the air fryer basket on the baking pan and slide into Rack Position 2, select Air Fry, set temperature to 400ºF (205ºC), and set time to 4 minutes.
6. When cooking is complete, the scallops should be firm and just opaque in the center. Remove from the oven to the bowl of vegetables and toss well. Serve warm.

341.Spinach & Tuna Balls With Ricotta

Servings:4
Cooking Time: 20 Minutes
Ingredients:
- 14 oz store-bought crescent dough
- ½ cup spinach, steamed
- 1 cup ricotta cheese, crumbled
- ¼ tsp garlic powder
- 1 tsp fresh oregano, chopped
- ½ cup canned tuna, drained

Directions:

1. Preheat on AirFry function to 350 F. Roll the dough onto a lightly floured flat surface. Combine the ricotta cheese, spinach, tuna,

oregano, salt, and garlic powder together in a bowl.

2. Cut the dough into 4 equal pieces. Divide the mixture between the dough pieces. Make sure to place the filling in the center. Fold the dough and secure with a fork. Place onto a lined baking dish and press Start. Cook for 12 minutes until lightly browned. Serve.

342.Delicious Fried Seafood

Servings: 4
Cooking Time: 15 Minutes
Ingredients:

- 1 lb fresh scallops, mussels, fish fillets, prawns, shrimp
- 2 eggs, lightly beaten
- Salt and black pepper to taste
- 1 cup breadcrumbs mixed with zest of 1 lemon

Directions:
1. Dip each piece of the seafood into the eggs and season with salt and pepper. Coat in the crumbs and spray with oil. Arrange into the frying basket and fit in the baking tray; cook for 10 minutes at 400 F on Air Fry function, turning once halfway through. Serve.

MEATLESS RECIPES

343.Cabbage Fritters(1)

Servings:x
Cooking Time:x
Ingredients:
- 1-2 tbsp. fresh coriander leaves
- 2 or 3 green chilies finely chopped
- 1 ½ tbsp. lemon juice
- Salt and pepper to taste
- 2 tbsp. garam masala
- 2 cups cabbage
- 1 ½ cup coarsely crushed peanuts
- 3 tsp. ginger finely chopped

Directions:
1. Mix the ingredients in a clean bowl.
2. Mold this mixture into round and flat fritters.
3. Wet the fritters slightly with water. Coat each fritter with the crushed peanuts.
4. Pre heat the oven at 160 degrees Fahrenheit for 5 minutes. Place the fritters in the fry basket and let them cook for another 25 minutes at the same temperature. Keep rolling them over to get a uniform cook. Serve either with mint sauce or ketchup.

344.Garlicky Fennel Cabbage Steaks

Servings: 3
Cooking Time: 25 Minutes
Ingredients:
- 1 cabbage head
- 1 tbsp garlic paste
- 1 tsp salt
- 2 tbsp olive oil
- ½ tsp black pepper
- 2 tsp fennel seeds

Directions:
1. Preheat on Air Fry function to 350 F. Slice the cabbage into 1 ½-inch slices. In a small bowl, combine all the other ingredients; brush cabbage with the mixture. Arrange the steaks on a greased baking dish and cook for 15 minutes, flipping once. Serve.

345.Beetroot Chips

Servings: 3
Cooking Time: 25 Minutes
Ingredients:
- 1lb golden beetroots, sliced
- 2 tbsp olive oil
- 1 tbsp yeast flakes
- 1 tsp vegan seasoning
- Salt to taste

Directions:
1. In a bowl, add the olive oil, beetroots, vegan seasoning, and yeast and mix well. Dump the coated chips in the basket.

2. Fit in the baking tray and cook in your for 15 minutes at 370 F on Air Fry function, shaking once halfway through. Serve.

346.Roasted Bell Peppers With Garlic

Servings:4
Cooking Time: 22 Minutes
Ingredients:
- 1 green bell pepper, sliced into 1-inch strips
- 1 red bell pepper, sliced into 1-inch strips
- 1 orange bell pepper, sliced into 1-inch strips
- 1 yellow bell pepper, sliced into 1-inch strips
- 2 tablespoons olive oil, divided
- ½ teaspoon dried marjoram
- Pinch salt
- Freshly ground black pepper, to taste
- 1 head garlic

Directions:
1. Toss the bell peppers with 1 tablespoon of olive oil in a large bowl until well coated. Season with the marjoram, salt, and pepper. Toss again and set aside.
2. Cut off the top of a head of garlic. Place the garlic cloves on a large square of aluminum foil. Drizzle the top with the remaining 1 tablespoon of olive oil and wrap the garlic cloves in foil.
3. Transfer the garlic to the air fryer basket.
4. Put the air fryer basket on the baking pan and slide into Rack Position 2, select Roast, set temperature to 330ºF (166ºC) and set time to 15 minutes.
5. After 15 minutes, remove from the oven and add the bell peppers. Return to the oven and set time to 7 minutes.
6. When cooking is complete or until the garlic is soft and the bell peppers are tender.
7. Transfer the cooked bell peppers to a plate. Remove the garlic and unwrap the foil. Let the garlic rest for a few minutes. Once cooled, squeeze the roasted garlic cloves out of their skins and add them to the plate of bell peppers. Stir well and serve immediately.

347.Garlicky Veggie Bake

Servings: 3
Cooking Time: 25 Minutes
Ingredients:
- 3 turnips, sliced
- 1 large red onion, cut into rings
- 1 large zucchini, sliced
- Salt and black pepper to taste
- 2 cloves garlic, crushed
- 1 bay leaf, cut in 6 pieces
- 1 tbsp olive oil

Directions:
1. Place the turnips, onion, and zucchini in a bowl. Toss with olive oil, salt, and pepper.
2. Preheat on Air Fry function to 380 F. Place the veggies into a baking pan. Slip the bay leaves in the different parts of the slices and tuck the garlic cloves in between the slices. Cook for 15 minutes. Serve warm with as a side to a meat dish or salad.

348.Chili Sweet Potato Fries

Servings:4
Cooking Time: 30 Minutes
Ingredients:
- ½ tsp salt
- ½ tsp garlic powder
- ½ tsp chili powder
- ¼ tsp ground cumin
- 3 tbsp olive oil
- 3 sweet potatoes, cut into thick strips

Directions:
1. In a bowl, mix salt, garlic powder, chili powder, and cumin, and whisk in oil. Coat in the potato strips and arrange them on the basket, without overcrowding. Press Start and cook for 20-25 minutes at 380 F on AirFry function or until crispy. Serve hot.

349.Traditional Jacket Potatoes

Servings: 4
Cooking Time: 30 Minutes
Ingredients:
- 4 potatoes, well washed
- 2 garlic cloves, minced
- Salt and black pepper to taste
- 1 tsp rosemary
- 1 tsp butter

Directions:
1. Preheat your Oven to 360 F on Air Fry function. Prick the potatoes with a fork. Place them into your Air fryer basket and fit in the baking tray; cook for 25 minutes. Cut the potatoes in half and top with butter and rosemary; season with salt and pepper. Serve immediately.

350.Mushroom Marinade Cutlet

Servings:x
Cooking Time:x
Ingredients:
- 2 cup fresh green coriander
- ½ cup mint leaves
- 4 tsp. fennel
- 2 tbsp. ginger-garlic paste
- 1 small onion
- 6-7 flakes garlic (optional)
- Salt to taste
- 2 cups sliced mushrooms
- 1 big capsicum (Cut this capsicum into big cubes)
- 1 onion (Cut it into quarters. Now separate the layers carefully.)
- 5 tbsp. gram flour
- A pinch of salt to taste
- 3 tbsp. lemon juice

Directions:
1. Take a clean and dry container. Put into it the coriander, mint, fennel, and ginger, onion/garlic, salt and lemon juice. Mix them.
2. Pour the mixture into a grinder and blend until you get a thick paste. Slit the mushroom almost till the end and leave them aside. Now stuff all the pieces with the paste and set aside. Take the sauce and add to it the gram flour and some salt. Mix them together properly. Rub this mixture all over the stuffed mushroom.
3. Now, to the leftover sauce, add the capsicum and onions. Apply the sauce generously on each of the pieces of capsicum and onion. Now take satay sticks and arrange the cottage cheese pieces and vegetables on separate sticks.
4. Pre heat the oven at 290 Fahrenheit for around 5 minutes. Open the basket. Arrange the satay sticks properly. Close the basket. Keep the sticks with the mushroom at 180 degrees for around half an hour while the sticks with the vegetables are to be kept at the same temperature for only 7 minutes. Turn the sticks in between so that one side does not get burnt and also to provide a uniform cook.

351.Asparagus Spicy Lemon Kebab

Servings:x
Cooking Time:x
Ingredients:
- 3 tsp. lemon juice
- 2 tsp. garam masala
- 3 eggs
- 2 ½ tbsp. white sesame seeds
- 2 cups sliced asparagus
- 3 onions chopped
- 5 green chilies-roughly chopped
- 1 ½ tbsp. ginger paste
- 1 ½ tsp. garlic paste
- 1 ½ tsp. salt

Directions:
1. Grind the ingredients except for the egg and form a smooth paste. Coat the asparagus in the paste. Now, beat the eggs and add a little salt to it.
2. Dip the coated apricots in the egg mixture and then transfer to the sesame seeds and coat the asparagus. Place the vegetables on a stick.

3. Pre heat the oven at 160 degrees Fahrenheit for around 5 minutes. Place the sticks in the basket and let them cook for another 25 minutes at the same temperature. Turn the sticks over in between the cooking process to get a uniform cook.

352.Mixed Vegetable Patties

Servings:x
Cooking Time:x
Ingredients:
- 1 tbsp. fresh coriander leaves
- ¼ tsp. red chili powder
- ¼ tsp. cumin powder
- 2.55 Cottage cheese Momo's Recipe
- 1 ½ cup all-purpose flour
- ½ tsp. salt
- 1 cup grated mixed vegetables
- A pinch of salt to taste
- ¼ tsp. ginger finely chopped
- 1 green chili finely chopped
- 1 tsp. lemon juice
- 5 tbsp. water
- 2 cups crumbled cottage cheese
- 2 tbsp. oil
- 2 tsp. ginger-garlic paste
- 2 tsp. soya sauce
- 2 tsp. vinegar

Directions:
1. Squeeze the dough and cover it with plastic wrap and set aside. Next, cook the ingredients for the filling and try to ensure that the cottage cheese is covered well with the sauce.
2. Roll the dough and cut it into a square. Place the filling in the center. Now, wrap the dough to cover the filling and pinch the edges together.
3. Pre heat the oven at 200° F for 5 minutes. Place the gnocchi's in the fry basket and close it. Let them cook at the same temperature for another 20 minutes. Recommended sides are chili sauce or ketchup.
4. Mix the ingredients together and ensure that the flavors are right. You will now make round patties with the mixture and roll them out well.
5. Pre heat the oven at 250 Fahrenheit for 5 minutes. Open the basket of the Fryer and arrange the patties in the basket. Close it carefully. Keep the fryer at 150 degrees for around 10 or 12 minutes. In between the cooking process, turn the patties over to get a uniform cook. Serve hot with mint sauce.

353.Cottage Cheese Pops

Servings:x

Cooking Time:x
Ingredients:
- 1 tsp. dry basil
- ½ cup hung curd
- 1 tsp. lemon juice
- 1 cup cottage cheese cut into 2" cubes
- 1 ½ tsp. garlic paste
- Salt and pepper to taste
- 1 tsp. dry oregano
- 1 tsp. red chili flakes

Directions:
1. Cut the cottage cheese into thick and long rectangular pieces.
2. Add the rest of the ingredients into a separate bowl and mix them well to get a consistent mixture.
3. Dip the cottage cheese pieces in the above mixture and leave them aside for some time.
4. Pre heat the oven at 180° C for around 5 minutes. Place the coated cottage cheese pieces in the fry basket and close it properly. Let them cook at the same temperature for 20 more minutes. Keep turning them over in the basket so that they are cooked properly. Serve with tomato ketchup.

354.Asparagus Flat Cakes

Servings:x
Cooking Time:x
Ingredients:
- 2 or 3 green chilies finely chopped
- 1 ½ tbsp. lemon juice
- Salt and pepper to taste
- 2 tbsp. garam masala
- 2 cups sliced asparagus
- 3 tsp. ginger finely chopped
- 1-2 tbsp. fresh coriander leaves

Directions:
1. Mix the ingredients in a clean bowl and add water to it. Make sure that the paste is not too watery but is enough to apply on the asparagus.
2. Pre heat the oven at 160 degrees Fahrenheit for 5 minutes. Place the French Cuisine Galettes in the fry basket and let them cook for another 25 minutes at the same temperature. Keep rolling them over to get a uniform cook. Serve either with mint sauce or ketchup.

355.Cottage Cheese Homemade Fried Sticks

Servings:x
Cooking Time:x
Ingredients:
- One or two poppadums'
- 4 or 5 tbsp. corn flour
- 1 cup of water
- 2 cups cottage cheese

- 1 big lemon-juiced
- 1 tbsp. ginger-garlic paste
- For seasoning, use salt and red chili powder in small amounts
- ½ tsp. carom

Directions:
1. Take the cottage cheese. Cut it into long pieces. Now, make a mixture of lemon juice, red chili powder, salt, ginger garlic paste and carom to use as a marinade. Let the cottage cheese pieces marinate in the mixture for some time and then roll them in dry corn flour. Leave them aside for around 20 minutes.
2. Take the poppadum into a pan and roast them. Once they are cooked, crush them into very small pieces. Now take another container and pour around 100 ml of water into it. Dissolve 2 tbsp. of corn flour in this water. Dip the cottage cheese pieces in this solution of corn flour and roll them on to the pieces of crushed poppadum so that the poppadum sticks to the cottage cheese
3. . Pre heat the oven for 10 minutes at 290 Fahrenheit. Then open the basket of the fryer and place the cottage cheese pieces inside it. Close the basket properly. Let the fryer stay at 160 degrees for another 20 minutes. Halfway through, open the basket and toss the cottage cheese around a bit to allow for uniform cooking. Once they are done, you can serve it either with ketchup or mint sauce. Another recommended side is mint sauce.

356.Parmesan Cabbage With Blue Cheese Sauce

Servings:4
Cooking Time: 25 Minutes
Ingredients:
- ½ head cabbage, cut into wedges
- 2 cups Parmesan cheese, chopped
- 4 tbsp butter, melted
- Salt and black pepper to taste
- ½ cup blue cheese sauce

Directions:
1. Drizzle cabbage wedges with butter and coat with Parmesan cheese. Place them in the frying basket and cook for 20 minutes at 380 F on AirFry setting. Serve topped with blue cheese sauce.

357.Veggie Mix Fried Chips

Servings:4
Cooking Time: 45 Minutes
Ingredients:
- 1 large eggplant, cut into strips
- 5 potatoes, peeled and cut into strips
- 3 zucchinis, cut into strips

- ½ cup cornstarch
- ½ cup olive oil
- Salt to taste

Directions:
1. Preheat on AirFry function to 390 F. In a bowl, stir cornstarch, ½ cup of water, salt, pepper, olive oil, eggplants, zucchini, and potatoes. Place the veggie mixture in the basket and press Start. Cook for 12 minutes. Serve warm.

358.Amazing Macadamia Delight

Servings:6
Cooking Time: 20 Minutes
Ingredients:
- 3 cups macadamia nuts
- 3 tbsp liquid smoke
- Salt to taste
- 2 tbsp molasses

Directions:
1. Preheat on Bake function to 360 F. In a bowl, add salt, liquid, molasses, and cashews and toss to coat. Place the cashews ina baking tray and press Start. Cook for 10 minutes, shaking the basket every 5 minutes. Serve.

359.Gorgonzola Cheese & Pumpkin Salad

Servings:2
Cooking Time: 30 Minutes + Chilling Time
Ingredients:
- ½ lb pumpkin
- 2 oz gorgonzola cheese, crumbled
- 2 tbsp pine nuts, toasted
- 1 tbsp olive oil
- ½ cup baby spinach
- 1 spring onion, sliced
- 2 radishes, thinly sliced
- 1 tsp apple cider vinegar

Directions:
1. Preheat on Bake function to 360 F. Peel the pumpkin and chop it into small pieces. Place in a greased baking dish and bake for 20 minutes. Let cool.
2. Add baby spinach, radishes, and spring onion in a serving bowl and toss with olive oil and vinegar. Top with the pumpkin and gorgonzola cheese and sprinkle with the pine nuts to serve.

360.Asian-inspired Broccoli

Servings:2
Cooking Time: 10 Minutes
Ingredients:
- 12 ounces (340 g) broccoli florets
- 2 tablespoons Asian hot chili oil
- 1 teaspoon ground Sichuan peppercorns (or black pepper)
- 2 garlic cloves, finely chopped

- 1 (2-inch) piece fresh ginger, peeled and finely chopped
- Kosher salt and freshly ground black pepper

Directions:
1. Toss the broccoli florets with the chili oil, Sichuan peppercorns, garlic, ginger, salt, and pepper in a mixing bowl until thoroughly coated.
2. Transfer the broccoli florets to the air fryer basket.
3. Put the air fryer basket on the baking pan and slide into Rack Position 2, select Air Fry, set temperature to 375ºF (190ºC), and set time to 10 minutes.
4. Stir the broccoli florets halfway through the cooking time.
5. When cooking is complete, the broccoli florets should be lightly browned and tender. Remove the broccoli from the oven and serve on a plate.

361.Vegetable Fried Mix Chips

Servings: 4
Cooking Time: 45 Minutes
Ingredients:
- 1 large eggplant
- 4 potatoes
- 3 zucchinis
- ½ cup cornstarch
- ½ cup olive oil
- Salt to season

Directions:
1. Preheat on Air Fry function to 390 F. Cut the eggplant and zucchini in long 3-inch strips. Peel and cut the potatoes into 3-inch strips; set aside.
2. In a bowl, stir in cornstarch, ½ cup of water, salt, pepper, oil, eggplant, zucchini, and potatoes. Place one-third of the veggie strips in the basket and fit in the baking tray; cook for 12 minutes, shaking once.
3. Once ready, transfer them to a serving platter. Repeat the cooking process for the remaining veggie strips. Serve warm.

362.Sago French Cuisine Galette

Servings:x
Cooking Time:x
Ingredients:
- 2 or 3 green chilies finely chopped
- 1 ½ tbsp. lemon juice
- Salt and pepper to taste
- 2 cup sago soaked
- 1 ½ cup coarsely crushed peanuts
- 3 tsp. ginger finely chopped
- 1-2 tbsp. fresh coriander leaves

Directions:

1. Wash the soaked sago and mix it with the rest of the ingredients in a clean bowl.
2. Mold this mixture into round and flat French Cuisine Galettes.
3. Wet the French Cuisine Galettes slightly with water. Coat each French Cuisine Galette with the crushed peanuts.
4. Pre heat the oven at 160 degrees Fahrenheit for 5 minutes. Place the French Cuisine Galettes in the fry basket and let them cook for another 25 minutes at the same temperature. Keep rolling them over to get a uniform cook. Serve either with mint sauce or ketchup.

363.Cauliflower Bites

Servings: 4
Cooking Time: 18 Minutes
Ingredients:
- 1 Head Cauliflower, cut into small florets
- Tsps Garlic Powder
- Pinch of Salt and Pepper
- 1 Tbsp Butter, melted
- 1/2 Cup Chili Sauce
- Olive Oil

Directions:
1. Preparing the Ingredients. Place cauliflower into a bowl and pour oil over florets to lightly cover.
2. Season florets with salt, pepper, and the garlic powder and toss well.
3. Air Frying. Place florets into the air fryer oven at 350 degrees for 14 minutes.
4. Remove cauliflower from the Air fryer oven.
5. Combine the melted butter with the chili sauce
6. Pour over the florets so that they are well coated.
7. Return to the air fryer oven and cook for additional 3 to 4 minutes
8. Serve as a side or with ranch or cheese dip as a snack.

364.Teriyaki Tofu

Servings:3
Cooking Time: 15 Minutes
Ingredients:
- Nonstick cooking spray
- 14 oz. firm or extra firm tofu, pressed & cut in 1-inch cubes
- ¼ cup cornstarch
- ½ tsp salt
- ½ tsp ginger
- ½ tsp white pepper
- 3 tbsp. olive oil
- 12 oz. bottle vegan teriyaki sauce

Directions:
1. Lightly spray baking pan with cooking spray.

2. In a shallow dish, combine cornstarch, salt, ginger, and pepper.
3. Heat oil in a large skillet over med-high heat.
4. Toss tofu cubes in cornstarch mixture then add to skillet. Cook 5 minutes, turning over halfway through, until tofu is nicely seared. Transfer the tofu to the prepared baking pan.
5. Set oven to convection bake on 350°F for 15 minutes.
6. Pour all but ½ cup teriyaki sauce over tofu and stir to coat. After oven has preheated for 5 minutes, place the baking pan in position 2 and bake tofu 10 minutes.
7. Turn tofu over, spoon the sauce in the pan over it and bake another 10 minutes. Serve with reserved sauce for dipping.
- **Nutrition Info:** Calories: 469, Total Fat 25g, Saturated Fat 4g, Total Carbs 33g, Net Carbs 30g, Protein 28g, Sugar 16g, Fiber 3g, Sodium 2424mg, Potassium 571mg, Phosphorus 428mg

365.Crispy Potato Lentil Nuggets

Servings: 4
Cooking Time: 10 Minutes
Ingredients:
- Nonstick cooking spray
- 1 cup red lentils
- 1 tbsp. olive oil
- 1 cup onion, grated
- 1 cup carrot, grated
- 1 cup potato, grated
- ½ cup flour
- ½ tsp salt
- ½ tsp garlic powder
- ¾ tsp paprika
- ¼ tsp pepper

Directions:
1. Place baking pan in position 2. Lightly spray fryer basket with cooking spray.
2. Soak lentils in just enough water to cover them for 25 minutes.
3. Heat oil in a large skillet over medium heat. Add onion, carrot, and potato. Cook, stirring frequently until vegetables are tender, 12-15 minutes.
4. Drain the lentils and place them in a food processor. Add flour and spices and pulse to combine, leave some texture to the mixture.
5. Add cooked veggies to the food processor and pulse just until combined. Mixture will be sticky, so oil your hands. Form mixture into nugget shapes and add to the fryer basket in a single layer.
6. Place basket in the oven and set air fry on 350°F for 10 minutes. Turn nuggets over halfway through cooking time. Repeat with remaining mixture. Serve with your favorite dipping sauce.
- **Nutrition Info:** Calories: 317, Total Fat 5g, Saturated Fat 1g, Total Carbs 54g, Net Carbs 46g, Protein 14g, Sugar 3g, Fiber 8g, Sodium 317mg, Potassium 625mg, Phosphorus 197mg

366.Onion French Cuisine Galette

Servings:x
Cooking Time:x
Ingredients:
- 2 or 3 green chilies finely chopped
- 1 ½ tbsp. lemon juice
- Salt and pepper to taste
- 2 tbsp. garam masala
- 2 medium onions (Cut long)
- 1 ½ cup coarsely crushed peanuts
- 3 tsp. ginger finely chopped
- 1-2 tbsp. fresh coriander leaves

Directions:
1. Mix the ingredients in a clean bowl.
2. Mold this mixture into round and flat French Cuisine Galettes.
3. Wet the French Cuisine Galettes slightly with water. Coat each French Cuisine Galette with the crushed peanuts.
4. Pre heat the oven at 160 degrees Fahrenheit for 5 minutes. Place the French Cuisine Galettes in the fry basket and let them cook for another 25 minutes at the same temperature. Keep rolling them over to get a uniform cook. Serve either with mint sauce or ketchup.

367.Cheesy Asparagus And Potato Platter

Servings:5
Cooking Time: 26 Minutes
Ingredients:
- 4 medium potatoes, cut into wedges
- Cooking spray
- 1 bunch asparagus, trimmed
- 2 tablespoons olive oil
- Salt and pepper, to taste
- Cheese Sauce:
- ¼ cup crumbled cottage cheese
- ¼ cup buttermilk
- 1 tablespoon whole-grain mustard
- Salt and black pepper, to taste

Directions:
1. Spritz the air fryer basket with cooking spray.
2. Put the potatoes in the air fryer basket.
3. Put the air fryer basket on the baking pan and slide into Rack Position 2, select Roast, set temperature to 400ºF (205ºC) and set time to 20 minutes.
4. Stir the potatoes halfway through.

5. When cooking is complete, the potatoes should be golden brown.
6. Remove the potatoes from the oven to a platter. Cover the potatoes with foil to keep warm. Set aside.
7. Place the asparagus in the air fryer basket and drizzle with the olive oil. Sprinkle with salt and pepper.
8. Put the air fryer basket on the baking pan and slide into Rack Position 2, select Roast, set temperature to 400ºF (205ºC) and set time to 6 minutes. Stir the asparagus halfway through.
9. When cooking is complete, the asparagus should be crispy.
10. Meanwhile, make the cheese sauce by stirring together the cottage cheese, buttermilk, and mustard in a small bowl. Season as needed with salt and pepper.
11. Transfer the asparagus to the platter of potatoes and drizzle with the cheese sauce. Serve immediately.

368. Rosemary Beets With Balsamic Glaze

Servings:2
Cooking Time: 10 Minutes
Ingredients:
- Beet:
- 2 beets, cubed
- 2 tablespoons olive oil
- 2 springs rosemary, chopped
- Salt and black pepper, to taste
- Balsamic Glaze:
- $1/3$ cup balsamic vinegar
- 1 tablespoon honey

Directions:
1. Combine the beets, olive oil, rosemary, salt, and pepper in a mixing bowl and toss until the beets are completely coated.
2. Place the beets in the air fryer basket.
3. Put the air fryer basket on the baking pan and slide into Rack Position 2, select Air Fry, set temperature to 400ºF (205ºC) and set time to 10 minutes.
4. Stir the vegetables halfway through.
5. When cooking is complete, the beets should be crisp and browned at the edges.
6. Meanwhile, make the balsamic glaze: Place the balsamic vinegar and honey in a small saucepan and bring to a boil over medium heat. When the sauce boils, reduce the heat to medium-low heat and simmer until the liquid is reduced by half.
7. When ready, remove the beets from the oven to a platter. Pour the balsamic glaze over the top and serve immediately.

369. Cottage Cheese French Cuisine Galette

Servings:x
Cooking Time:x

Ingredients:
- 1-2 tbsp. fresh coriander leaves
- 2 or 3 green chilies finely chopped
- 1 ½ tbsp. lemon juice
- Salt and pepper to taste
- 2 tbsp. garam masala
- 2 cups grated cottage cheese
- 1 ½ cup coarsely crushed peanuts
- 3 tsp. ginger finely chopped

Directions:
1. Mix the ingredients in a clean bowl.
2. Mold this mixture into round and flat French Cuisine Galettes.
3. Wet the French Cuisine Galettes slightly with water. Coat each French Cuisine Galette with the crushed peanuts.
4. Pre heat the oven at 160 degrees Fahrenheit for 5 minutes. Place the French Cuisine Galettes in the fry basket and let them cook for another 25 minutes at the same temperature. Keep rolling them over to get a uniform cook. Serve either with mint sauce or ketchup.

370. Vegetable Skewer

Servings:x
Cooking Time:x
Ingredients:
- 3 tbsp. cream
- 3 eggs
- 2 cups mixed vegetables
- 3 onions chopped
- 5 green chilies
- 1 ½ tbsp. ginger paste
- 1 ½ tsp. garlic paste
- 1 ½ tsp. salt
- 2 ½ tbsp. white sesame seeds

Directions:
1. Grind the ingredients except for the egg and form a smooth paste. Coat the vegetables in the paste. Now, beat the eggs and add a little salt to it.
2. Dip the coated vegetables in the egg mixture and then transfer to the sesame seeds and coat the vegetables well. Place the vegetables on a stick.
3. Pre heat the oven at 160 degrees Fahrenheit for around 5 minutes. Place the sticks in the basket and let them cook for another 25 minutes at the same temperature. Turn the sticks over in between the cooking process to get a uniform cook.

371. Cheesy Cauliflower Fritters

Servings: 8
Cooking Time: 7 Minutes
Ingredients:
- ½ C. chopped parsley

- 1 C. Italian breadcrumbs
- 1/3 C. shredded mozzarella cheese
- 1/3 C. shredded sharp cheddar cheese
- 1 egg
- 2 minced garlic cloves
- 3 chopped scallions
- 1 head of cauliflower

Directions:
1. Preparing the Ingredients. Cut the cauliflower up into florets. Wash well and pat dry. Place into a food processor and pulse 20-30 seconds till it looks like rice.
2. Place cauliflower rice in a bowl and mix with pepper, salt, egg, cheeses, breadcrumbs, garlic, and scallions.
3. With hands, form 15 patties of the mixture. Add more breadcrumbs if needed.
4. Air Frying. With olive oil, spritz patties, and place into your air fryer oven in a single layer. Set temperature to 390°F, and set time to 7 minutes, flipping after 7 minutes.
- **Nutrition Info:** CALORIES: 209; FAT: 17G; PROTEIN: 6G; SUGAR:0.5

372.Mushroom Pasta

Servings:x
Cooking Time:x
Ingredients:
- 2 cups sliced mushroom
- 2 tbsp. all-purpose flour
- 2 cups of milk
- 1 tsp. dried oregano
- ½ tsp. dried basil
- ½ tsp. dried parsley
- 1 cup pasta
- 1 ½ tbsp. olive oil
- A pinch of salt
- For tossing pasta:
- 1 ½ tbsp. olive oil
- Salt and pepper to taste
- ½ tsp. oregano
- ½ tsp. basil
- 2 tbsp. olive oil
- Salt and pepper to taste

Directions:
1. Boil the pasta and sieve it when done. You will need to toss the pasta in the ingredients mentioned above and set aside.
2. For the sauce, add the ingredients to a pan and bring the ingredients to a boil. Stir the sauce and continue to simmer to make a thicker sauce. Add the pasta to the sauce and transfer this into a glass bowl garnished with cheese.
3. Pre heat the oven at 160 degrees for 5 minutes. Place the bowl in the basket and close it. Let it continue to cook at the same temperature for 10 minutes more. Keep stirring the pasta in between.

373.Simple Ratatouille

Servings:2
Cooking Time: 16 Minutes
Ingredients:
- 2 Roma tomatoes, thinly sliced
- 1 zucchini, thinly sliced
- 2 yellow bell peppers, sliced
- 2 garlic cloves, minced
- 2 tablespoons olive oil
- 2 tablespoons herbes de Provence
- 1 tablespoon vinegar
- Salt and black pepper, to taste

Directions:
1. Place the tomatoes, zucchini, bell peppers, garlic, olive oil, herbes de Provence, and vinegar in a large bowl and toss until the vegetables are evenly coated. Sprinkle with salt and pepper and toss again. Pour the vegetable mixture into the baking pan.
2. Slide the baking pan into Rack Position 2, select Roast, set temperature to 390ºF (199ºC) and set time to 16 minutes.
3. Stir the vegetables halfway through.
4. When cooking is complete, the vegetables should be tender.
5. Let the vegetable mixture stand for 5 minutes in the oven before removing and serving.

374.Bean, Salsa, And Cheese Tacos

Servings:4
Cooking Time: 7 Minutes
Ingredients:
- 1 (15-ounce / 425-g) can black beans, drained and rinsed
- ½ cup prepared salsa
- 1½ teaspoons chili powder
- 4 ounces (113 g) grated Monterey Jack cheese
- 2 tablespoons minced onion
- 8 (6-inch) flour tortillas
- 2 tablespoons vegetable or extra-virgin olive oil
- Shredded lettuce, for serving

Directions:
1. In a medium bowl, add the beans, salsa and chili powder. Coarsely mash them with a potato masher. Fold in the cheese and onion and stir until combined.
2. Arrange the flour tortillas on a cutting board and spoon 2 to 3 tablespoons of the filling into each tortilla. Fold the tortillas over, pressing lightly to even out the filling. Brush the tacos on one side with half the olive oil and put them, oiled side down, in the air fryer basket. Brush the top side with the remaining olive oil.
3. Put the air fryer basket on the baking pan and slide into Rack Position 2, select Air Fry,

set temperature to 400ºF (205ºC), and set time to 7 minutes.

4. Flip the tacos halfway through the cooking time.
5. Remove from the oven and allow to cool for 5 minutes. Serve with the shredded lettuce on the side.

375.Grandma´s Ratatouille

Servings:2
Cooking Time: 30 Minutes
Ingredients:
- 1 tbsp olive oil
- 3 Roma tomatoes, thinly sliced
- 2 garlic cloves, minced
- 1 zucchini, thinly sliced
- 2 yellow bell peppers, sliced
- 1 tbsp vinegar
- 2 tbsp herbs de Provence
- Salt and black pepper to taste

Directions:
1. Preheat on AirFry function to 390 F. Place all ingredients in a bowl. Season with salt and pepper and stir to coat. Arrange the vegetable on a baking dish and place in the oven. Cook for 15 minutes, shaking occasionally. Let sit for 5 more minutes after the timer goes off.

376.Green Chili Flat Cakes

Servings:x
Cooking Time:x
Ingredients:
- 2 or 3 green chilies finely chopped
- 1 ½ tbsp. lemon juice
- Salt and pepper to taste
- 2 tbsp. garam masala
- 10–12 green chilies
- 3 tsp. ginger finely chopped
- 1-2 tbsp. fresh coriander leaves

Directions:
1. Mix the ingredients in a clean bowl and add water to it. Make sure that the paste is not too watery but is enough to apply to the green chilies.
2. Pre heat the oven at 160 degrees Fahrenheit for 5 minutes. Place the French Cuisine Galettes in the fry basket and let them cook for another 25 minutes at the same temperature. Keep rolling them over to get a uniform cook. Serve either with mint sauce or ketchup.

377.Garlicky Sesame Carrots

Servings:4 To 6
Cooking Time: 16 Minutes
Ingredients:
- 1 pound (454 g) baby carrots
- 1 tablespoon sesame oil
- ½ teaspoon dried dill
- Pinch salt
- Freshly ground black pepper, to taste
- 6 cloves garlic, peeled
- 3 tablespoons sesame seeds

Directions:
1. In a medium bowl, drizzle the baby carrots with the sesame oil. Sprinkle with the dill, salt, and pepper and toss to coat well.
2. Place the baby carrots in the air fryer basket.
3. Put the air fryer basket on the baking pan and slide into Rack Position 2, select Roast, set temperature to 380ºF (193ºC), and set time to 16 minutes.
4. After 8 minutes, remove from the oven and stir in the garlic. Return the pan to the oven and continue roasting for 8 minutes more.
5. When cooking is complete, the carrots should be lightly browned. Remove from the oven and serve sprinkled with the sesame seeds.

378.Cheese Stuffed Green Peppers With Tomato Sauce

Servings:4
Cooking Time: 35 Minutes
Ingredients:
- 2 cans green chili peppers
- 1 cup cheddar cheese, shredded
- 1 cup Monterey Jack cheese, shredded
- 2 tbsp all-purpose flour
- 2 large eggs, beaten
- ½ cup milk
- 1 can tomato sauce

Directions:
1. Preheat on AirFry function to 380 F. Spray a baking dish with cooking spray. Take half of the chilies and arrange them in the baking dish. Top with half of the cheese and cover with the remaining chilies. In a medium bowl, combine eggs, milk, and flour and pour over the chilies.
2. Press Start and cook for 20 minutes. Remove the chilies and pour the tomato sauce over them; cook for 15 more minutes. Top with the remaining cheese and serve.

379.Rosemary Butternut Squash Roast

Servings: 2
Cooking Time: 30 Minutes
Ingredients:
- 1 butternut squash
- 1 tbsp dried rosemary
- 2 tbsp maple syrup
- Salt to taste

Directions:
1. Place the squash on a cutting board and peel. Cut in half and remove the seeds and pulp. Slice into wedges and season with salt.

Preheat on Air Fry function to 350 F. Spray the wedges with cooking spray and sprinkle with rosemary. Place the wedges in the basket without overlapping and fit in the baking tray. Cook for 20 minutes, flipping once halfway through. Serve with maple syrup and goat cheese.

380.French Bean Toast

Servings:x
Cooking Time:x
Ingredients:
- 1 tsp. sugar for every 2 slices
- Crushed cornflakes
- 2 cups baked beans
- Bread slices (brown or white)
- 1 egg white for every 2 slices

Directions:
1. Put two slices together and cut them along the diagonal.
2. In a bowl, whisk the egg whites and add some sugar.
3. Dip the bread triangles into this mixture and then coat them with the crushed cornflakes.
4. Pre heat the oven at 180° C for 4 minutes. Place the coated bread triangles in the fry basket and close it. Let them cook at the same temperature for another 20 minutes at least. Halfway through the process, turn the triangles over so that you get a uniform cook. Top with baked beans and serve.

381.Speedy Vegetable Pizza

Servings: 1
Cooking Time: 15 Minutes
Ingredients:
- 1 ½ tbsp tomato paste
- ¼ cup grated cheddar cheese
- ¼ cup grated mozzarella cheese
- 1 tbsp cooked sweet corn
- 4 zucchini slices
- 4 eggplant slices
- 4 red onion rings
- ½ green bell pepper, chopped
- 3 cherry tomatoes, quartered
- 1 pizza crust
- ¼ tsp basil
- ¼ tsp oregano

Directions:
1. Preheat on Bake function to 350 F. Spread the tomato paste on the pizza crust. Top with zucchini and eggplant slices first, then green peppers, and onion rings. Cover with cherry tomatoes and scatter the corn. Sprinkle with oregano and basil and sprinkle with cheddar and mozzarella cheeses. Cook for 10-12 minutes until golden brown on top. Serve.

382.Herby Tofu

Servings: 2
Cooking Time: 30 Minutes
Ingredients:
- 6 oz extra firm tofu
- Black pepper to taste
- 1 tbsp vegetable broth
- 1 tbsp soy sauce
- ⅓ tsp dried oregano
- ⅓ tsp garlic powder
- ⅓ tsp dried basil
- ⅓ tsp onion powder

Directions:
1. Place the tofu on a cutting board and cut it into 3 lengthwise slices with a knife. Line a side of the cutting board with paper towels, place the tofu on it, and cover with a paper towel. Use your hands to press the tofu gently until as much liquid has been extracted from it. Chop the tofu into 8 cubes; set aside.
2. In another bowl, add the soy sauce, vegetable broth, oregano, basil, garlic powder, onion powder, and black pepper and mix well with a spoon. Rub the spice mixture on the tofu. Let it marinate for 10 minutes.
3. Preheat on Air Fry function to 390 F. Place the tofu in the fryer's basket in a single layer and fit in the baking tray. Cook for 10 minutes, flipping it at the 6-minute mark. Remove to a plate and serve with green salad.

383.Vegetable Spring Rolls

Servings: 4
Cooking Time: 15 Minutes
Ingredients:
- ½ cabbage head, grated
- 2 carrots, grated
- 1 tsp minced ginger
- 1 tsp minced garlic
- 1 tsp sesame oil
- 1 tsp soy sauce
- 1 tsp sesame seeds
- ½ tsp salt
- 1 tsp olive oil
- 1 package spring roll wrappers

Directions:
1. Combine all ingredients except for the wrappers in a large bowl. Divide the mixture between the spring roll wrappers and roll them up. Arrange on a greased baking tray and cook in your for 5 minutes on Bake function at 370 F. Serve.

384.Garlic Stuffed Mushrooms

Servings:2
Cooking Time: 12 Minutes
Ingredients:
- 18 medium-sized white mushrooms
- 1 small onion, peeled and chopped

- 4 garlic cloves, peeled and minced
- 2 tablespoons olive oil
- 2 teaspoons cumin powder
- A pinch ground allspice
- Fine sea salt and freshly ground black pepper, to taste

Directions:
1. On a clean work surface, remove the mushroom stems. Using a spoon, scoop out the mushroom gills and discard.
2. Thoroughly combine the onion, garlic, olive oil, cumin powder, allspice, salt, and pepper in a mixing bowl. Stuff the mushrooms evenly with the mixture.
3. Place the stuffed mushrooms in the air fryer basket.
4. Put the air fryer basket on the baking pan and slide into Rack Position 2, select Roast, set temperature to 345ºF (174ºC) and set time to 12 minutes.
5. When cooking is complete, the mushroom should be browned.
6. Cool for 5 minutes before serving.

385.Balsamic Asparagus

Servings:4
Cooking Time: 10 Minutes
Ingredients:
- 4 tablespoons olive oil, plus more for greasing
- 4 tablespoons balsamic vinegar
- 1½ pounds (680 g) asparagus spears, trimmed
- Salt and freshly ground black pepper, to taste

Directions:
1. Grease the air fryer basket with olive oil.
2. In a shallow bowl, stir together the 4 tablespoons of olive oil and balsamic vinegar to make a marinade.
3. Put the asparagus spears in the bowl so they are thoroughly covered by the marinade and allow to marinate for 5 minutes.
4. Put the asparagus in the greased basket in a single layer and season with salt and pepper.
5. Put the air fryer basket on the baking pan and slide into Rack Position 2, select Air Fry, set temperature to 350ºF (180ºC), and set time to 10 minutes.
6. Flip the asparagus halfway through the cooking time.
7. When done, the asparagus should be tender and lightly browned. Cool for 5 minutes before serving.

386.Green Chili Taquitos

Servings: 3
Cooking Time: 10 Minutes
Ingredients:
- Nonstick cooking spray
- 6 corn tortillas

- ¾ cup vegan cream cheese
- 1 cup vegan cheddar cheese, grated
- 4 oz. green chilies, diced & drained

Directions:
1. Place baking pan in position 2. Lightly spray fryer basket with cooking spray.
2. Wrap tortillas in paper towels and microwave 1 minute.
3. Spread the cream cheese over tortillas. Top with cheddar cheese and chilies. Roll up tightly. Place, seam side down, in fryer basket.
4. Place the basket on the baking pan and set oven to air fry on 350°F for 10 minutes or until tortillas are browned and crispy. Turn taquitos over halfway through cooking time. Serve immediately.
- **Nutrition Info:** Calories: 706, Total Fat 34g, Saturated Fat 18g, Total Carbs 51g, Net Carbs 35g, Protein 24g, Sugar 11g, Fiber 16g, Sodium 2371mg, Potassium 1074mg, Phosphorus 850mg

387.Tofu & Pea Cauli Rice

Servings:4
Cooking Time: 30 Minutes
Ingredients:
- Tofu:
- ½ block tofu
- ½ cup onions, chopped
- 2 tbsp soy sauce
- 1 tsp turmeric
- 1 cup carrots, chopped
- Cauliflower:
- 3 cups cauliflower rice
- 2 tbsp soy sauce
- ½ cup broccoli, chopped
- 2 garlic cloves, minced
- 1 ½ tsp toasted sesame oil
- 1 tbsp fresh ginger, minced
- ½ cup frozen peas
- 1 tbsp rice vinegar

Directions:
1. Preheat on AirFry function to 370 F. Crumble the tofu and combine it with all tofu ingredients. Place in a baking dish and cook for 10 minutes.
2. Meanwhile, place all cauliflower ingredients in a large bowl; mix to combine. Add the cauliflower mixture to the tofu and stir to combine. Press Start and cook for 12 minutes. Serve.

388.Mixed Vegetable Pancakes

Servings:x
Cooking Time:x
Ingredients:
- 2 cups shredded vegetables
- Salt and Pepper to taste
- 3 tbsp. Butter
- 1 ½ cups almond flour
- 3 eggs

- 2 tsp. dried basil
- 2 tsp. dried parsley

Directions:
1. Preheat the air fryer to 250 Fahrenheit.
2. In a small bowl, mix the ingredients together. Ensure that the mixture is smooth and well balanced.
3. Take a pancake mold and grease it with butter. Add the batter to the mold and place it in the air fryer basket.
4. Cook till both the sides of the pancake have browned on both sides and serve with maple syrup.

389.Cauliflower French Cuisine Galette

Servings:x
Cooking Time:x
Ingredients:
- 3 tsp. ginger finely chopped
- 1-2 tbsp. fresh coriander leaves
- 2 or 3 green chilies finely chopped
- 1 ½ tbsp. lemon juice
- Salt and pepper to taste
- 2 tbsp. garam masala
- 2 cups cauliflower
- 1 ½ cup coarsely crushed peanuts

Directions:
1. Mix the ingredients in a clean bowl.
2. Mold this mixture into round and flat French Cuisine Galettes.
3. Wet the French Cuisine Galettes slightly with water. Coat each French Cuisine Galette with the crushed peanuts.
4. Pre heat the oven at 160 degrees Fahrenheit for 5 minutes. Place the French Cuisine Galettes in the fry basket and let them cook for another 25 minutes at the same temperature. Keep rolling them over to get a uniform cook. Serve either with mint sauce or ketchup.

390.Cumin Sweet Potatoes Wedges

Servings:4
Cooking Time: 30 Minutes
Ingredients:
- ½ tsp garlic powder
- ½ tsp cayenne pepper powder
- ¼ tsp ground cumin
- 3 tbsp olive oil
- 3 sweet potatoes, cut into ½-inch thick wedges
- 2 tbsp fresh parsley, chopped
- Sea salt to taste

Directions:
1. In a bowl, mix salt, garlic powder, cayenne pepper powder, and cumin. Whisk in olive oil and coat in the potatoes. Arrange them on the basket, without overcrowding and press Start. Cook for 20-25 minutes at 380 F on AirFry function. Sprinkle with parsley and sea salt and serve.

391.Rosemary Squash With Cheese

Servings: 2
Cooking Time: 20 Minutes
Ingredients:
- 1 pound (454 g) butternut squash, cut into wedges
- 2 tablespoons olive oil
- 1 tablespoon dried rosemary
- Salt, to salt
- 1 cup crumbled goat cheese
- 1 tablespoon maple syrup

Directions:
1. Toss the squash wedges with the olive oil, rosemary, and salt in a large bowl until well coated.
2. Transfer the squash wedges to the air fryer basket, spreading them out in as even a layer as possible.
3. Put the air fryer basket on the baking pan and slide into Rack Position 2, select Air Fry, set temperature to 350ºF (180ºC), and set time to 20 minutes.
4. After 10 minutes, remove from the oven and flip the squash. Return the pan to the oven and continue cooking for 10 minutes.
5. When cooking is complete, the squash should be golden brown. Remove from the oven. Sprinkle the goat cheese on top and serve drizzled with the maple syrup.

392.Broccoli Marinade Cutlet

Servings:x
Cooking Time:x
Ingredients:
- 1 ½ tsp. salt
- 3 tsp. lemon juice
- 2 tsp. garam masala
- 3 eggs
- 2 ½ tbsp. white sesame seeds
- 2 cups broccoli florets
- 3 onions chopped
- 5 green chilies-roughly chopped
- 1 ½ tbsp. ginger paste
- 1 ½ tsp. garlic paste

Directions:
1. Grind the ingredients except for the egg and form a smooth paste. Coat the florets in the paste. Now, beat the eggs and add a little salt to it.
2. Dip the coated florets in the egg mixture and then transfer to the sesame seeds and coat the florets well. Place the vegetables on a stick.
3. Pre heat the oven at 160 degrees Fahrenheit for around 5 minutes. Place the sticks in the basket and let them cook for another 25 minutes at the same temperature. Turn the sticks over in between the cooking process to get a uniform cook.

393.Cheesy Spinach Toasties

Servings:x
Cooking Time:x
Ingredients:
- 1 tsp. coarsely crushed green chilies
- 2 tbsp. grated pizza cheese
- 1 cup milk
- 2 toasted bread slices cut into triangles
- 1 tbsp. butter
- 1 tbsp. all-purpose flour
- 1 small onion finely chopped
- 1-2 flakes garlic finely chopped
- Half a bunch of spinach that has been boiled and crushed (does not have to
- be crushed finely)
- 1 tbsp. fresh cream
- Some salt and pepper to taste

Directions:
1. Take a pan and melt some butter in it. Also add some onions and garlic.
2. Now keep roasting them in the butter until the onions are caramelized or attain a golden-brown color.
3. Into this pan add the required amount of all-purpose flour. Continue to roast for 3 minutes or so. Add milk and keep stirring until you bring it to a boil.
4. Add green chilies, cream, spinach and seasoning. Mix the ingredients properly and let it cook until the mixture thickens. Toast some bread. Apply the paste made in the previous step on the bread.
5. Sprinkle some grated cheese on top of the paste.
6. Pre heat the oven at 290 Fahrenheit for around 4 minutes. Put the toasts in the Fry basket and let it continue to cook for another 10 minutes at the same temperature.

394.Vegetable Dumpling

Servings:x
Cooking Time:x
Ingredients:
- 2 tbsp. oil
- 2 tsp. ginger-garlic paste
- 2 tsp. soya sauce
- 2 tsp. vinegar
- 1 ½ cup all-purpose flour
- ½ tsp. salt or to taste
- 5 tbsp. water
- 2 cup carrots grated
- 2 cup cabbage grated

Directions:
1. Squeeze the dough and cover it with plastic wrap and set aside. Next, cook the ingredients for the filling and try to ensure that the vegetables are covered well with the sauce.
2. Roll the dough and place the filling in the center. Now, wrap the dough to cover the filling and pinch the edges together. Pre

heat the oven at 200° F for 5 minutes. Place the dumplings in the fry basket and close it. Let them cook at the same temperature for another 20 minutes. Recommended sides are chili sauce or ketchup.

395.Cilantro Roasted Carrots With Cumin Seeds

Servings:4
Cooking Time: 15 Minutes
Ingredients:
- 1 lb carrots, julienned
- 1 tbsp olive oil
- 1 tsp cumin seeds
- 2 tbsp fresh cilantro, chopped

Directions:
1. Preheat on AirFry function to 350 F. In a bowl, mix oil, carrots, and cumin seeds. Gently stir to coat the carrots well. Place the carrots in a baking tray and press Star. Cook for 10 minutes. Scatter fresh coriander over the carrots and serve.

396.Paprika Cauliflower

Servings:4
Cooking Time: 20 Minutes
Ingredients:
- 1 large head cauliflower, broken into small florets
- 2 teaspoons smoked paprika
- 1 teaspoon garlic powder
- Salt and freshly ground black pepper, to taste
- Cooking spray

Directions:
1. Spray the air fryer basket with cooking spray.
2. In a medium bowl, toss the cauliflower florets with the smoked paprika and garlic powder until evenly coated. Sprinkle with salt and pepper.
3. Place the cauliflower florets in the basket and lightly mist with cooking spray.
4. Put the air fryer basket on the baking pan and slide into Rack Position 2, select Air Fry, set temperature to 400ºF (205ºC), and set time to 20 minutes.
5. Stir the cauliflower four times during cooking.
6. Remove the cauliflower from the oven and serve hot.

397.Mediterranean Baked Eggs With Spinach

Servings:2
Cooking Time: 10 Minutes
Ingredients:
- 2 tablespoons olive oil
- 4 eggs, whisked
- 5 ounces (142 g) fresh spinach, chopped
- 1 medium-sized tomato, chopped
- 1 teaspoon fresh lemon juice

- ½ teaspoon ground black pepper
- ½ teaspoon coarse salt
- ½ cup roughly chopped fresh basil leaves, for garnish

Directions:
1. Generously grease the baking pan with olive oil.
2. Stir together the remaining ingredients except the basil leaves in the greased baking pan until well incorporated.
3. Slide the baking pan into Rack Position 1, select Convection Bake, set temperature to 280ºF (137ºC), and set time to 10 minutes.
4. When cooking is complete, the eggs should be completely set and the vegetables should be tender. Remove from the oven and serve garnished with the fresh basil leaves.

398.Sesame-thyme Whole Maitake Mushrooms

Servings:2
Cooking Time: 15 Minutes
Ingredients:
- 1 tablespoon soy sauce
- 2 teaspoons toasted sesame oil
- 3 teaspoons vegetable oil, divided
- 1 garlic clove, minced
- 7 ounces (198 g) maitake (hen of the woods) mushrooms
- ½ teaspoon flaky sea salt
- ½ teaspoon sesame seeds
- ½ teaspoon finely chopped fresh thyme leaves

Directions:
1. Whisk together the soy sauce, sesame oil, 1 teaspoon of vegetable oil, and garlic in a small bowl.
2. Arrange the mushrooms in the air fryer basket in a single layer. Drizzle the soy sauce mixture over the mushrooms.
3. Put the air fryer basket on the baking pan and slide into Rack Position 2, select Roast, set temperature to 300ºF (150ºC), and set time to 15 minutes.
4. After 10 minutes, remove from the oven. Flip the mushrooms and sprinkle the sea

salt, sesame seeds, and thyme leaves on top. Drizzle the remaining 2 teaspoons of vegetable oil all over. Return to the oven and continue roasting for an additional 5 minutes.
5. When cooking is complete, remove the mushrooms from the oven to a plate and serve hot.

399.Honey Chili Potatoes

Servings:x
Cooking Time:x
Ingredients:
- 1 capsicum, cut into thin and long pieces (lengthwise).
- 2 tbsp. olive oil
- 2 onions. Cut them into halves.
- 1 ½ tbsp. sweet chili sauce
- 1 ½ tsp. ginger garlic paste
- ½ tbsp. red chili sauce.
- 2 tbsp. tomato ketchup
- 3 big potatoes (Cut into strips or cubes)
- 2 ½ tsp. ginger-garlic paste
- ¼ tsp. salt
- 1 tsp. red chili sauce
- ¼ tsp. red chili powder/black pepper
- A few drops of edible orange food coloring
- 2 tsp. soya sauce
- 2 tsp. vinegar
- A pinch of black pepper powder
- 1-2 tsp. red chili flakes

Directions:
1. Create the mix for the potato Oregano Fingers and coat the chicken well with it.
2. Pre heat the oven at 250 Fahrenheit for 5 minutes or so. Open the basket of the Fryer. Place the Oregano Fingers inside the basket. Now let the fryer stay at 290 Fahrenheit for another 20 minutes. Keep tossing the Oregano Fingers periodically through the cook to get a uniform cook.
3. Add the ingredients to the sauce and cook it with the vegetables till it thickens. Add the Oregano Fingers to the sauce and cook till the flavors have blended.

SNACKS AND DESSERTS RECIPES

400.Walnut Carrot Cake

Servings: 4
Cooking Time: 25 Minutes
Ingredients:
- 1 egg
- 1/2 cup sugar
- 1/4 cup canola oil
- 1/4 cup walnuts, chopped
- 1/2 tsp baking powder
- 1/2 cup flour
- 1/4 cup grated carrot
- 1/2 tsp vanilla
- 1/2 tsp cinnamon

Directions:
1. Fit the oven with the rack in position
2. In a medium bowl, beat sugar and oil for 1 minute. Add vanilla, cinnamon, and egg and beat for 30 seconds.
3. Add remaining ingredients and stir everything well until just combined.
4. Pour batter into the greased baking dish.
5. Set to bake at 350 F for 30 minutes. After 5 minutes place the baking dish in the preheated oven.
6. Serve and enjoy.
- **Nutrition Info:** Calories: 340 Fat 20 g Carbohydrates 40 g Sugar 25 g Protein 5 g Cholesterol 41 mg

401.Honey And Oats Cookie

Servings:x
Cooking Time:x
Ingredients:
- ½ cup milk
- 1 tbsp. unsalted butter
- 2 tsp. honey
- 1 cup all-purpose flour
- 1 cups flour
- ½ cup oats
- 1 tsp. baking powder
- 1 tbsp. liquid glucose
- 2 tbsp. powdered sugar

Directions:
1. Mix the dry ingredients together in a large bowl and warm the glucose with a little water. Mix the glucose, honey and the butter to the bowl followed by the milk. You will need to roll the dough using a pin. Now, create cookies and set them on a prepared baking tray.
2. Preheat the fryer to 300 Fahrenheit for five minutes. Place the baking tray in the basket and reduce the temperature to 250 Fahrenheit. Turn the cookies in the tray to ensure that they are cooked uniformly. When the cookies have cooled, store them in an airtight container.

402.Strawberry Cobbler

Servings: 6
Cooking Time: 45 Minutes
Ingredients:
- 2 cups strawberries, diced
- 1 cup milk
- 1 cup self-rising flour
- 1 1/4 cup sugar
- 1 tsp vanilla
- 1/2 cup butter, melted

Directions:
1. Fit the oven with the rack in position
2. In a bowl, mix together flour and 1 cup sugar.
3. Add milk and whisk until smooth.
4. Add vanilla and butter and mix well.
5. Pour mixture into the greased baking dish and sprinkle with strawberries and top with remaining sugar.
6. Set to bake at 350 F for 50 minutes. After 5 minutes place the baking dish in the preheated oven.
7. Serve and enjoy.
- **Nutrition Info:** Calories: 405 Fat 16.5 g Carbohydrates 63.4 g Sugar 46 g Protein 4 g Cholesterol 44 mg

403.Fried Bananas With Chocolate Sauce

Servings: 2
Cooking Time: 10 Minutes
Ingredients:
- 1 large egg
- ¼ cup cornstarch
- ¼ cup plain bread crumbs
- 3 bananas, halved crosswise
- Cooking oil
- Chocolate sauce (see Ingredient tip)

Directions:
1. Preparing the Ingredients. In a small bowl, beat the egg. In another bowl, place the cornstarch. Place the bread crumbs in a third bowl. Dip the bananas in the cornstarch, then the egg, and then the bread crumbs.
2. Spray the air fryer rack/basket with cooking oil. Place the bananas in the basket and spray them with cooking oil.
3. Air Frying. Cook for 5 minutes. Open the air fryer oven and flip the bananas. Cook for an additional 2 minutes. Transfer the bananas to plates.
4. Drizzle the chocolate sauce over the bananas, and serve.
5. You can make your own chocolate sauce using 2 tablespoons milk and ¼ cup chocolate chips. Heat a saucepan over medium-high heat. Add the milk and stir for

1 to 2 minutes. Add the chocolate chips. Stir for 2 minutes, or until the chocolate has melted.

- **Nutrition Info:** CALORIES: 203; FAT:6G; PROTEIN:3G; FIBER:3G

404.Stuffed Mushrooms With Sour Cream

Servings: 12
Cooking Time: 8 Minutes
Ingredients:

- ¼ orange bell pepper, diced
- ¾ cup Cheddar cheese, shredded
- 12 mushrooms caps, stems diced
- ½ onion, diced
- ½ small carrot, diced
- ¼ cup sour cream

Directions:

1. Preheat the Air fryer to 350 degree F and grease a baking tray.
2. Place mushroom stems, onion, orange bell pepper and carrot over medium heat in a skillet.
3. Cook for about 5 minutes until softened and stir in ½ cup Cheddar cheese and sour cream.
4. Stuff this mixture in the mushroom caps and arrange them on the baking tray.
5. Top with rest of the cheese and place the baking tray in the Air fryer basket.
6. Cook for about 8 minutes until cheese is melted and serve warm.

- **Nutrition Info:** Calories: 43, Fat: 3.1g, Carbohydrates: 1.7g, Sugar: 1g, Protein: 2.4g, Sodium: 55mg

405.Easy Mocha Cake

Servings:2
Cooking Time: 30 Minutes
Ingredients:

- ¼ cup butter
- ½ tsp instant coffee
- 1 tbsp black coffee, brewed
- 1 egg
- ¼ cup sugar
- ¼ cup flour
- 1 tsp cocoa powder
- Powdered sugar for icing

Directions:

1. Preheat on Bake function to 330 F. Beat the sugar and egg together in a bowl. Beat in cocoa, instant and black coffees; stir in flour. Transfer the batter to a greased cake pan and press Start. Bake for 15 minutes. Dust with powdered sugar and serve.

406.Delicious Jalapeno Poppers

Servings: 10
Cooking Time: 7 Minutes
Ingredients:

- 10 jalapeno peppers, cut in half, remove seeds & membranes
- 1/2 cup cheddar cheese, shredded
- 4 oz cream cheese
- 1/4 tsp paprika
- 1 tsp ground cumin
- 1 tsp salt

Directions:

1. Fit the oven with the rack in position 2.
2. In a small bowl, mix together cream cheese, cheddar cheese, cumin, paprika, and salt.
3. Stuff cream cheese mixture into each jalapeno half.
4. Place stuffed jalapeno peppers in air fryer basket then place air fryer basket in baking pan.
5. Place a baking pan on the oven rack. Set to air fry at 350 F for 7 minutes.
6. Serve and enjoy.

- **Nutrition Info:** Calories: 69 Fat 6.1 g Carbohydrates 1.5 g Sugar 0.5 g Protein 2.5 g Cholesterol 18 mg

407.Blueberry Cakes

Servings:x
Cooking Time:x
Ingredients:

- 1 cup sugar
- 3 tsp. vinegar
- 2 cups blueberries
- ½ tsp. vanilla essence
- 2 cups All-purpose flour
- 1 ½ cup milk
- ½ tsp. baking powder
- ½ tsp. baking soda
- 2 tbsp. butter
- Muffin cups or butter paper cups.

Directions:

1. Mix the ingredients together and use your Oregano Fingers to get a crumbly mixture.
2. Add the baking soda and the vinegar to the milk and mix continuously. Add this milk to the mixture and create a batter that you will need to transfer to the muffin cups.
3. Preheat the fryer to 300 Fahrenheit for five minutes. You will need to place the muffin cups in the basket and cover it. Cook the muffins for fifteen minutes and check whether or not the muffins are cooked using a toothpick.
4. Remove the cups and serve hot.

408.Mozzarella And Tomato Salad

Servings: 6
Cooking Time: 15 Minutes
Ingredients:

- 1 lb. tomatoes; sliced
- 1 cup mozzarella; shredded
- 1 tbsp. ginger; grated

- 1 tbsp. balsamic vinegar
- 1 tsp. sweet paprika
- 1 tsp. chili powder
- ½ tsp. coriander, ground

Directions:
1. In a pan that fits your air fryer, mix all the ingredients except the mozzarella, toss, introduce the pan in the air fryer and cook at 360°F for 12 minutes
2. Divide into bowls and serve cold as an appetizer with the mozzarella sprinkled all over.
- **Nutrition Info:** Calories: 185; Fat: 8g; Fiber: 2g; Carbs: 4g; Protein: 8g

409.Italian Pork Skewers

Servings:x
Cooking Time:x
Ingredients:
- ¼ cup finely minced onion
- 1 teaspoon dried Italian seasoning
- ½ teaspoon salt
- teaspoon pepper
- 2 pounds pork tenderloin
- ¼ cup balsamic vinegar
- ¼ cup olive oil

Directions:
1. Trim excess fat from tenderloin. Cut pork, on a slant, into ¼-inch-thick slices, each about 4 inches long. In large bowl, combine remaining ingredients and mix well with wire whisk. Add tenderloin slices and mix gently to coat. Cover and refrigerate for 2 to 3 hours. Meanwhile, soak 8-inch wooden skewers in cold water.
2. Remove pork from marinade and thread onto soaked skewers. Flash freeze on baking sheet in single layer. When frozen solid, pack skewers in rigid containers, with layers separated by waxed paper. Label skewers and freeze.
3. To thaw and reheat: Thaw overnight in refrigerator. Cook skewers 4 to 6 inches from medium coals on grill, or broil 4 to 6 inches from heat source, for about 4 to 6 minutes or until cooked (160ºF on an instant-read thermometer), turning once.

410.Easy Blueberry Muffins

Servings: 12
Cooking Time: 30 Minutes
Ingredients:
- 5.5 oz plain yogurt
- ½ cup fresh blueberries
- 2 tsp baking powder, gluten-free
- ¼ cup Swerve
- 2 ½ cups almond flour
- ½ tsp vanilla
- 3 eggs
- Pinch of salt

Directions:
1. Fit the oven with the rack in position
2. Line 6-cups muffin tin with cupcake liners and set aside.
3. In a bowl, whisk egg, yogurt, vanilla, and salt until smooth.
4. Add flour, swerve and baking powder and blend again until smooth.
5. Add blueberries and stir well.
6. Pour batter into the prepared muffin tin.
7. Set to bake at 325 F for 35 minutes. After 5 minutes place muffin tin in the preheated oven.
8. Serve and enjoy.
- **Nutrition Info:** Calories: 63 Fat 4.2 g Carbohydrates 3.6 g Sugar 1.8 g Protein 3.4 g Cholesterol 42 mg

411.Easy Egg Custard

Servings: 6
Cooking Time: 40 Minutes
Ingredients:
- 2 egg yolks
- 1 tsp nutmeg
- 1/2 cup erythritol
- 2 cups heavy whipping cream
- 3 eggs
- 1/2 tsp vanilla

Directions:
1. Fit the oven with the rack in position
2. Add all ingredients into the large mixing bowl and beat until just well combined.
3. Pour custard mixture into the greased pie dish.
4. Set to bake at 350 F for 40 minutes. After 5 minutes place the pie dish in the preheated oven.
5. Serve.
- **Nutrition Info:** Calories: 190 Fat 18.6 g Carbohydrates 1.7 g Sugar 0.4 g Protein 4.5 g Cholesterol 207 mg

412.Coffee Flavored Doughnuts

Servings: 6
Cooking Time: 6 Minutes
Ingredients:
- Coconut sugar, ¼ cup
- White all-purpose flour, 1 cup
- Baking powder, 1 tsp.
- Salt, ½ tsp.
- Sunflower oil, 1 tbsp.
- Coffee, ¼ cup
- Aquafaba, 2 tbsps.

Directions:
1. Combine the sugar, flour, baking powder, salt in a mixing bowl.
2. In another bowl, combine the aquafaba, sunflower oil, and coffee.

3. Mix to form a dough.
4. Let the dough rest inside the fridge.
5. Preheat the air fryer to 4000 F.
6. Knead the dough and create doughnuts.
7. Arrange inside the air fryer in single layer and cook for 6 minutes.
8. Do not shake so that the donut maintains its shape.
- **Nutrition Info:** Calories: 113 Protein: 2.16g Fat: 2.54g Carbs: 20.45g

413.Almond Cranberry Muffins

Servings: 6
Cooking Time: 30 Minutes
Ingredients:
- 2 eggs
- 1 tsp vanilla
- 1/4 cup sour cream
- 1/2 cup cranberries
- 1 1/2 cups almond flour
- 1/4 tsp cinnamon
- 1 tsp baking powder
- 1/4 cup Swerve
- Pinch of salt

Directions:
1. Fit the oven with the rack in position
2. Line 6-cups muffin tin with cupcake liners and set aside.
3. In a bowl, beat sour cream, vanilla, and eggs.
4. Add remaining ingredients except for cranberries and beat until smooth.
5. Add cranberries and fold well.
6. Pour batter into the prepared muffin tin.
7. Set to bake at 325 F for 30 minutes. After 5 minutes place muffin tin in the preheated oven.
8. Serve and enjoy.
- **Nutrition Info:** Calories: 218 Fat 16 g Carbohydrates 18 g Sugar 10 g Protein 8 g Cholesterol 59 mg

414.Coconut Broccoli Pop-corn

Servings: 4
Cooking Time: 6 Minutes
Ingredients:
- 2 cups broccoli florets
- 4 eggs yolks
- 2 cups coconut flour
- 1/4 cup butter, melted
- Pepper
- Salt

Directions:
1. Fit the oven with the rack in position 2.
2. In a bowl whisk egg yolks with melted butter, pepper, and salt. Add coconut flour and stir to combine.
3. Coat each broccoli floret with egg mixture and place in the air fryer basket then place an air fryer basket in the baking pan.

4. Place a baking pan on the oven rack. Set to air fry at 400 F for 6 minutes.
5. Serve and enjoy.
- **Nutrition Info:** Calories: 201 Fat 17.2 g Carbohydrates 7.7 g Sugar 1.4 g Protein 5.1 g Cholesterol 240 mg

415.Crunchy Parmesan And Garlic Zucchini

Servings:x
Cooking Time:x
Ingredients:
- 1 cup panko crumbs, seasoned with salt, pepper and paprika
- 1 cup freshly grated parmesan
- 3 Tbsp olive oil
- 4-6 small green zucchini, sliced into spears by cutting into ½
- lengthwise and then into thirds
- Coarse salt and pepper, to taste
- 4 garlic cloves, sliced thin

Directions:
1. Preheat oven to 450°F.
2. Heat oil in a large oven on medium-low heat.
3. Add zucchini and let brown on one side for 3 minutes and flip over pieces. Cook for another 3 minutes.
4. Sprinkle with salt and pepper.
5. Add sliced garlic and saute for 1 minute.
6. Sprinkle panko crumbs and grated cheese on top.
7. Transfer to oven until brown and bubbly, about 5-10 minutes.

416.Saffron Pudding

Servings:x
Cooking Time:x
Ingredients:
- 3 tbsp. powdered sugar
- 3 tbsp. unsalted butter
- 2 cups milk
- 2 tbsp. saffron
- 2 cups almond flour
- 2 tbsp. custard powder

Directions:
1. Boil the milk and the sugar in a pan and add the custard powder followed by the almond flour and stir till you get a thick mixture. Mix the saffron into the mixture and stir till the color has spread well.
2. Preheat the fryer to 300 Fahrenheit for five minutes. Place the dish in the basket and reduce the temperature to 250 Fahrenheit. Cook for ten minutes and set aside to cool.

417.Nutty Parmesan Homemade Fried Sticks

Servings:x

Cooking Time:x
Ingredients:
- ½ cup grated Parmesan cheese
- Teas
- 1 package frozen puff pastry sheets, thawed
- ½ cup ground almonds

Directions:
1. Preheat oven to 375ºF. In a small bowl, combine almonds, cheese, and pepper; blend well. Sprinkle half of this mixture over work surface and cover with one sheet puff pastry. Using a rolling pin, gently press pastry into cheese mixture. Turn pastry over and press cheese mixture into other side of pastry. Repeat with other half of cheese mixture and second sheet of puff pastry.
2. Using pastry cutter or sharp knife, cut pastry into ½-inch strips. Place on parchment paper- or foil-lined baking sheets, twisting each strip several times. Bake at 375ºF for 10 to 15 minutes or until browned and crisp, being careful not to burn sticks. Remove from baking sheet and cool completely on wire racks. Pack carefully into rigid containers, separating layers with waxed paper. Label containers and freeze.
3. To thaw and reheat: Thaw sticks at room temperature and serve, or carefully place frozen sticks on baking sheet and bake at 350ºF for 4 to 5 minutes or until hotpot cayenne pepper

418.Artichoke Cashews Spinach Dip

Servings: 10
Cooking Time: 20 Minutes
Ingredients:
- 28 oz can artichokes, drained and rinsed
- 1 small onion, diced
- 4 garlic cloves
- 1 1/2 cups cashews
- 1 tsp olive oil
- 4 cups fresh spinach
- 2 tbsp fresh lemon juice
- 1/4 cup nutritional yeast
- 1 1/2 cups milk
- 1 1/2 tsp salt

Directions:
1. Fit the oven with the rack in position 2.
2. Soak cashews in boiling water for 5 minutes. Drain well.
3. Heat oil in a pan over medium heat. Add onion and garlic and sauté for 2-3 minutes.
4. Remove pan from heat and set aside.
5. Add soaked cashews, milk, nutritional yeast, lemon juice, and salt into the blender and blend until smooth.

6. Add sautéed garlic onion, artichokes, and spinach and blend for few minutes until getting chunky texture.
7. Transfer blended mixture into the baking dish.
8. Set to bake at 425 F for 25 minutes. After 5 minutes place the baking dish in the preheated oven.
9. Serve and enjoy.
- **Nutrition Info:** Calories: 205 Fat 11.3 g Carbohydrates 21.4 g Sugar 3.9 g Protein 9 g Cholesterol 3 mg

419.Vanilla Brownie Squares

Servings: 2
Cooking Time: 25 Minutes
Ingredients:
- 1 whole egg, beaten
- ¼ cup chocolate chips
- 2 tbsp white sugar
- ⅓ cup flour
- 2 tbsp safflower oil
- 1 tsp vanilla
- ¼ cup cocoa powder

Directions:
1. Preheat on Bake function to 360 F. In a bowl, mix the egg, sugar, olive oil, and vanilla. In another bowl, mix cocoa powder and flour. Add the flour mixture to the vanilla mixture and stir until fully incorporated.
2. Pour the mixture into a greased baking pan and sprinkle chocolate chips on top. Cook for 20 minutes. Chill and cut into squares to serve.

420.Baked Cream

Servings:x
Cooking Time:x
Ingredients:
- 1 cup fresh blueberries
- 1 cup blackberries
- Handful of mint leaves
- 3 tsp. sugar
- 2 cups condensed milk
- 2 cups fresh cream
- 1 cup fresh strawberries
- 4 tsp. water

Directions:
1. Blend the cream and add the milk to it. Whisk the ingredients well together and transfer this mixture into small baking bowls ensuring you do not overfill the bowls.
2. Preheat the fryer to 300 Fahrenheit for five minutes. You will need to place the bowls in the basket and cover it. Cook it for fifteen minutes. When you shake the bowls, the mixture should just shake but not break.

Leave it in the refrigerator to set and then arrange the fruits, garnish and serve.

421.Air Fryer Cinnamon Rolls

Servings: 8
Cooking Time: 5 Minutes
Ingredients:
- 1 ½ tbsp. cinnamon
- ¾ C. brown sugar
- ¼ C. melted coconut oil
- 1 pound frozen bread dough, thawed
- Glaze:
- ½ tsp. vanilla
- 1 ¼ C. powdered erythritol
- 2 tbsp. softened ghee
- 3 ounces softened cream cheese

Directions:
1. Preparing the Ingredients. Lay out bread dough and roll out into a rectangle. Brush melted ghee over dough and leave a 1-inch border along edges.
2. Mix cinnamon and sweetener together and then sprinkle over the dough.
3. Roll dough tightly and slice into 8 pieces. Let sit 1-2 hours to rise.
4. To make the glaze, simply mix ingredients together till smooth.
5. Air Frying. Once rolls rise, place into the air fryer oven and cook 5 minutes at 350 degrees.
6. Serve rolls drizzled in cream cheese glaze. Enjoy!
- **Nutrition Info:** CALORIES: 390; FAT:8G; PROTEIN:1G; SUGAR:7G

422.Chocolate Pudding

Servings: 6
Cooking Time: 20 Minutes
Ingredients:
- 24 ounces cream cheese, soft
- 2 tablespoons almond meal
- ¼ cup erythritol
- 3 eggs, whisked
- 1 tablespoon vanilla extract
- ½ cup heavy cream
- 12 ounces dark chocolate, melted

Directions:
1. In a bowl mix all the ingredients and whisk well.
2. Divide this into 6 ramekins, put them in your air fryer and cook at 320 degrees F for 20 minutes.
3. Keep in the fridge for 1 hour before serving.
- **Nutrition Info:** calories 200, fat 7, fiber 2, carbs 4, protein 6

423.Fruity Oreo Muffins

Servings: 6
Cooking Time: 10 Minutes

Ingredients:
- 1 cup milk
- 1 pack Oreo biscuits, crushed
- ¾ teaspoon baking powder
- 1 banana, peeled and chopped
- 1 apple, peeled, cored and chopped
- 1 teaspoon cocoa powder
- 1 teaspoon honey
- 1 teaspoon fresh lemon juice
- A pinch of ground cinnamon

Directions:
1. Preheat the Air fryer to 320 degree F and grease 6 muffin cups lightly.
2. Mix milk, biscuits, cocoa powder, baking soda, and baking powder in a bowl until well combined.
3. Transfer the mixture into the muffin cups and cook for about 10 minutes.
4. Remove from the Air fryer and invert the muffin cups onto a wire rack to cool.
5. Meanwhile, mix the banana, apple, honey, lemon juice, and cinnamon in another bowl.
6. Scoop some portion of muffins from the center and fill with fruit mixture to serve.
- **Nutrition Info:** Calories: 182, Fat: 3.1g, Carbohydrates: 31.4g, Sugar: 19.5g, Protein: 3.1g, Sodium: 196mg

424.Delicious Raspberry Cobbler

Servings: 6
Cooking Time: 10 Minutes
Ingredients:
- 1 egg, lightly beaten
- 1 cup raspberries, sliced
- 2 tsp swerve
- 1/2 tsp vanilla
- 1 tbsp butter, melted
- 1 cup almond flour

Directions:
1. Fit the oven with the rack in position
2. Add raspberries into the baking dish.
3. Sprinkle sweetener over raspberries.
4. Mix together almond flour, vanilla, and butter in the bowl.
5. Add egg in almond flour mixture and stir well to combine.
6. Spread almond flour mixture over sliced raspberries.
7. Set to bake at 350 F for 15 minutes. After 5 minutes place the baking dish in the preheated oven.
8. Serve and enjoy.
- **Nutrition Info:** Calories: 66 Fat 5 g Carbohydrates 3 g Sugar 1 g Protein 2 g Cholesterol 32 mg

425.Hot Coconut 'n Cocoa Buns

Servings: 8
Cooking Time: 15 Minutes

Ingredients:
- Eggs, 4.
- Coconut flour, 1/3 cup
- Cacao powder, 3 tbsps.
- Coconut milk, 1 cup
- Cacao nibs, ¼ cup

Directions:
1. Preheat the air fryer for 5 minutes.
2. Combine all ingredients in a mixing bowl.
3. Form buns using your hands and place in a baking dish that will fit in the air fryer.
4. Bake for 15 minutes for 375 °F.
5. Once air fryer turns off, leave the buns in the air fryer until it cools completely.
- **Nutrition Info:** Calories: 161 Carbs: 4g Protein: 5.7g Fat: 13.6g

426.Fruit Medley

Servings:x
Cooking Time:x
Ingredients:
- 2 large peaches or nectarines, cut into wedges
- 12 strawberries, quartered
- 12 large plums
- 6 apricots
- 2 tsp fresh lime juice
- 2 Tbsp chopped mint
- Cooking spray
- 2 Tbsp avocado oil
- 1½ Tbsp sugar
- ¼ tsp sea salt
- 1 cup blueberries

Directions:
1. Heat oven over medium-high heat. Spray with cooking spray.
2. Dab a small amount of oil onto fruit. Sprinkle on sugar and sea salt.
3. Place peach wedges, plums and apricots into oven, working in batches. Cook for 1-2 minutes on each side, until slightly charred and softened.
4. Place fruit on a serving plate and sprinkle with lime juice, chopped mint and blueberries.

427.Chocolate Ramekins

Servings: 4
Cooking Time: 12 Minutes
Ingredients:
- ½ cup butter
- 2/3 cup dark chocolate, chopped
- ¼ cup caster sugar
- 2 medium eggs
- 2 teaspoons fresh orange rind, finely grated
- ¼ cup fresh orange juice
- 2 tablespoons self-rising flour

Directions:

1. In a microwave-safe bowl, add the butter, and chocolate and microwave on high heat for about 2 minutes or until melted completely, stirring after every 30 seconds.
2. Remove from microwave and stir the mixture until smooth.
3. Add the sugar, and eggs and whisk until frothy.
4. Add the orange rind and juice, followed by flour and mix until well combined.
5. Divide mixture into 4 greased ramekins about ¾ full.
6. Press "Power Button" of Air Fry Oven and turn the dial to select the "Air Fry" mode.
7. Press the Time button and again turn the dial to set the cooking time to 12 minutes.
8. Now push the Temp button and rotate the dial to set the temperature at 355 degrees F.
9. Press "Start/Pause" button to start.
10. When the unit beeps to show that it is preheated, open the lid.
11. Arrange the ramekins in "Air Fry Basket" and insert in the oven.
12. Place the ramekins set aside to cool completely before serving.
- **Nutrition Info:** Calories 454 Total Fat 33.6 g Saturated Fat 21.1 g Cholesterol 149 mg Sodium 217 mg Total Carbs 34.2 g Fiber 1.2 g Sugar 28.4g Protein 5.7 g

428.Tasty Pumpkin Cookies

Servings: 27
Cooking Time: 25 Minutes
Ingredients:
- 1 egg
- 2 cups almond flour
- 1/2 tsp baking powder
- 1 tsp vanilla
- 1/2 cup butter
- 1 tsp liquid stevia
- 1/2 tsp pumpkin pie spice
- 1/2 cup pumpkin puree

Directions:
1. Fit the oven with the rack in position
2. In a large bowl, add all ingredients and mix until well combined.
3. Make cookies from mixture and place onto a parchment-lined baking pan.
4. Set to bake at 300 F for 30 minutes. After 5 minutes place the baking dish in the preheated oven.
5. Serve and enjoy.
- **Nutrition Info:** Calories: 46 Fat 4.6 g Carbohydrates 0.9 g Sugar 0.3 g Protein 0.7 g Cholesterol 15 mg

429.Polenta Fries With Chili-lime Mayo

Servings:4
Cooking Time: 28 Minutes
Ingredients:

- Polenta Fries:
- 2 teaspoons vegetable or olive oil
- ¼ teaspoon paprika
- 1 pound (454 g) prepared polenta, cut into 3-inch × ½-inch strips
- Salt and freshly ground black pepper, to taste
- Chili-Lime Mayo:
- ½ cup mayonnaise
- 1 teaspoon chili powder
- 1 teaspoon chopped fresh cilantro
- ¼ teaspoon ground cumin
- Juice of ½ lime
- Salt and freshly ground black pepper, to taste

Directions:
1. Mix the oil and paprika in a bowl. Add the polenta strips and toss until evenly coated. Transfer the polenta strips to the air fryer basket.
2. Put the air fryer basket on the baking pan and slide into Rack Position 2, select Air Fry, set temperature to 400ºF (205ºC), and set time to 28 minutes.
3. Stir the polenta strips halfway through the cooking time.
4. Meanwhile, whisk together all the ingredients for the chili-lime mayo in a small bowl.
5. When cooking is complete, remove the polenta fries from the oven to a plate. Season as desired with salt and pepper. Serve alongside the chili-lime mayo as a dipping sauce.

430.Habanero Chicken Wings

Servings: 6
Cooking Time: 16 Minutes
Ingredients:
- 1 1/2 lbs chicken wings
- 2 tbsp habanero hot sauce
- 2 garlic cloves, chopped
- 1 tsp pepper
- 1 tsp garlic salt
- 1 tsp cayenne pepper
- 1/2 tbsp soy sauce

Directions:
1. Fit the oven with the rack in position 2.
2. Add chicken wings into the large bowl and toss with remaining ingredients.
3. Transfer chicken wings in air fryer basket then place air fryer basket in baking pan.
4. Place a baking pan on the oven rack. Set to air fry at 360 F for 16 minutes.
5. Serve and enjoy.
- **Nutrition Info:** Calories: 226 Fat 8.5 g Carbohydrates 2.2 g Sugar 0.2 g Protein 33.1 g Cholesterol 101 mg

431.Pita Bread Cheese Pizza

Servings: 4
Cooking Time: 6 Minutes
Ingredients:
- 1 pita bread
- ¼ cup Mozzarella cheese
- 7 slices pepperoni
- ¼ cup sausage
- 1 tablespoon yellow onion, sliced thinly
- 1 tablespoon pizza sauce
- 1 drizzle extra-virgin olive oil
- ½ teaspoon fresh garlic, minced

Directions:
1. Preheat the Air fryer to 350 degree F and grease an Air fryer basket.
2. Spread pizza sauce on the pita bread and add sausages, pepperoni, onions, garlic and cheese.
3. Drizzle with olive oil and place it in the Air fryer basket.
4. Cook for about 6 minutes and dish out to serve warm.
- **Nutrition Info:** Calories: 56, Fat: 3.6g, Carbohydrates: 6.7g, Sugar: 3.6g, Protein: 0.3g, Sodium: 0mg

432.Lemon-butter Shortbread

Servings: 4 Dozen Cookies
Cooking Time: 36 To 40 Minutes
Ingredients:
- 1 tablespoon grated lemon zest
- 1 cup granulated sugar
- 1 pound (454 g) unsalted butter, at room temperature
- ¼ teaspoon fine salt
- 4 cups all-purpose flour
- $1/3$ cup cornstarch
- Cooking spray

Directions:
1. Add the lemon zest and sugar to a stand mixer fitted with the paddle attachment and beat on medium speed for 1 to 2 minute. Let stand for about 5 minutes. Fold in the butter and salt and blend until fluffy.
2. Mix together the flour and cornstarch in a large bowl. Add to the butter mixture and mix to combine.
3. Spritz the baking pan with cooking spray and spread a piece of parchment paper onto the bottom. Scrape the dough into the pan until even and smooth.
4. Slide the baking pan into Rack Position 1, select Convection Bake, set temperature to 325ºF (160ºC), and set time to 36 minutes.
5. After 20 minutes, check the shortbread. Continue cooking for another 16 minutes until lightly browned.

6. When done, remove from the oven. Slice and allow to cool for 5 minutes before serving.

433.Shrimp Cheese Quiches

Servings:x
Cooking Time:x
Ingredients:
- 1 (6-ounce) can tiny shrimp, drained
- ½ teaspoon dried marjoram leaves
- ½ teaspoon salt
- ½ teaspoon pepper
- ¾ cup shredded Havarti cheese
- 2 9-inch Pie Crusts
- ½ cup chopped leek, rinsed
- 1 tablespoon olive oil
- 2 eggs
- ½ cup cream

Directions:
1. Using a 2-inch cookie cutter, cut 36 rounds from pie crusts. Place each in a 1¾-inch mini muffin cup, pressing to bottom and sides. Set aside.
2. Sauté leek in olive oil until tender. Beat eggs with cream in medium bowl. Add drained shrimp, cooked leek, marjoram, salt, and pepper, and mix well.
3. Sprinkle 1 teaspoon cheese into each muffin cup and fill cups with shrimp mixture. Bake at 375ºF for 15 to 18 minutes or until pastry is golden and filling is set. Cool in refrigerator until cold, then freeze.
4. Freeze in single layer on baking sheet. When frozen solid, pack in rigid containers, using waxed paper to separate layers. Label and freeze.
5. To reheat: Place frozen quiches on baking sheet and bake at 375ºF for 8 to 11 minutes or until hot.

434.Cherry Apple Risotto

Servings: 4
Cooking Time: 12 Minutes
Ingredients:
- 1 tablespoon of butter
- ¼ cup of brown sugar
- ½ cup of apple juice
- 1½ cups of milk
- ¾ cup of Arborio rice, boiled
- 1 apple, diced
- 2 pinches salt
- ¾ teaspoon of cinnamon powder
- ¼ cup of dried cherries
- 1½ tablespoons of almonds, roasted and sliced
- ¼ cup of whipped cream

Directions:
1. Set the Instant Vortex on Air fryer to 375 degrees F for 12 minutes. Combine rice with butter, sugar, apple juice, milk, apple, salt, and cinnamon in a bowl. Pour the rice mixture into the cooking tray. Insert the cooking tray in the Vortex when it displays "Add Food". Toss the food when it displays "Turn Food". Remove from the oven when cooking time is complete. Top with the dried cherries, almonds, and whipped cream to serve.
- **Nutrition Info:** Calories: 317 Cal Total Fat: 8.5 g Saturated Fat: 0 g Cholesterol: 0 mg Sodium: 0 mg Total Carbs: 54.8 g Fiber: 0 g Sugar: 0 g Protein: 6.2 g

435.Strawberry Shortcake Quickie

Servings: 4
Cooking Time: 25 Minutes
Ingredients:
- Almond flour, 2/3 cup
- Eggs, 3
- Liquid stevia, ¼ tsp.
- Salt, ¼ tsp.
- Butter, ½ cup
- Baking powder, ½ tsp.
- Halved strawberries, 1 cup
- Vanilla extract, 1 tsp.
- Erythritol, 1/3 cup

Directions:
1. Preheat the air fryer for 5 minutes.
2. Mix all ingredients in a bowl with the exception of the strawberries.
3. Use a hand mixer to mix everything.
4. Pour into greased mugs.
5. Top with sliced strawberries
6. Place the mugs in the fryer basket.
7. Bake for 25 minutes at 350 °F.
8. Chill in the refrigerator before serving.
- **Nutrition Info:** Calories:: 265 Carbs: 3.7g Protein: 2.5 g Fat: 26.7g

436.Rustic Blackberry Galette

Servings:x
Cooking Time:x
Ingredients:
- Pinch of salt
- ¼ tsp cinnamon
- 1 tsp vanilla extract
- 1 package store-bought puff pastry, thawed
- 1 egg white, slightly beaten
- 2 lbs. fresh blackberries, rinsed and dried
- ¾ cup granulated sugar
- 2 Tbsp fresh lime juice
- 2 tsp chopped fresh basil
- 1 tsp chopped fresh mint

Directions:
1. Preheat oven to 375°F.
2. Roll out puff pastry and place in greased oven. Allow pastry to hang over the sides slightly.

3. Toss together blackberries, sugar, lime juice, basil, mint, salt, cinnamon and vanilla extract.
4. Spread fruit mixture inside pastry dough in oven.
5. Fold pastry over the berries to cover edges and about ½ way up. Brush egg white over pastry.
6. Place the pot in oven and bake about 40 minutes, until pastry browns.

437.Tiny Filled Puffs

Servings:x
Cooking Time:x
Ingredients:
- 3 eggs
- ½ cup grated Parmesan cheese
- 1 tablespoon dried chives
- 1 cup water
- ½ cup butter
- ½ teaspoon salt
- 1 cup flour

Directions:
1. Preheat oven to 375ºF. Line baking sheet with parchment paper and set aside. In heavy saucepan, combine water and butter. Bring to a rolling boil that cannot be stirred down. Add salt and flour all at once. Cook and stir over medium heat until dough forms a ball and cleans sides of pan. Remove from heat and beat in eggs, one at a time, until well combined. Stir in cheese and chives.
2. Drop dough by teaspoons onto prepared baking sheet. Bake at 375ºF for 18 to 22 minutes or until dough is puffed, golden brown, and firm. Remove from baking sheet and cool on wire rack.
3. Flash freeze puffs in single layer on baking sheet. Then carefully pack into rigid containers. Label puffs and freeze.
4. To reheat: Place frozen puffs on baking sheet. Bake in preheated 400ºF oven for 5 to 8 minutes, until hot. Let cool slightly, then cut puffs in half and fill with desired filling.

438.Banana Butter Brownie

Servings: 4
Cooking Time: 16 Minutes
Ingredients:
- 1 scoop protein powder
- 2 tbsp cocoa powder
- 1 cup bananas, overripe
- 1/2 cup almond butter, melted

Directions:
1. Fit the oven with the rack in position
2. Add all ingredients into the blender and blend until smooth.

3. Pour batter into the greased cake pan.
4. Set to bake at 325 F for 21 minutes. After 5 minutes place the cake pan in the preheated oven.
5. Serve and enjoy.
- **Nutrition Info:** Calories: 83 Fat 2 g Carbohydrates 10 g Sugar 5 g Protein 7 g Cholesterol 16 mg

439.Air Fried Banana With Sesame Seeds

Servings:5
Cooking Time: 15 Minutes
Ingredients:
- 1 ½ cups flour
- 5 bananas, sliced
- 1 tsp salt
- 3 tbsp sesame seeds
- 1 cup water
- 2 eggs, beaten
- 1 tsp baking powder
- ½ tbsp sugar

Directions:
1. Preheat on Bake function to 340 F. In a bowl, mix salt, sesame seeds, flour, baking powder, eggs, sugar, and water. Coat sliced bananas with the flour mixture and place the prepared slices in the basket. Press Start. Bake cook for 8-10 minutes. Serve chilled.

440.Blueberry Apple Crumble

Servings: 6
Cooking Time: 15 Minutes
Ingredients:
- 1 medium apple, finely diced
- 1/2 cup of frozen blueberries strawberries
- 2/3 cup of rice flour
- 2 tablespoons of sugar
- 1/2 teaspoon of ground cinnamon
- 2 tablespoons of nondairy butter

Directions:
1. Set the Instant Vortex on Air fryer to 350 degrees F for 15 minutes. Combine apple with blueberries in a bowl. Mingle butter with flour, cinnamon, and sugar in another bowl. Pour the butter mixture into the apple mixture. Transfer this mixture on the cooking tray. Insert the cooking tray in the Vortex when it displays "Add Food". Flip the sides when it displays "Turn Food". Remove from the oven when cooking time is complete. Serve warm.
- **Nutrition Info:** Calories: 379 Cal Total Fat: 29.7 g Saturated Fat: 0 g Cholesterol: 0 mg Sodium: 0 mg Total Carbs: 23.7 g Fiber: 0 g Sugar: 0 g Protein: 5.2 g

441.Orange Citrus Blend

Servings:x
Cooking Time:x

Ingredients:
- 3 tbsp. powdered sugar
- 3 tbsp. unsalted butter
- 2 oranges (sliced)
- 2 persimmons (sliced)
- 2 cups milk
- 2 cups almond flour
- 2 tbsp. custard powder

Directions:
1. Boil the milk and the sugar in a pan and add the custard powder followed by the almond flour and stir till you get a thick mixture. Add the sliced fruits to the mixture.
2. Preheat the fryer to 300 Fahrenheit for five minutes. Place the dish in the basket and reduce the temperature to 250 Fahrenheit. Cook for ten minutes and set aside to cool.

442.Mushroom And Spinach calzones

Servings:4
Cooking Time: 26 To 27 Minutes
Ingredients:
- 2 tablespoons olive oil
- 1 onion, chopped
- 2 garlic cloves, minced
- ¼ cup chopped mushrooms
- 1 pound (454 g) spinach, chopped
- 1 tablespoon Italian seasoning
- ½ teaspoon oregano
- Salt and black pepper, to taste
- 1½ cups marinara sauce
- 1 cup ricotta cheese, crumbled
- 1 (13-ounce / 369-g) pizza crust
- Cooking spray

Directions:
1. Make the Filling:
2. Heat the olive oil in a pan over medium heat until shimmering.
3. Add the onion, garlic, and mushrooms and sauté for 4 minutes, or until softened.
4. Stir in the spinach and sauté for 2 to 3 minutes, or until the spinach is wilted. Sprinkle with the Italian seasoning, oregano, salt, and pepper and mix well.
5. Add the marinara sauce and cook for about 5 minutes, stirring occasionally, or until the sauce is thickened.
6. Remove the pan from the heat and stir in the ricotta cheese. Set aside.
7. Make the Calzones:
8. Spritz the air fryer basket with cooking spray. Set aside.
9. Roll the pizza crust out with a rolling pin on a lightly floured work surface, then cut it into 4 rectangles.
10. Spoon ¼ of the filling into each rectangle and fold in half. Crimp the edges with a fork to seal. Mist them with cooking spray. Transfer the calzones to the basket.
11. Put the air fryer basket on the baking pan and slide into Rack Position 2, select Air Fry, set temperature to 375ºF (190ºC), and set time to 15 minutes.
12. Flip the calzones halfway through the cooking time.
13. When cooking is complete, the calzones should be golden brown and crisp. Transfer the calzones to a paper towel-lined plate and serve.

443.Baked Almonds

Servings: 6
Cooking Time: 20 Minutes
Ingredients:
- 1 1/2 cups raw almonds
- 1/2 tsp cayenne
- 1/4 tsp onion powder
- 1/4 tsp dried basil
- 2 tbsp butter, melted
- 1/2 tsp garlic powder
- 1/2 tsp cumin
- 1 1/2 tsp chili powder
- 1/2 tsp sea salt

Directions:
1. Fit the oven with the rack in position
2. Add almonds and remaining ingredients into the mixing bowl and toss well.
3. Spread almonds in baking pan.
4. Set to bake at 350 F for 25 minutes. After 5 minutes place the baking pan in the preheated oven.
5. Serve and enjoy.
- **Nutrition Info:** Calories: 176 Fat 15.9 g Carbohydrates 5.9 g Sugar 1.2 g Protein 5.2 g Cholesterol 10 mg

444.Plum Cream(2)

Servings: 4
Cooking Time: 15 Minutes
Ingredients:
- 1 lb. plums, pitted and chopped.
- 1 ½ cups heavy cream
- ¼ cup swerve
- 1 tbsp. lemon juice

Directions:
1. Take a bowl and mix all the ingredients and whisk really well.
2. Divide this into 4 ramekins, put them in the air fryer and cook at 340°F for 20 minutes. Serve cold
- **Nutrition Info:** Calories: 171; Fat: 4g; Fiber: 2g; Carbs: 4g; Protein: 4g

445.Poppy Seed Pound Cake

Servings: 8
Cooking Time: 20 Minutes
Ingredients:
- Large eggs, 2.
- Coconut milk, ½ cup

- Unsalted butter, 1/3 cup
- Vanilla extract, ¼ tsp.
- Psyllium husk powder, 2 tbsps.
- Baking powder, 1 ½ tsps.
- Poppy seeds, 2 tbsps.
- Almond flour, 1 ½ cup

Directions:
1. Preheat the air fryer for 5 minutes.
2. In a mixing bowl, combine all ingredients.
3. Use a hand mixer to mix everything.
4. Pour into a small loaf pan that will fit in the air fryer.
5. Bake for 20 minutes at 3750 F or until a toothpick inserted in the middle comes out clean.
- **Nutrition Info:** Calories: 145 Carbs: 3.6 Protein: 2.1g Fat: 13.6g

446.Easy Ricotta Cake

Servings: 8
Cooking Time: 45 Minutes
Ingredients:
- 2 eggs
- 1/2 cup erythritol
- 1/4 cup coconut flour
- 15 oz ricotta
- Pinch of salt

Directions:
1. Fit the oven with the rack in position
2. In a bowl whisk eggs.
3. Add remaining ingredients and mix until well combined.
4. Transfer batter in greased cake pan.
5. Set to bake at 350 F for 50 minutes. After 5 minutes place the cake pan in the preheated oven.
6. Slice and serve.
- **Nutrition Info:** Calories: 91 Fat 5.4 g Carbohydrates 3.1 g Sugar 0.3 g Protein 7.5 g Cholesterol 57 mg

447.Bacon Cheese Jalapeno Poppers

Servings: 5
Cooking Time: 5 Minutes
Ingredients:
- 10 fresh jalapeno peppers, cut in half and remove seeds
- 1/4 cup cheddar cheese, shredded
- 5 oz cream cheese, softened
- ¼ tsp paprika
- 2 bacon slices, cooked and crumbled

Directions:
1. Fit the oven with the rack in position 2.
2. In a bowl, mix bacon, cream cheese, paprika and cheddar cheese.
3. Stuff cheese mixture into each jalapeno.
4. Place stuffed jalapeno halved in air fryer basket then place air fryer basket in baking pan.
5. Place a baking pan on the oven rack. Set to air fry at 370 F for 5 minutes.
6. Serve and enjoy.

- **Nutrition Info:** Calories: 176 Fat 15.7 g Carbohydrates 3.2 g Sugar 1 g Protein 6.2 g Cholesterol 47 mg

448.Perfectly Puffy Coconut Cookies

Servings: 12
Cooking Time: 15 Minutes
Ingredients:
- 1 cup butter, melted
- 1 ¾ cups granulated swerve
- 3 eggs
- 2 tablespoons coconut milk
- 1 teaspoon coconut extract
- 1 teaspoon vanilla extract
- 1 cup coconut flour
- 1 ¼ cups almond flour
- 1/2 teaspoon baking powder
- 1/2 teaspoon baking soda
- 1/2 teaspoon fine table salt
- 1/2 cups coconut chips, unsweetened

Directions:
1. Begin by preheating your Air Fryer to 350 degrees F.
2. In the bowl of an electric mixer, beat the butter and swerve until well combined. Now, add the eggs one at a time, and mix well; add the coconut milk, coconut extract, and vanilla; beat until creamy and uniform.
3. Mix the flour with baking powder, baking soda, and salt. Then, stir the flour mixture into the butter mixture and stir until everything is well incorporated.
4. Finally, fold in the coconut chips and mix again. Scoop out 1 tablespoon size balls of the batter on a cookie pan, leaving 2 inches between each cookie.
5. Bake for 10 minutes or until golden brown, rotating the pan once or twice through the cooking time. Let your cookies cool on wire racks.
- **Nutrition Info:** 304 Calories; 17g Fat; 32g Carbs; 3g Protein; 16g Sugars; 2g Fiber

449.Walnut Zucchini Bread

Servings: 8
Cooking Time: 20 Minutes
Ingredients:
- 1½ cups all-purpose flour
- ½ teaspoon baking soda
- ½ teaspoon baking powder
- ½ tablespoon ground cinnamon
- ½ teaspoon salt
- 2¼ cups white sugar
- ½ cup vegetable oil
- 1½ eggs
- 1½ teaspoons vanilla extract
- 1 cup zucchini, grated
- ½ cup walnuts, chopped

Directions:
1. In a bowl and mix together the flour, baking powder, baking soda, cinnamon, and salt.

2. In another large bowl, add the sugar, oil, eggs, and vanilla extract and whisk until well combined.
3. Add the flour mixture and mix until just combined.
4. Gently, fold in the zucchini and walnuts.
5. Place the mixture into a lightly greased loaf pan.
6. Press "Power Button" of Air Fry Oven and turn the dial to select the "Air Crisp" mode.
7. Press the Time button and again turn the dial to set the cooking time to 20 minutes.
8. Now push the Temp button and rotate the dial to set the temperature at 320 degrees F.
9. Press "Start/Pause" button to start.
10. When the unit beeps to show that it is preheated, open the lid.
11. Arrange the pan in "Air Fry Basket" and insert in the oven.
12. Place the pan onto a wire rack to cool for about 10 minutes.
13. Carefully, invert the bread onto wire rack to cool completely before slicing.
14. Cut the bread into desired-sized slices and serve.
- **Nutrition Info:** Calories 483 Total Fat 19.3 g Saturated Fat 3.2 g Cholesterol 31mg Sodium 241 mg Total Carbs 76 g Fiber 1.6 g Sugar 56.8 g Protein 5.5 g

450.Coconut Bars

Servings: 12
Cooking Time: 40 Minutes
Ingredients:
- 1 and ¼ cups almond flour
- 1 cup swerve
- 1 cup butter, melted
- ½ cup coconut cream
- 1 and ½ cups coconut, flaked
- 1 egg yolk
- ¾ cup walnuts, chopped
- ½ teaspoon vanilla extract

Directions:
1. In a bowl, mix the flour with half of the swerve and half of the butter, stir well and press this on the bottom of a baking pan that fits the air fryer.
2. Introduce this in the air fryer and cook at 350 degrees F for 15 minutes.
3. Meanwhile, heat up a pan with the rest of the butter over medium heat, add the remaining swerve and the rest of the Ingredients:, whisk, cook for 1-2 minutes, take off the heat and cool down.
4. Spread this well over the crust, put the pan in the air fryer again and cook at 350 degrees F for 25 minutes.
5. Cool down, cut into bars and serve.
- **Nutrition Info:** Calories 182, fat 12, fiber 2, carbs 4, protein 4

451.Radish Chips

Servings: 6

Cooking Time: 18 Minutes
Ingredients:
- Garlic powder
- Avocado oil
- Radish slices, 1 lb.
- Pepper
- Onion powder
- Salt

Directions:
1. Toss the washed radish slices with oil, salt, pepper, onion powder, and garlic powder.
2. Spread these slices in the air fryer basket and return the basket to the fryer.
3. Air fry them for 5 minutes at 370 degrees F then toss them well.
4. Air fry the slices again for 5 more minutes.
5. Adjust seasoning with more spices and cooking oil.
6. Air fry these slices again for 5 minutes then toss them.
7. Cook for another 3 minutes and serve.
- **Nutrition Info:** Calories: 72 Fat: 6.6 g Carbs: 3.6 g Protein: 0.8 g

452.Brownies

Servings:x
Cooking Time:x
Ingredients:
- ½ cup condensed milk
- 1 tbsp. unsalted butter
- 2 tbsp. water
- ½ cup chopped nuts
- 3 tbsp. melted dark chocolate
- 1 cup all-purpose flour

Directions:
1. Add the ingredients together and whisk till you get a smooth mixture.
2. Prepare a tin by greasing it with butter. Transfer the mixture into the tin.
3. Preheat the fryer to 300 Fahrenheit for five minutes. You will need to place the tin in the basket and cover it. Check whether the brownies have been cooked using a knife or a toothpick and remove the tray. When the brownies have cooled, cut them and serve with a dollop of ice cream.

453.Spiced Apple Chips

Servings:4
Cooking Time: 10 Minutes
Ingredients:
- 4 medium apples (any type will work), cored and thinly sliced
- ¼ teaspoon nutmeg
- ¼ teaspoon cinnamon
- Cooking spray

Directions:
1. Place the apple slices in a large bowl and sprinkle the spices on top. Toss to coat.
2. Put the apple slices in the air fryer basket in a single layer and spray them with cooking spray.

3. Put the air fryer basket on the baking pan and slide into Rack Position 2, select Air Fry, set temperature to 360ºF (182ºC), and set time to 10 minutes.
4. Stir the apple slices halfway through.
5. When cooking is complete, the apple chips should be crispy. Transfer the apple chips to a paper towel-lined plate and rest for 5 minutes before serving.

454.Coconut Pumpkin Bars

Servings: 16
Cooking Time: 28 Minutes
Ingredients:
- 2 eggs
- 1/4 cup coconut flour
- 8 oz pumpkin puree
- 1/2 cup coconut oil, melted
- 1/3 cup Swerve
- 1 1/2 tsp pumpkin pie spice
- 1/2 tsp baking soda
- 1 tsp baking powder
- Pinch of salt

Directions:
1. Fit the oven with the rack in position
2. In a bowl, beat eggs, sweetener, coconut oil, pumpkin pie spice, and pumpkin puree until well combined.
3. In another bowl, mix together baking powder, coconut flour, salt, and baking soda.
4. Add coconut flour mixture to the egg mixture and mix well.
5. Pour the bar mixture into the prepared baking pan and spread evenly.
6. Set to bake at 350 F for 33 minutes. After 5 minutes place the baking dish in the preheated oven.
7. Slice and serve.
- **Nutrition Info:** Calories: 73 Fat 7.5 g Carbohydrates 1.6 g Sugar 0.5 g Protein 0.9 g Cholesterol 20 mg

455.Eggplant Stacks

Servings: 4

Cooking Time: 15 Minutes
Ingredients:
- 2 large tomatoes; cut into ¼-inch slices
- ¼ cup fresh basil, sliced
- 4 oz. fresh mozzarella; cut into ½-oz. slices
- 1 medium eggplant; cut into ¼-inch slices
- 2 tbsp. olive oil

Directions:
1. In a 6-inch round baking dish, place four slices of eggplant on the bottom. Place a slice of tomato on top of each eggplant round, then mozzarella, then eggplant. Repeat as necessary.
2. Drizzle with olive oil. Cover dish with foil and place dish into the air fryer basket. Adjust the temperature to 350 Degrees F and set the timer for 12 minutes.
3. When done, eggplant will be tender. Garnish with fresh basil to serve.
- **Nutrition Info:** Calories: 195; Protein: 8.5g; Fiber: 5.2g; Fat: 12.7g; Carbs: 12.7g

456.Lemon Cookies

Servings: 12
Cooking Time: 15 Minutes
Ingredients:
- ¼ cup cashew butter, soft
- 1 egg, whisked
- ¾ cup swerve
- 1 cup coconut cream
- Juice of 1 lemon
- 1 tsp. baking powder
- 1 tsp. lemon peel, grated

Directions:
1. In a bowl, combine all the ingredients gradually and stir well.
2. Spoon balls this on a cookie sheet lined with parchment paper and flatten them.
3. Put the cookie sheet in the fryer and cook at 350°F for 20 minutes. Serve the cookies cold
- **Nutrition Info:** Calories: 121; Fat: 5g; Fiber: 1g; Carbs: 4g; Protein: 2g

OTHER FAVORITE RECIPES

457.Easy Corn And Bell Pepper Casserole

Servings:4
Cooking Time: 20 Minutes
Ingredients:
- 1 cup corn kernels
- ¼ cup bell pepper, finely chopped
- ½ cup low-fat milk
- 1 large egg, beaten
- ½ cup yellow cornmeal
- ½ cup all-purpose flour
- ½ teaspoon baking powder
- 2 tablespoons melted unsalted butter
- 1 tablespoon granulated sugar
- Pinch of cayenne pepper
- ¼ teaspoon kosher salt
- Cooking spray

Directions:
1. Spritz the baking pan with cooking spray.
2. Combine all the ingredients in a large bowl. Stir to mix well. Pour the mixture into the baking pan.
3. Slide the baking pan into Rack Position 1, select Convection Bake, set temperature to 330ºF (166ºC) and set time to 20 minutes.
4. When cooking is complete, the casserole should be lightly browned and set.
5. Remove from the oven and serve immediately.

458.Jewish Blintzes

Servings: 8 Blintzes
Cooking Time: 10 Minutes
Ingredients:
- 2 (7½-ounce / 213-g) packages farmer cheese, mashed
- ¼ cup cream cheese
- ¼ teaspoon vanilla extract
- ¼ cup granulated white sugar
- 8 egg roll wrappers
- 4 tablespoons butter, melted

Directions:
1. Combine the farmer cheese, cream cheese, vanilla extract, and sugar in a bowl. Stir to mix well.
2. Unfold the egg roll wrappers on a clean work surface, spread ¼ cup of the filling at the edge of each wrapper and leave a ½-inch edge uncovering.
3. Wet the edges of the wrappers with water and fold the uncovered edge over the filling. Fold the left and right sides in the center, then tuck the edge under the filling and fold to wrap the filling.
4. Brush the wrappers with melted butter, then arrange the wrappers in a single layer in the air fryer basket, seam side down.

Leave a little space between each two wrappers.
5. Put the air fryer basket on the baking pan and slide into Rack Position 2, select Air Fry, set temperature to 375ºF (190ºC) and set time to 10 minutes.
6. When cooking is complete, the wrappers will be golden brown.
7. Serve immediately.

459.Sweet Air Fried Pecans

Servings: 4 Cups
Cooking Time: 10 Minutes
Ingredients:
- 2 egg whites
- 1 tablespoon cumin
- 2 teaspoons smoked paprika
- ½ cup brown sugar
- 2 teaspoons kosher salt
- 1 pound (454 g) pecan halves
- Cooking spray

Directions:
1. Spritz the air fryer basket with cooking spray.
2. Combine the egg whites, cumin, paprika, sugar, and salt in a large bowl. Stir to mix well. Add the pecans to the bowl and toss to coat well.
3. Transfer the pecans to the basket.
4. Put the air fryer basket on the baking pan and slide into Rack Position 2, select Air Fry, set temperature to 300ºF (150ºC) and set time to 10 minutes.
5. Stir the pecans at least two times during the cooking.
6. When cooking is complete, the pecans should be lightly caramelized. Remove from the oven and serve immediately.

460.Kale Salad Sushi Rolls With Sriracha Mayonnaise

Servings:12
Cooking Time: 10 Minutes
Ingredients:
- Kale Salad:
- 1½ cups chopped kale
- 1 tablespoon sesame seeds
- ¾ teaspoon soy sauce
- ¾ teaspoon toasted sesame oil
- ½ teaspoon rice vinegar
- ¼ teaspoon ginger
- ⅛ teaspoon garlic powder
- Sushi Rolls:
- 3 sheets sushi nori
- 1 batch cauliflower rice
- ½ avocado, sliced
- Sriracha Mayonnaise:

- ¼ cup Sriracha sauce
- ¼ cup vegan mayonnaise
- Coating:
- ½ cup panko bread crumbs

Directions:
1. In a medium bowl, toss all the ingredients for the salad together until well coated and set aside.
2. Place a sheet of nori on a clean work surface and spread the cauliflower rice in an even layer on the nori. Scoop 2 to 3 tablespoon of kale salad on the rice and spread over. Place 1 or 2 avocado slices on top. Roll up the sushi, pressing gently to get a nice, tight roll. Repeat to make the remaining 2 rolls.
3. In a bowl, stir together the Sriracha sauce and mayonnaise until smooth. Add bread crumbs to a separate bowl.
4. Dredge the sushi rolls in Sriracha Mayonnaise, then roll in bread crumbs till well coated.
5. Place the coated sushi rolls in the air fryer basket.
6. Put the air fryer basket on the baking pan and slide into Rack Position 2, select Air Fry, set temperature to 390ºF (199ºC) and set time to 10 minutes.
7. Flip the sushi rolls halfway through the cooking time.
8. When cooking is complete, the sushi rolls will be golden brown and crispy. .
9. Transfer to a platter and rest for 5 minutes before slicing each roll into 8 pieces. Serve warm.

461.Chicken Sausage And Broccoli Casserole

Servings:8
Cooking Time: 20 Minutes
Ingredients:
- 10 eggs
- 1 cup Cheddar cheese, shredded and divided
- ¾ cup heavy whipping cream
- 1 (12-ounce / 340-g) package cooked chicken sausage
- 1 cup broccoli, chopped
- 2 cloves garlic, minced
- ½ tablespoon salt
- ¼ tablespoon ground black pepper
- Cooking spray

Directions:
1. Spritz the baking pan with cooking spray.
2. Whisk the eggs with Cheddar and cream in a large bowl to mix well.
3. Combine the cooked sausage, broccoli, garlic, salt, and ground black pepper in a separate bowl. Stir to mix well.
4. Pour the sausage mixture into the baking pan, then spread the egg mixture over to cover.
5. Slide the baking pan into Rack Position 1, select Convection Bake, set temperature to 400ºF (205ºC) and set time to 20 minutes.
6. When cooking is complete, the egg should be set and a toothpick inserted in the center should come out clean.
7. Serve immediately.

462.Parmesan Cauliflower Fritters

Servings:6
Cooking Time: 8 Minutes
Ingredients:
- 2 cups cooked cauliflower
- 1 cup panko bread crumbs
- 1 large egg, beaten
- ½ cup grated Parmesan cheese
- 1 tablespoon chopped fresh chives Spritz the air fryer basket with cooking spray
- Cooking spray.

Directions:
1. Put the cauliflower, panko bread crumbs, egg, Parmesan, and chives in a food processor, then pulse to lightly mash and combine the mixture until chunky and thick.
2. Shape the mixture into 6 flat patties, then arrange them in the basket and spritz with cooking spray.
3. Put the air fryer basket on the baking pan and slide into Rack Position 2, select Air Fry, set temperature to 390ºF (199ºC) and set time to 8 minutes.
4. Flip the patties halfway through the cooking time.
5. When done, the patties should be crispy and golden brown. Remove from the oven and serve immediately.

463.Hillbilly Broccoli Cheese Casserole

Servings:6
Cooking Time: 30 Minutes
Ingredients:
- 4 cups broccoli florets
- ¼ cup heavy whipping cream
- ½ cup sharp Cheddar cheese, shredded
- ¼ cup ranch dressing
- Kosher salt and ground black pepper, to taste

Directions:
1. Combine all the ingredients in a large bowl. Toss to coat well broccoli well.
2. Pour the mixture into the baking pan.
3. Slide the baking pan into Rack Position 1, select Convection Bake, set temperature to 375ºF (190ºC) and set time to 30 minutes.
4. When cooking is complete, the broccoli should be tender.

5. Remove the baking pan from the oven and serve immediately.

464.Oven Baked Rice

Servings: About 4 Cups
Cooking Time: 35 Minutes
Ingredients:
- 1 cup long-grain white rice, rinsed and drained
- 1 tablespoon unsalted butter, melted, or 1 tablespoon extra-virgin olive oil
- 2 cups water
- 1 teaspoon kosher salt or ½ teaspoon fine salt

Directions:
1. Add the butter and rice to the baking pan and stir to coat. Pour in the water and sprinkle with the salt. Stir until the salt is dissolved.
2. Select Bake, set the temperature to 325ºF (163ºC), and set the time for 35 minutes. Select Start to begin preheating.
3. Once the unit has preheated, place the pan in the oven.
4. After 20 minutes, remove the pan from the oven. Stir the rice. Transfer the pan back to the oven and continue cooking for 10 to 15 minutes, or until the rice is mostly cooked through and the water is absorbed.
5. When done, remove the pan from the oven and cover with aluminum foil. Let stand for 10 minutes. Using a fork, gently fluff the rice.
6. Serve immediately.

465.Garlicky Olive Stromboli

Servings:8
Cooking Time: 25 Minutes
Ingredients:
- 4 large cloves garlic, unpeeled
- 3 tablespoons grated Parmesan cheese
- ½ cup packed fresh basil leaves
- ½ cup marinated, pitted green and black olives
- ¼ teaspoon crushed red pepper
- ½ pound (227 g) pizza dough, at room temperature
- 4 ounces (113 g) sliced provolone cheese (about 8 slices)
- Cooking spray

Directions:
1. Spritz the air fryer basket with cooking spray. Put the unpeeled garlic in the basket.
2. Put the air fryer basket on the baking pan and slide into Rack Position 2, select Air Fry, set temperature to 370ºF (188ºC) and set time to 10 minutes.
3. When cooked, the garlic will be softened completely. Remove from the oven and allow to cool until you can handle.
4. Peel the garlic and place into a food processor with 2 tablespoons of Parmesan, basil, olives, and crushed red pepper. Pulse to mix well. Set aside.
5. Arrange the pizza dough on a clean work surface, then roll it out with a rolling pin into a rectangle. Cut the rectangle in half.
6. Sprinkle half of the garlic mixture over each rectangle half, and leave ½-inch edges uncover. Top them with the provolone cheese.
7. Brush one long side of each rectangle half with water, then roll them up. Spritz the basket with cooking spray. Transfer the rolls to the basket. Spritz with cooking spray and scatter with remaining Parmesan.
8. Select Air Fry and set time to 15 minutes.
9. Flip the rolls halfway through the cooking time. When done, the rolls should be golden brown.
10. Remove the rolls from the oven and allow to cool for a few minutes before serving.

466.Simple Air Fried Okra Chips

Servings:6
Cooking Time: 16 Minutes
Ingredients:
- 2 pounds (907 g) fresh okra pods, cut into 1-inch pieces
- 2 tablespoons canola oil
- 1 teaspoon coarse sea salt

Directions:
1. Stir the oil and salt in a bowl to mix well. Add the okra and toss to coat well. Place the okra in the air fryer basket.
2. Put the air fryer basket on the baking pan and slide into Rack Position 2, select Air Fry, set temperature to 400ºF (205ºC) and set time to 16 minutes.
3. Flip the okra at least three times during cooking.
4. When cooked, the okra should be lightly browned. Remove from the oven and serve immediately.

467.Banana Cake

Servings:8
Cooking Time: 20 Minutes
Ingredients:
- 1 cup plus 1 tablespoon all-purpose flour
- ¼ teaspoon baking soda
- ¾ teaspoon baking powder
- ¼ teaspoon salt
- 9½ tablespoons granulated white sugar
- 5 tablespoons butter, at room temperature
- 2½ small ripe bananas, peeled
- 2 large eggs
- 5 tablespoons buttermilk
- 1 teaspoon vanilla extract

- Cooking spray

Directions:
1. Spritz the baking pan with cooking spray.
2. Combine the flour, baking soda, baking powder, and salt in a large bowl. Stir to mix well.
3. Beat the sugar and butter in a separate bowl with a hand mixer on medium speed for 3 minutes.
4. Beat in the bananas, eggs, buttermilk, and vanilla extract into the sugar and butter mix with a hand mixer.
5. Pour in the flour mixture and whip with hand mixer until sanity and smooth.
6. Scrape the batter into the pan and level the batter with a spatula.
7. Slide the baking pan into Rack Position 1, select Convection Bake, set temperature to 325ºF (163ºC) and set time to 20 minutes.
8. After 15 minutes, remove the pan from the oven. Check the doneness. Return the pan to the oven and continue cooking.
9. When done, a toothpick inserted in the center should come out clean.
10. Invert the cake on a cooling rack and allow to cool for 15 minutes before slicing to serve.

468.Sumptuous Beef And Bean Chili Casserole

Servings:4
Cooking Time: 31 Minutes
Ingredients:
- 1 tablespoon olive oil
- ½ cup finely chopped bell pepper
- ½ cup chopped celery
- 1 onion, chopped
- 2 garlic cloves, minced
- 1 pound (454 g) ground beef
- 1 can diced tomatoes
- ½ teaspoon parsley
- ½ tablespoon chili powder
- 1 teaspoon chopped cilantro
- 1½ cups vegetable broth
- 1 (8-ounce / 227-g) can cannellini beans
- Salt and ground black pepper, to taste

Directions:
1. Heat the olive oil in a nonstick skillet over medium heat until shimmering.
2. Add the bell pepper, celery, onion, and garlic to the skillet and sauté for 5 minutes or until the onion is translucent.
3. Add the ground beef and sauté for an additional 6 minutes or until lightly browned.
4. Mix in the tomatoes, parsley, chili powder, cilantro and vegetable broth, then cook for 10 more minutes. Stir constantly.

5. Pour them in the baking pan, then mix in the beans and sprinkle with salt and ground black pepper.
6. Slide the baking pan into Rack Position 1, select Convection Bake, set temperature to 350ºF (180ºC) and set time to 10 minutes.
7. When cooking is complete, the vegetables should be tender and the beef should be well browned.
8. Remove from the oven and serve immediately.

469.Citrus Avocado Wedge Fries

Servings: 12 Fries
Cooking Time: 8 Minutes
Ingredients:
- 1 cup all-purpose flour
- 3 tablespoons lime juice
- ¾ cup orange juice
- 1¼ cups plain dried bread crumbs
- 1 cup yellow cornmeal
- 1½ tablespoons chile powder
- 2 large Hass avocados, peeled, pitted, and cut into wedges
- Coarse sea salt, to taste
- Cooking spray

Directions:
1. Spritz the air fryer basket with cooking spray.
2. Pour the flour in a bowl. Mix the lime juice with orange juice in a second bowl. Combine the bread crumbs, cornmeal, and chile powder in a third bowl.
3. Dip the avocado wedges in the bowl of flour to coat well, then dredge the wedges into the bowl of juice mixture, and then dunk the wedges in the bread crumbs mixture. Shake the excess off.
4. Arrange the coated avocado wedges in a single layer in the basket. Spritz with cooking spray.
5. Put the air fryer basket on the baking pan and slide into Rack Position 2, select Air Fry, set temperature to 400ºF (205ºC) and set time to 8 minutes.
6. Stir the avocado wedges and sprinkle with salt halfway through the cooking time.
7. When cooking is complete, the avocado wedges should be tender and crispy.
8. Serve immediately.

470.Greek Frittata

Servings:2
Cooking Time: 8 Minutes
Ingredients:
- 1 cup chopped mushrooms
- 2 cups spinach, chopped
- 4 eggs, lightly beaten
- 3 ounces (85 g) feta cheese, crumbled

- 2 tablespoons heavy cream
- A handful of fresh parsley, chopped
- Salt and ground black pepper, to taste
- Cooking spray

Directions:
1. Spritz the baking pan with cooking spray.
2. Whisk together all the ingredients in a large bowl. Stir to mix well.
3. Pour the mixture in the prepared baking pan.
4. Slide the baking pan into Rack Position 1, select Convection Bake, set temperature to 350ºF (180ºC) and set time to 8 minutes.
5. Stir the mixture halfway through.
6. When cooking is complete, the eggs should be set.
7. Serve immediately.

471.Supplì Al Telefono (risotto Croquettes)

Servings:6
Cooking Time: 54 Minutes
Ingredients:
- Risotto Croquettes:
- 4 tablespoons unsalted butter
- 1 small yellow onion, minced
- 1 cup Arborio rice
- 3½ cups chicken stock
- ½ cup dry white wine
- 3 eggs
- Zest of 1 lemon
- ½ cup grated Parmesan cheese
- 2 ounces (57 g) fresh Mozzarella cheese
- ¼ cup peas
- 2 tablespoons water
- ½ cup all-purpose flour
- 1½ cups panko bread crumbs
- Kosher salt and ground black pepper, to taste
- Cooking spray
- Tomato Sauce:
- 2 tablespoons extra-virgin olive oil
- 4 cloves garlic, minced
- ¼ teaspoon red pepper flakes
- 1 (28-ounce / 794-g) can crushed tomatoes
- 2 teaspoons granulated sugar
- Kosher salt and ground black pepper, to taste

Directions:
1. Melt the butter in a pot over medium heat, then add the onion and salt to taste. Sauté for 5 minutes or until the onion in translucent.
2. Add the rice and stir to coat well. Cook for 3 minutes or until the rice is lightly browned. Pour in the chicken stock and wine.
3. Bring to a boil. Then cook for 20 minutes or until the rice is tender and liquid is almost absorbed.
4. Make the risotto: When the rice is cooked, break the egg into the pot. Add the lemon zest and Parmesan cheese. Sprinkle with salt and ground black pepper. Stir to mix well.
5. Pour the risotto in a baking sheet, then level with a spatula to spread the risotto evenly. Wrap the baking sheet in plastic and refrigerate for1 hour.
6. Meanwhile, heat the olive oil in a saucepan over medium heat until shimmering.
7. Add the garlic and sprinkle with red pepper flakes. Sauté for a minute or until fragrant.
8. Add the crushed tomatoes and sprinkle with sugar. Stir to mix well. Bring to a boil. Reduce the heat to low and simmer for 15 minutes or until lightly thickened. Sprinkle with salt and pepper to taste. Set aside until ready to serve.
9. Remove the risotto from the refrigerator. Scoop the risotto into twelve 2-inch balls, then flatten the balls with your hands.
10. Arrange a about ½-inch piece of Mozzarella and 5 peas in the center of each flattened ball, then wrap them back into balls.
11. Transfer the balls to a baking sheet lined with parchment paper, then refrigerate for 15 minutes or until firm.
12. Whisk the remaining 2 eggs with 2 tablespoons of water in a bowl. Pour the flour in a second bowl and pour the panko in a third bowl.
13. Dredge the risotto balls in the bowl of flour first, then into the eggs, and then into the panko. Shake the excess off.
14. Transfer the balls to the baking pan and spritz with cooking spray.
15. Slide the baking pan into Rack Position 1, select Convection Bake, set temperature to 400ºF (205ºC) and set time to 10 minutes.
16. Flip the balls halfway through the cooking time.
17. When cooking is complete, the balls should be until golden brown.
18. Serve the risotto balls with the tomato sauce.

472.Herbed Cheddar Frittata

Servings:4
Cooking Time: 20 Minutes
Ingredients:
- ½ cup shredded Cheddar cheese
- ½ cup half-and-half
- 4 large eggs
- 2 tablespoons chopped scallion greens
- 2 tablespoons chopped fresh parsley
- ½ teaspoon kosher salt
- ½ teaspoon ground black pepper
- Cooking spray

Directions:

1. Spritz the baking pan with cooking spray.
2. Whisk together all the ingredients in a large bowl, then pour the mixture into the prepared baking pan.
3. Slide the baking pan into Rack Position 1, select Convection Bake, set temperature to 300ºF (150ºC) and set time to 20 minutes.
4. Stir the mixture halfway through.
5. When cooking is complete, the eggs should be set.
6. Serve immediately.

473.Air Fried Crispy Brussels Sprouts

Servings:4
Cooking Time: 20 Minutes
Ingredients:
- ¼ teaspoon salt
- ⅛ teaspoon ground black pepper
- 1 tablespoon extra-virgin olive oil
- 1 pound (454 g) Brussels sprouts, trimmed and halved
- Lemon wedges, for garnish

Directions:
1. Combine the salt, black pepper, and olive oil in a large bowl. Stir to mix well.
2. Add the Brussels sprouts to the bowl of mixture and toss to coat well. Arrange the Brussels sprouts in the air fryer basket.
3. Put the air fryer basket on the baking pan and slide into Rack Position 2, select Air Fry, set temperature to 350ºF (180ºC) and set time to 20 minutes.
4. Stir the Brussels sprouts two times during cooking.
5. When cooked, the Brussels sprouts will be lightly browned and wilted. Transfer the cooked Brussels sprouts to a large plate and squeeze the lemon wedges on top to serve.

474.Keto Cheese Quiche

Servings:8
Cooking Time: 1 Hour
Ingredients:
- Crust:
- 1¼ cups blanched almond flour
- 1 large egg, beaten
- 1¼ cups grated Parmesan cheese
- ¼ teaspoon fine sea salt
- Filling:
- 4 ounces (113 g) cream cheese
- 1 cup shredded Swiss cheese
- $^1/_3$ cup minced leeks
- 4 large eggs, beaten
- ½ cup chicken broth
- ⅛ teaspoon cayenne pepper
- ¾ teaspoon fine sea salt
- 1 tablespoon unsalted butter, melted
- Chopped green onions, for garnish
- Cooking spray

Directions:
1. Spritz the baking pan with cooking spray.
2. Combine the flour, egg, Parmesan, and salt in a large bowl. Stir to mix until a satiny and firm dough forms.
3. Arrange the dough between two grease parchment papers, then roll the dough into a $^1/_{16}$-inch thick circle.
4. Make the crust: Transfer the dough into the prepared pan and press to coat the bottom.
5. Slide the baking pan into Rack Position 1, select Convection Bake, set temperature to 325ºF (163ºC) and set time to 12 minutes.
6. When cooking is complete, the edges of the crust should be lightly browned.
7. Meanwhile, combine the ingredient for the filling, except for the green onions in a large bowl.
8. Pour the filling over the cooked crust and cover the edges of the crust with aluminum foil.
9. Slide the baking pan into Rack Position 1, select Convection Bake, set time to 15 minutes.
10. When cooking is complete, reduce the heat to 300ºF (150ºC) and set time to 30 minutes.
11. When cooking is complete, a toothpick inserted in the center should come out clean.
12. Remove from the oven and allow to cool for 10 minutes before serving.

475.Cauliflower And Pumpkin Casserole

Servings:6
Cooking Time: 50 Minutes
Ingredients:
- 1 cup chicken broth
- 2 cups cauliflower florets
- 1 cup canned pumpkin purée
- ¼ cup heavy cream
- 1 teaspoon vanilla extract
- 2 large eggs, beaten
- $^1/_3$ cup unsalted butter, melted, plus more for greasing the pan
- ¼ cup sugar
- 1 teaspoon fine sea salt
- Chopped fresh parsley leaves, for garnish
- TOPPING:
- ½ cup blanched almond flour
- 1 cup chopped pecans
- $^1/_3$ cup unsalted butter, melted
- ½ cup sugar

Directions:
1. Pour the chicken broth in the baking pan, then add the cauliflower.
2. Slide the baking pan into Rack Position 1, select Convection Bake, set temperature to 350ºF (180ºC) and set time to 20 minutes.

3. When cooking is complete, the cauliflower should be soft.
4. Meanwhile, combine the ingredients for the topping in a large bowl. Stir to mix well.
5. Pat the cauliflower dry with paper towels, then place in a food processor and pulse with pumpkin purée, heavy cream, vanilla extract, eggs, butter, sugar, and salt until smooth.
6. Clean the baking pan and grease with more butter, then pour the purée mixture in the pan. Spread the topping over the mixture.
7. Put the baking pan back to the oven. Select Bake and set time to 30 minutes.
8. When baking is complete, the topping of the casserole should be lightly browned.
9. Remove the casserole from the oven and serve with fresh parsley on top.

476.Crispy Cheese Wafer

Servings:2
Cooking Time: 5 Minutes
Ingredients:
- 1 cup shredded aged Manchego cheese
- 1 teaspoon all-purpose flour
- ½ teaspoon cumin seeds
- ¼ teaspoon cracked black pepper

Directions:
1. Line the air fryer basket with parchment paper.
2. Combine the cheese and flour in a bowl. Stir to mix well. Spread the mixture in the pan into a 4-inch round.
3. Combine the cumin and black pepper in a small bowl. Stir to mix well. Sprinkle the cumin mixture over the cheese round.
4. Put the air fryer basket on the baking pan and slide into Rack Position 2, select Air Fry, set temperature to 375ºF (190ºC) and set time to 5 minutes.
5. When cooked, the cheese will be lightly browned and frothy.
6. Use tongs to transfer the cheese wafer onto a plate and slice to serve.

477.Classic Churros

Servings: 12 Churros
Cooking Time: 10 Minutes
Ingredients:
- 4 tablespoons butter
- ¼ teaspoon salt
- ½ cup water
- ½ cup all-purpose flour
- 2 large eggs
- 2 teaspoons ground cinnamon
- ¼ cup granulated white sugar
- Cooking spray

Directions:

1. Put the butter, salt, and water in a saucepan. Bring to a boil until the butter is melted on high heat. Keep stirring.
2. Reduce the heat to medium and fold in the flour to form a dough. Keep cooking and stirring until the dough is dried out and coat the pan with a crust.
3. Turn off the heat and scrape the dough in a large bowl. Allow to cool for 15 minutes.
4. Break and whisk the eggs into the dough with a hand mixer until the dough is sanity and firm enough to shape.
5. Scoop up 1 tablespoon of the dough and roll it into a ½-inch-diameter and 2-inch-long cylinder. Repeat with remaining dough to make 12 cylinders in total.
6. Combine the cinnamon and sugar in a large bowl and dunk the cylinders into the cinnamon mix to coat.
7. Arrange the cylinders on a plate and refrigerate for 20 minutes.
8. Spritz the air fryer basket with cooking spray. Place the cylinders in the basket and spritz with cooking spray.
9. Put the air fryer basket on the baking pan and slide into Rack Position 2, select Air Fry, set temperature to 375ºF (190ºC) and set time to 10 minutes.
10. Flip the cylinders halfway through the cooking time.
11. When cooked, the cylinders should be golden brown and fluffy.
12. Serve immediately.

478.Crunchy And Beery Onion Rings

Servings:2 To 4
Cooking Time: 16 Minutes
Ingredients:
- $^2/_3$ cup all-purpose flour
- 1 teaspoon paprika
- ½ teaspoon baking soda
- 1 teaspoon salt
- ½ teaspoon freshly ground black pepper
- 1 egg, beaten
- ¾ cup beer
- 1½ cups bread crumbs
- 1 tablespoons olive oil
- 1 large Vidalia onion, peeled and sliced into ½-inch rings
- Cooking spray

Directions:
1. Spritz the air fryer basket with cooking spray.
2. Combine the flour, paprika, baking soda, salt, and ground black pepper in a bowl. Stir to mix well.
3. Combine the egg and beer in a separate bowl. Stir to mix well.

4. Make a well in the center of the flour mixture, then pour the egg mixture in the well. Stir to mix everything well.
5. Pour the bread crumbs and olive oil in a shallow plate. Stir to mix well.
6. Dredge the onion rings gently into the flour and egg mixture, then shake the excess off and put into the plate of bread crumbs. Flip to coat the both sides well. Arrange the onion rings in the basket.
7. Put the air fryer basket on the baking pan and slide into Rack Position 2, select Air Fry, set temperature to 360ºF (182ºC) and set time to 16 minutes.
8. Flip the rings and put the bottom rings to the top halfway through.
9. When cooked, the rings will be golden brown and crunchy. Remove from the oven and serve immediately.

479. Traditional Latkes

Servings: 4 Latkes
Cooking Time: 10 Minutes
Ingredients:
- 1 egg
- 2 tablespoons all-purpose flour
- 2 medium potatoes, peeled and shredded, rinsed and drained
- ¼ teaspoon granulated garlic
- ½ teaspoon salt
- Cooking spray

Directions:
1. Spritz the air fryer basket with cooking spray.
2. Whisk together the egg, flour, potatoes, garlic, and salt in a large bowl. Stir to mix well.
3. Divide the mixture into four parts, then flatten them into four circles. Arrange the circles onto the basket and spritz with cooking spray.
4. Put the air fryer basket on the baking pan and slide into Rack Position 2, select Air Fry, set temperature to 380ºF (193ºC) and set time to 10 minutes.
5. Flip the latkes halfway through.
6. When cooked, the latkes will be golden brown and crispy. Remove from the oven and serve immediately.

480. Lemony And Garlicky Asparagus

Servings: 10 Spears
Cooking Time: 10 Minutes
Ingredients:
- 10 spears asparagus (about ½ pound / 227 g in total), snap the ends off
- 1 tablespoon lemon juice
- 2 teaspoons minced garlic
- ½ teaspoon salt
- ¼ teaspoon ground black pepper
- Cooking spray

Directions:
1. Line the air fryer basket with parchment paper.
2. Put the asparagus spears in a large bowl. Drizzle with lemon juice and sprinkle with minced garlic, salt, and ground black pepper. Toss to coat well.
3. Transfer the asparagus to the basket and spritz with cooking spray.
4. Put the air fryer basket on the baking pan and slide into Rack Position 2, select Air Fry, set temperature to 400ºF (205ºC) and set time to 10 minutes.
5. Flip the asparagus halfway through cooking.
6. When cooked, the asparagus should be wilted and soft. Remove from the oven and serve immediately.

481. Broccoli, Carrot, And Tomato Quiche

Servings: 4
Cooking Time: 14 Minutes
Ingredients:
- 4 eggs
- 1 teaspoon dried thyme
- 1 cup whole milk
- 1 steamed carrots, diced
- 2 cups steamed broccoli florets
- 2 medium tomatoes, diced
- ¼ cup crumbled feta cheese
- 1 cup grated Cheddar cheese
- 1 teaspoon chopped parsley
- Salt and ground black pepper, to taste
- Cooking spray

Directions:
1. Spritz the baking pan with cooking spray.
2. Whisk together the eggs, thyme, salt, and ground black pepper in a bowl and fold in the milk while mixing.
3. Put the carrots, broccoli, and tomatoes in the prepared baking pan, then spread with feta cheese and ½ cup Cheddar cheese. Pour the egg mixture over, then scatter with remaining Cheddar on top.
4. Slide the baking pan into Rack Position 1, select Convection Bake, set temperature to 350ºF (180ºC) and set time to 14 minutes.
5. When cooking is complete, the egg should be set and the quiche should be puffed.
6. Remove the quiche from the oven and top with chopped parsley, then slice to serve.

482. Milky Pecan Tart

Servings: 8
Cooking Time: 26 Minutes
Ingredients:
- Tart Crust:
- ¼ cup firmly packed brown sugar

- $^1/_3$ cup butter, softened
- 1 cup all-purpose flour
- ¼ teaspoon kosher salt
- Filling:
- ¼ cup whole milk
- 4 tablespoons butter, diced
- ½ cup packed brown sugar
- ¼ cup pure maple syrup
- 1½ cups finely chopped pecans
- ¼ teaspoon pure vanilla extract
- ¼ teaspoon sea salt

Directions:
1. Line the baking pan with aluminum foil, then spritz the pan with cooking spray.
2. Stir the brown sugar and butter in a bowl with a hand mixer until puffed, then add the flour and salt and stir until crumbled.
3. Pour the mixture in the prepared baking pan and tilt the pan to coat the bottom evenly.
4. Slide the baking pan into Rack Position 1, select Convection Bake, set temperature to 350ºF (180ºC) and set time to 13 minutes.
5. When done, the crust will be golden brown.
6. Meanwhile, pour the milk, butter, sugar, and maple syrup in a saucepan. Stir to mix well. Bring to a simmer, then cook for 1 more minute. Stir constantly.
7. Turn off the heat and mix the pecans and vanilla into the filling mixture.
8. Pour the filling mixture over the golden crust and spread with a spatula to coat the crust evenly.
9. Select Bake and set time to 12 minutes. When cooked, the filling mixture should be set and frothy.
10. Remove the baking pan from the oven and sprinkle with salt. Allow to sit for 10 minutes or until cooled.
11. Transfer the pan to the refrigerator to chill for at least 2 hours, then remove the aluminum foil and slice to serve.

483.Chicken Ham Casserole

Servings:4 To 6
Cooking Time: 15 Minutes
Ingredients:
- 2 cups diced cooked chicken
- 1 cup diced ham
- ¼ teaspoon ground nutmeg
- ½ cup half-and-half
- ½ teaspoon ground black pepper
- 6 slices Swiss cheese
- Cooking spray

Directions:
1. Spritz the baking pan with cooking spray.
2. Combine the chicken, ham, nutmeg, half-and-half, and ground black pepper in a large bowl. Stir to mix well.

3. Pour half of the mixture into the baking pan, then top the mixture with 3 slices of Swiss cheese, then pour in the remaining mixture and top with remaining cheese slices.
4. Slide the baking pan into Rack Position 1, select Convection Bake, set temperature to 350ºF (180ºC) and set time to 15 minutes.
5. When cooking is complete, the egg should be set and the cheese should be melted.
6. Serve immediately.

484.Dehydrated Bananas With Coconut Sprnikles

Servings:x
Cooking Time:x
Ingredients:
- 5 very ripe bananas, peeled
- 1 cup shredded coconut

Directions:
1. Place coconut in a large shallow dish. Cut Press banana wedges in the coconut and organize in one layer on the dehydrating basket.
2. Hours Put basket in rack place 4 and then press START.
3. Dehydrate for 26 hours or until peanuts are Dry to the touch but still garnish with a sweet, intense banana taste.
4. Let bananas cool completely before storing in an Airtight container for up to 5 months.

485.Oven Grits

Servings: About 4 Cups
Cooking Time: 1 Hour 5 Minutes
Ingredients:
- 1 cup grits or polenta (not instant or quick cook)
- 2 cups chicken or vegetable stock
- 2 cups milk
- 2 tablespoons unsalted butter, cut into 4 pieces
- 1 teaspoon kosher salt or ½ teaspoon fine salt

Directions:
1. Add the grits to the baking pan. Stir in the stock, milk, butter, and salt.
2. Select Bake, set the temperature to 325ºF (163ºC), and set the time for 1 hour and 5 minutes. Select Start to begin preheating.
3. Once the unit has preheated, place the pan in the oven.
4. After 15 minutes, remove the pan from the oven and stir the polenta. Return the pan to the oven and continue cooking.
5. After 30 minutes, remove the pan again and stir the polenta again. Return the pan to the oven and continue cooking for 15 to 20 minutes, or until the polenta is soft and creamy and the liquid is absorbed.
6. When done, remove the pan from the oven.

7. Serve immediately.

486. Chocolate Buttermilk Cake

Servings:8
Cooking Time: 20 Minutes
Ingredients:
- 1 cup all-purpose flour
- $^2/_3$ cup granulated white sugar
- ¼ cup unsweetened cocoa powder
- ¾ teaspoon baking soda
- ¼ teaspoon salt
- $^2/_3$ cup buttermilk
- 2 tablespoons plus 2 teaspoons vegetable oil
- 1 teaspoon vanilla extract
- Cooking spray

Directions:
1. Spritz the baking pan with cooking spray.
2. Combine the flour, cocoa powder, baking soda, sugar, and salt in a large bowl. Stir to mix well.
3. Mix in the buttermilk, vanilla, and vegetable oil. Keep stirring until it forms a grainy and thick dough.
4. Scrape the chocolate batter from the bowl and transfer to the pan, level the batter in an even layer with a spatula.
5. Slide the baking pan into Rack Position 1, select Convection Bake, set temperature to 325ºF (163ºC) and set time to 20 minutes.
6. After 15 minutes, remove the pan from the oven. Check the doneness. Return the pan to the oven and continue cooking.
7. When done, a toothpick inserted in the center should come out clean.
8. Invert the cake on a cooling rack and allow to cool for 15 minutes before slicing to serve.

487. Shrimp With Sriracha And Worcestershire Sauce

Servings:4
Cooking Time: 10 Minutes
Ingredients:
- 1 tablespoon Sriracha sauce
- 1 teaspoon Worcestershire sauce
- 2 tablespoons sweet chili sauce
- ¾ cup mayonnaise
- 1 egg, beaten
- 1 cup panko bread crumbs
- 1 pound (454 g) raw shrimp, shelled and deveined, rinsed and drained
- Lime wedges, for serving
- Cooking spray

Directions:
1. Spritz the air fryer basket with cooking spray.
2. Combine the Sriracha sauce, Worcestershire sauce, chili sauce, and mayo in a bowl. Stir to mix well. Reserve $^1/_3$ cup of the mixture as the dipping sauce.
3. Combine the remaining sauce mixture with the beaten egg. Stir to mix well. Put the panko in a separate bowl.
4. Dredge the shrimp in the sauce mixture first, then into the panko. Roll the shrimp to coat well. Shake the excess off.
5. Place the shrimp in the basket, then spritz with cooking spray.
6. Put the air fryer basket on the baking pan and slide into Rack Position 2, select Air Fry, set temperature to 360ºF (182ºC) and set time to 10 minutes.
7. Flip the shrimp halfway through the cooking time.
8. When cooking is complete, the shrimp should be opaque.
9. Remove the shrimp from the oven and serve with reserve sauce mixture and squeeze the lime wedges over.

488. Potato Chips With Lemony Cream Dip

Servings:2 To 4
Cooking Time: 15 Minutes
Ingredients:
- 2 large russet potatoes, sliced into ⅛-inch slices, rinsed
- Sea salt and freshly ground black pepper, to taste
- Cooking spray
- Lemony Cream Dip:
- ½ cup sour cream
- ¼ teaspoon lemon juice
- 2 scallions, white part only, minced
- 1 tablespoon olive oil
- ¼ teaspoon salt
- Freshly ground black pepper, to taste

Directions:
1. Soak the potato slices in water for 10 minutes, then pat dry with paper towels.
2. Transfer the potato slices in the air fryer basket. Spritz the slices with cooking spray.
3. Put the air fryer basket on the baking pan and slide into Rack Position 2, select Air Fry, set temperature to 300ºF (150ºC) and set time to 15 minutes.
4. Stir the potato slices three times during cooking. Sprinkle with salt and ground black pepper in the last minute.
5. Meanwhile, combine the ingredients for the dip in a small bowl. Stir to mix well.
6. When cooking is complete, the potato slices will be crispy and golden brown. Remove from the oven and serve the potato chips immediately with the dip.

489. Roasted Carrot Chips

Servings: 3 Cups
Cooking Time: 15 Minutes

Ingredients:
- 3 large carrots, peeled and sliced into long and thick chips diagonally
- 1 tablespoon granulated garlic
- 1 teaspoon salt
- ¼ teaspoon ground black pepper
- 1 tablespoon olive oil
- 1 tablespoon finely chopped fresh parsley

Directions:
1. Toss the carrots with garlic, salt, ground black pepper, and olive oil in a large bowl to coat well. Place the carrots in the air fryer basket.
2. Put the air fryer basket on the baking pan and slide into Rack Position 2, select Roast, set temperature to 360ºF (182ºC) and set time to 15 minutes.
3. Stir the carrots halfway through the cooking time.
4. When cooking is complete, the carrot chips should be soft. Remove from the oven. Serve the carrot chips with parsley on top.

490.Southwest Corn And Bell Pepper Roast

Servings:4
Cooking Time: 10 Minutes
Ingredients:
- Corn:
- 1½ cups thawed frozen corn kernels
- 1 cup mixed diced bell peppers
- 1 jalapeño, diced
- 1 cup diced yellow onion
- ½ teaspoon ancho chile powder
- 1 tablespoon fresh lemon juice
- 1 teaspoon ground cumin
- ½ teaspoon kosher salt
- Cooking spray
- For Serving:
- ¼ cup feta cheese
- ¼ cup chopped fresh cilantro
- 1 tablespoon fresh lemon juice

Directions:
1. Spritz the air fryer basket with cooking spray.
2. Combine the ingredients for the corn in a large bowl. Stir to mix well.
3. Pour the mixture into the basket.
4. Put the air fryer basket on the baking pan and slide into Rack Position 2, select Air Fry, set temperature to 375ºF (190ºC) and set time to 10 minutes.
5. Stir the mixture halfway through the cooking time.
6. When done, the corn and bell peppers should be soft.
7. Transfer them onto a large plate, then spread with feta cheese and cilantro. Drizzle with lemon juice and serve.

491.Baked Cherry Tomatoes With Basil

Servings:2
Cooking Time: 5 Minutes
Ingredients:
- 2 cups cherry tomatoes
- 1 clove garlic, thinly sliced
- 1 teaspoon olive oil
- ⅛ teaspoon kosher salt
- 1 tablespoon freshly chopped basil, for topping
- Cooking spray

Directions:
1. Spritz the baking pan with cooking spray and set aside.
2. In a large bowl, toss together the cherry tomatoes, sliced garlic, olive oil, and kosher salt. Spread the mixture in an even layer in the prepared pan.
3. Slide the baking pan into Rack Position 1, select Convection Bake, set temperature to 360ºF (182ºC) and set time to 5 minutes.
4. When cooking is complete, the tomatoes should be the soft and wilted.
5. Transfer to a bowl and rest for 5 minutes. Top with the chopped basil and serve warm.

492.Mediterranean Quiche

Servings:4
Cooking Time: 30 Minutes
Ingredients:
- 4 eggs
- ¼ cup chopped Kalamata olives
- ½ cup chopped tomatoes
- ¼ cup chopped onion
- ½ cup milk
- 1 cup crumbled feta cheese
- ½ tablespoon chopped oregano
- ½ tablespoon chopped basil
- Salt and ground black pepper, to taste
- Cooking spray

Directions:
1. Spritz the baking pan with cooking spray.
2. Whisk the eggs with remaining ingredients in a large bowl. Stir to mix well.
3. Pour the mixture into the prepared baking pan.
4. Slide the baking pan into Rack Position 1, select Convection Bake, set temperature to 340ºF (171ºC) and set time to 30 minutes.
5. When cooking is complete, the eggs should be set and a toothpick inserted in the center should come out clean.
6. Serve immediately.

493.Teriyaki Shrimp Skewers

Servings: 12 Skewered Shrimp
Cooking Time: 6 Minutes
Ingredients:
- 1½ tablespoons mirin

- 1½ teaspoons ginger juice
- 1½ tablespoons soy sauce
- 12 large shrimp (about 20 shrimps per pound), peeled and deveined
- 1 large egg
- ¾ cup panko bread crumbs
- Cooking spray

Directions:
1. Combine the mirin, ginger juice, and soy sauce in a large bowl. Stir to mix well.
2. Dunk the shrimp in the bowl of mirin mixture, then wrap the bowl in plastic and refrigerate for 1 hour to marinate.
3. Spritz the air fryer basket with cooking spray.
4. Run twelve 4-inch skewers through each shrimp.
5. Whisk the egg in the bowl of marinade to combine well. Pour the bread crumbs on a plate.
6. Dredge the shrimp skewers in the egg mixture, then shake the excess off and roll over the bread crumbs to coat well.
7. Arrange the shrimp skewers in the basket and spritz with cooking spray.
8. Put the air fryer basket on the baking pan and slide into Rack Position 2, select Air Fry, set temperature to 400ºF (205ºC) and set time to 6 minutes.
9. Flip the shrimp skewers halfway through the cooking time.
10. When done, the shrimp will be opaque and firm.
11. Serve immediately.

494.Apple Fritters With Sugary Glaze

Servings: 15 Fritters
Cooking Time: 8 Minutes
Ingredients:
- Apple Fritters:
- 2 firm apples, peeled, cored, and diced
- ½ teaspoon cinnamon
- Juice of 1 lemon
- 1 cup all-purpose flour
- 1½ teaspoons baking powder
- ½ teaspoon kosher salt
- 2 eggs
- ¼ cup milk
- 2 tablespoons unsalted butter, melted
- 2 tablespoons granulated sugar
- Cooking spray
- Glaze:
- ½ teaspoon vanilla extract
- 1¼ cups powdered sugar, sifted
- ¼ cup water

Directions:
1. Line the air fryer basket with parchment paper.
2. Combine the apples with cinnamon and lemon juice in a small bowl. Toss to coat well.
3. Combine the flour, baking powder, and salt in a large bowl. Stir to mix well.
4. Whisk the egg, milk, butter, and sugar in a medium bowl. Stir to mix well.
5. Make a well in the center of the flour mixture, then pour the egg mixture into the well and stir to mix well. Mix in the apple until a dough forms.
6. Use an ice cream scoop to scoop 15 balls from the dough onto the pan. Spritz with cooking spray.
7. Put the air fryer basket on the baking pan and slide into Rack Position 2, select Air Fry, set temperature to 360ºF (182ºC) and set time to 8 minutes.
8. Flip the apple fritters halfway through the cooking time.
9. Meanwhile, combine the ingredients for the glaze in a separate small bowl. Stir to mix well.
10. When cooking is complete, the apple fritters will be golden brown. Serve the fritters with the glaze on top or use the glaze for dipping.

495.Spinach And Chickpea Casserole

Servings:4
Cooking Time: 21 To 22 Minutes
Ingredients:
- 2 tablespoons olive oil
- 2 garlic cloves, minced
- 1 tablespoon ginger, minced
- 1 onion, chopped
- 1 chili pepper, minced
- Salt and ground black pepper, to taste
- 1 pound (454 g) spinach
- 1 can coconut milk
- ½ cup dried tomatoes, chopped
- 1 (14-ounce / 397-g) can chickpeas, drained

Directions:
1. Heat the olive oil in a saucepan over medium heat. Sauté the garlic and ginger in the olive oil for 1 minute, or until fragrant.
2. Add the onion, chili pepper, salt and pepper to the saucepan. Sauté for 3 minutes.
3. Mix in the spinach and sauté for 3 to 4 minutes or until the vegetables become soft. Remove from heat.
4. Pour the vegetable mixture into the baking pan. Stir in coconut milk, dried tomatoes and chickpeas until well blended.
5. Slide the baking pan into Rack Position 1, select Convection Bake, set temperature to 370ºF (188ºC) and set time to 15 minutes.
6. When cooking is complete, transfer the casserole to a serving dish. Let cool for 5 minutes before serving.

496. Southwest Seasoning

Servings: About ¾ Cups
Cooking Time: 0 Minutes
Ingredients:
- 3 tablespoons ancho chile powder
- 3 tablespoons paprika
- 2 tablespoons dried oregano
- 2 tablespoons freshly ground black pepper
- 2 teaspoons cayenne
- 2 teaspoons cumin
- 1 tablespoon granulated onion
- 1 tablespoon granulated garlic

Directions:
1. Stir together all the ingredients in a small bowl.
2. Use immediately or place in an airtight container in the pantry.

497. Spicy Air Fried Old Bay Shrimp

Servings: 2 Cups
Cooking Time: 10 Minutes
Ingredients:
- ½ teaspoon Old Bay Seasoning
- 1 teaspoon ground cayenne pepper
- ½ teaspoon paprika
- 1 tablespoon olive oil
- ⅛ teaspoon salt
- ½ pound (227 g) shrimps, peeled and deveined
- Juice of half a lemon

Directions:
1. Combine the Old Bay Seasoning, cayenne pepper, paprika, olive oil, and salt in a large bowl, then add the shrimps and toss to coat well.
2. Put the shrimps in the air fryer basket.
3. Put the air fryer basket on the baking pan and slide into Rack Position 2, select Air Fry, set temperature to 390ºF (199ºC) and set time to 10 minutes.
4. Flip the shrimps halfway through the cooking time.
5. When cooking is complete, the shrimps should be opaque. Serve the shrimps with lemon juice on top.

498. Sweet Cinnamon Chickpeas

Servings: 2
Cooking Time: 10 Minutes
Ingredients:
- 1 tablespoon cinnamon
- 1 tablespoon sugar
- 1 cup chickpeas, soaked in water overnight, rinsed and drained

Directions:
1. Combine the cinnamon and sugar in a bowl. Stir to mix well.
2. Add the chickpeas to the bowl, then toss to coat well.

3. Pour the chickpeas in the air fryer basket.
4. Put the air fryer basket on the baking pan and slide into Rack Position 2, select Air Fry, set temperature to 390ºF (199ºC) and set time to 10 minutes.
5. Stir the chickpeas three times during cooking.
6. When cooked, the chickpeas should be golden brown and crispy. Remove from the oven and serve immediately.

499. Crunchy Green Tomatoes Slices

Servings: 12 Slices
Cooking Time: 8 Minutes
Ingredients:
- ½ cup all-purpose flour
- 1 egg
- ½ cup buttermilk
- 1 cup cornmeal
- 1 cup panko
- 2 green tomatoes, cut into ¼-inch-thick slices, patted dry
- ½ teaspoon salt
- ½ teaspoon ground black pepper
- Cooking spray

Directions:
1. Spritz a baking sheet with cooking spray.
2. Pour the flour in a bowl. Whisk the egg and buttermilk in a second bowl. Combine the cornmeal and panko in a third bowl.
3. Dredge the tomato slices in the bowl of flour first, then into the egg mixture, and then dunk the slices into the cornmeal mixture. Shake the excess off.
4. Transfer the well-coated tomato slices in the baking sheet and sprinkle with salt and ground black pepper. Spritz the tomato slices with cooking spray.
5. Put the air fryer basket on the baking pan and slide into Rack Position 2, select Air Fry, set temperature to 400ºF (205ºC) and set time to 8 minutes.
6. Flip the slices halfway through the cooking time.
7. When cooking is complete, the tomato slices should be crispy and lightly browned. Remove the baking sheet from the oven.
8. Serve immediately.

500. Chocolate And Coconut Macaroons

Servings: 24 Macaroons
Cooking Time: 8 Minutes
Ingredients:
- 3 large egg whites, at room temperature
- ¼ teaspoon salt
- ¾ cup granulated white sugar
- 4½ tablespoons unsweetened cocoa powder
- 2¼ cups unsweetened shredded coconut

Directions:

1. Line the air fryer basket with parchment paper.
2. Whisk the egg whites with salt in a large bowl with a hand mixer on high speed until stiff peaks form.
3. Whisk in the sugar with the hand mixer on high speed until the mixture is thick. Mix in the cocoa powder and coconut.
4. Scoop 2 tablespoons of the mixture and shape the mixture in a ball. Repeat with remaining mixture to make 24 balls in total.
5. Arrange the balls in a single layer in the basket and leave a little space between each two balls.
6. Put the air fryer basket on the baking pan and slide into Rack Position 2, select Air Fry, set temperature to 375ºF (190ºC) and set time to 8 minutes.
7. When cooking is complete, the balls should be golden brown.
8. Serve immediately.

CPSIA information can be obtained
at www.ICGtesting.com
Printed in the USA
LVHW021449090121
676042LV00008B/464

9 781801 246286